# ADA
## Yearbook 1991

***Ada Byron, Countess of Lovelace***
(Crown copyright – The National Physical Laboratory)

# ADA

## Yearbook 1991

Edited by
**FRED LONG**
*Lecturer in Computer Science*
*University College of Wales, Aberystwyth*

## CHAPMAN & HALL

LONDON · NEW YORK · TOKYO · MELBOURNE · MADRAS

| UK | Chapman & Hall, 2–6 Boundary Row, London SE1 8HN |
|---|---|
| USA | Van Nostrand Reinhold, 115 5th Avenue, New York NY10003 |
| JAPAN | Chapman & Hall Japan, Thomson Publishing Japan, Hirakawacho Nemoto Building, 7F, 1-7-11 Hirakawa-cho, Chiyoda-ku, Tokyo 102 |
| AUSTRALIA | Chapman & Hall Australia, Thomas Nelson Australia, 102 Dodds Street, South Melbourne, Victoria 3205 |
| INDIA | Chapman & Hall India, R. Seshadri, 32 Second Main Road, CIT East, Madras 600 035 |

First edition 1991

© 1991 Ada Language UK Ltd

Printed in Great Britain by
St Edmundsbury Press Ltd, Bury St Edmunds, Suffolk

ISBN 0-412-39830-3    0 442 30836 1 (USA)
ISSN 0961-5350

The publisher makes no representation, express or implied, with regard to the accuracy of the information contained in this book and cannot accept any legal responsibility or liability for any errors or omissions that may be made.

**British Library Cataloguing in Publication Data**

ADA yearbook.
1991 –
1. Computer systems. Programming languages: Ada language
005.133
ISBN 0-412-39830-3

**Library of Congress Cataloging-in-Publication Data**

available

# Contents

# List of trademarks

VAX, VMS, ULTRIX, MicroVAX are trademarks of Digital Equipment Corporation.

AIX, OS/2, PC/AT, PC/RT, RISC SYSTEM/6000, MVS, VM/CMS are registered trademarks of International Business Machines Corporation.

MS-DOS is a registered trademark of Microsoft Corporation.

UNIX is a registered trademark of UNIX Systems Laboratories Corporation.

SunOS, SunView are trademarks of Sun Microsystems Incorporated.

TeamWORK is a trademark of Cadre Technologies.

All other products and brandnames are trademarks of their respective companies or organisations.

# Foreword

Ada UK has been publishing information about the Ada programming language, its use and the associated innovations in software engineering for well over a decade. At first, the information was provided in *ad hoc* ways by copying relevant papers and reports, with annual conferences for general background. Then the quarterly newsletter, which subsequently became the journal "Ada User", gave the growing Ada community a regular source of technical and commercial information. The conference was enlarged to provide an exhibition, with associated sessions covering managerial and training issues, as well as a forum for technical discussions.

The Ada Yearbook now provides another source of information about Ada in a conveniently accessible form. As the world of Ada has matured, the volume of information has grown larger and less volatile; in consequence we have decided to publish lists of Ada compilers, software components, organisations, and other references in a consolidated form annually rather than separately. At the same time, more people have become involved with Ada, and need to find out about its origins and significance. We have therefore combined introductory information for newcomers to Ada with reference material that everyone involved with Ada will find useful.

The preparation of the Ada Yearbook has been a major undertaking, and we thank all contributors for their efforts. The most important thanks are to Fred Long, who has coordinated the contributions and edited the whole work. In a remarkable short time, Fred has brought together a valuable package and laid the foundations for the series.

As the title indicates, we intend to publish a book like this every year. The details will change, but we hope each time to give a general introduction to the world of Ada as it currently is, and useful lists of information about everything to do with Ada. We welcome comments and suggestions, and invite readers to send feedback to us for future improvements.

Ian Pyle
Founder of Ada UK

Ada UK is the commonly-used name of Ada Language UK Limited, which is a not-for-profit company registered in the United Kingdom. The objectives of the company include promoting the development and use of Ada, and representing the needs and interests of its users. Membership is open to anyone, regardless of nationality. Further details about the benefits of membership may be obtained from Helen Byard, the Ada UK Administrator, PO Box 322, York, YO1 3GY, UK, tel. +44 904 412740.

# Preface

This is the first issue of what is planned to be an annual publication, organised by Ada UK. It is complementary to the quarterly "Ada User". Hopefully, the Yearbook will contain something of interest to everyone associated with Ada, from the novice who should find the "Ten of the most frequently asked questions about Ada" in chapter 2 helpful, to the Ada expert wondering what is happening in the Ada 9X project (chapters 6 and 18).

The Yearbook is divided into two parts. The intention is that the first part should contain information of a general, readable nature, such as the ten questions already referred to, letters from various Ada organisations around the world, etc. The second part is intended to be reference material, such as the list of validated Ada compilers, information about Ada products and projects, surveys on the use of Ada, reports on standards associated with Ada and with the development of Ada itself, and so forth. I have attempted to compile a short index of the Ada systems and support tools referenced in the second part. This appears at the end of the book. Unfortunately, I have not had time to produce a complete index of the whole book.

Readers of this book will be familiar with the concept of Configuration Management and the need for Baselines. It is inevitable that some new information will become available after the publication cut-off, whenever that is fixed. Regretfully, a few of our intended contributions did not arrive in time for this year's edition, so could not be included in this baseline. We hope to be able to have them (suitably updated) in next year's Yearbook.

I hope the Yearbook will develop and improve over the years. In order to do this we need feedback from you, the reader. Please let me know what you like about the book *and* what you do not like. What sort of articles or features would you like to see in future issues? Should the present format be retained, or revised? Only you can answer these questions. My address is to be found at the end of the book.

Many people have helped make this Yearbook possible and I would particularly like to thank the following:

- **Ian Pyle** and **John Barnes** who started the project going and made many things happen;

- **Judy Bishop**, **John Hole** and **Tony Orme** who organised surveys, collected information and prepared material for the Yearbook;

- **Judy Bamberger** who gave permission for inclusion of some "Ada Follies", provided the cartoons (drawn by **Steve Hoffman**) and proved a useful contact on the other side of the "pond";

- within my department I would like to thank my colleagues **Chris Loftus**, who wrote the Ada (what else?!) program which processed the list of validated compilers into the form in which it appears in the Yearbook, and **Andy Ormsby** who generated some TEX fonts in the sizes I needed. Also, the secretaries, **Ruth Scott**, **Rosemary Law** and **Donna Lansley**, who keyboarded much of the material included in the book, and the support staff, **Dave Price**, **Tim Cairnes**, **Gavin Harrold** and **Esther Phillips**, who helped with electronic mail problems, read floppies and tapes for me, kept the machines running and found more and more disc space as I needed it!

- At Chapman and Hall, I would like to thank **Ellen Taylor**, **Liz Carr** and **Martin Tribe** who advised about editorial matters, publication details, etc.

- Naturally, I thank all those who contributed letters and articles and who are acknowledged appropriately in the Yearbook.

- Finally, the support and encouragement of my long suffering, patient and, just lately, rather neglected, dear wife, **Ann**, should not go unrecognised.

Fred Long,
Aberystwyth

# Part One

# Reading material

*Range Checking*

# 1

# Guest introduction

I was very pleased to be invited to write an introduction to this first edition of the Ada Yearbook.

The expanding use of Ada in the 1980s has created a diverse community with many players involved in all aspects of Ada — training, developing and using being the prime components. The community has grown to such an extent that it is now quite hard to keep in touch with all that is going on. This Yearbook will prove of much assistance in keeping in touch; not only does it fulfil the need for a reference work containing informative lists of various kinds but the letters and articles give a good flavour of many aspects of the Ada scene which will be of assistance to both old and new members of the Ada community.

Ada is now well established in aerospace and defence communities around the world. But Ada is about Software Engineering and is applicable in all areas of programming where the importance of good design, reusability and reliability are appreciated.

The excellence of Ada, its portability, and the richness and variety of the tools supporting the language bring real rewards to those who use it. The reputation that Ada has built is well deserved and is now being enjoyed by a growing number of commercial areas. This Yearbook will be of special use to those using Ada for the first time by placing at their fingertips innumerable contacts which would otherwise take time to establish. It is thus much to be welcomed in assisting the move of Ada into new areas.

Ada UK has initiated a number of ventures that have been of value to the Ada community; they are to be congratulated on this latest venture, the publication of the Yearbook, which I am sure will become a permanent feature of the Ada infrastructure.

Jean D. Ichbiah

# 2

# Ten of the most frequently asked questions about Ada

## Tony Orme, AEG (UK) Limited

## 2.1 What is Ada?

Ada is the most recent conventional programming language, developed with modern software engineering principles in mind in response to the Software Crisis of late, expensive and poor-quality software. Originally created by the U.S. military, it has now spread outside the U.S. and outside defence to applications in space, air traffic control, the post office, banking, computer-aided design, etc. As well as being designed to meet the goals of software engineering such as understandability, modifiability, reusability and portability, there are two particular distinguishing features to Ada. These are the high degree of standardisation of the language together with compiler validation to assure conformance, and the incorporation of features such as tasking and exceptions which in other languages are only provided as non-standard, proprietary additions.

## 2.2 How did Ada arise?

In 1973 the U.S. Department of Defence found that, at current rates of increase, its projected software bill for 1985 would approach $5 billion per year. That, and the general lateness and poor quality of current military software, caused a number of initiatives to be taken, the most famous of which was an international competition to design a new programming language. This single language, in order to meet the DoD's future requirements and to replace some 450 languages then in U.S. military use, had to feature the latest ideas of software engineering and to support good design and coding practices. The main benefits were to be found in software maintenance, a particularly costly item for the DoD. The winning language was based on Pascal. Originally codenamed Green, it is now called Ada (in honour of Ada Augusta, Countess Lovelace, who was Charles Babbage's assistant and the first person to express concisely the scope of programming).

Ada was standardised in 1983 with the publication of MIL-STD-1815A (1815 was deliberately chosen as being the year of birth of the original Ada). There are also ANSI and ISO standards for Ada, and all are *exactly* the same. The name Ada was trademarked by the DoD, with a requirement that vendors had to meet certain conditions to use it.

Ada has been the mandatory programming language for all new deployed U.S. military projects since January 1984, except in cases where sound reasons for alternatives could be found and documented. NATO has a similar ruling that took effect in January 1986, and the MoD has effectively replaced Coral with Ada for new projects from July 1987.

The Commission of the European Communities intended to create a new European Systems Language in about 1984, but on hearing that Ada was mainly designed in the EC, switched its support behind Ada with study projects, compilers, etc.

## 2.3   Who was the original Ada?

Augusta Ada (1815–1852) was the daughter of Lord Byron. She married the Earl of Lovelace and largely followed the traditional way of life of an English aristocrat's wife of that period. Her claim to fame lies in her unusual mathematical talents, which led to her association with Charles Babbage, a professor at Cambridge University.

Babbage, a difficult but brilliant man years ahead of his time, had completed a mechanical Difference Engine for the automatic computation of tables. He now embarked on a much more difficult project, never to be completed: a programmable Analytical Engine. Augusta Ada was one of the few to understand precisely what the Analytical Engine was about, and her assessment of it would remain unaltered if she were talking of the computers of today:

> "The Analytical Engine has no pretensions whatever to originate anything. It can do whatever we know how to order it to perform".

Augusta Ada, in writing an untested program for the Engine to compute Bernoulli numbers, may be regarded as the world's first programmer.

## 2.4 How is Ada considered a Software Engineering language?

Different writers have taken different views of exactly what software engineering is. However, it may be said that:

1. software development should be conducted as an engineering discipline, particularly via the use of standards, including standard methods and tools;

2. specific principles should be applied to achieve the aims of software engineering.

The aim of the traditional engineering disciplines is uniformity in order to reduce cost and risk. Software engineers, at the design stage, use a methodology, and Ada well supports all methodologies, whether based on functional, data, process or object-based abstractions. At the code and test stage, Ada promotes a different culture to other (particularly older) languages, in terms of, for example, meaningful naming of variables, and judicious commenting. It has been found that consistency of design practice facilitates maintainability, and uniformity of coding style most readily permits code to be maintained in line with the original. The Ada recompilation rules greatly facilitate smooth integration. It is traditional for Ada compilers to come with sets of software tools, again improving consistency of development and maintenance.

Because software engineering is conveyed in a logical, rather than physical, medium, the specific principles are somewhat different from those of hardware engineering.

Some of these principles are:

**Abstraction:** Ada adds abstraction of data to the abstraction of expression and of control found in the older languages such as Cobol and Algol;

**Modularity:** Ada's strong typing, package construct, exceptions and nesting (of packages and procedures) all contribute to achieve a good partitioning of coherent units, which greatly helps maintainability;

**Reuse:** a principle shared with traditional engineering, and an area where Ada's language standardisation, generic construct and high degree of portability give it a tremendous advantage. Some very large libraries of reusable Ada software are now being created, and developments in this field are likely to occur first in Ada implementations.

Of necessity, this has been a brief analysis, but it is found that Ada has made considerable contributions towards achieving the aims of software engineering, namely cost containment, and improvement in maintainability, reliability and efficiency. Ada also gives us much more confidence to tackle large, complex systems.

## 2.5   What is an APSE?

At the same time that the competition to design a new language was in progress, it was realised that whichever language was chosen would need to be complemented by a set of high-quality tools to assist in the discipline and practices of software engineering, and aid program (and programmer) portability. The technology of tools to support these activities was not as far advanced as that of language design, and the Stoneman report, published in 1980, was a wish-list rather than a precise specification. It proposed that tools be integrated in an Ada Programming Support Environment (APSE), with a program database accessed by powerful configuration control tools (amongst others).

The APSE concept attracted much interest within the computing community. A slightly different emphasis led to the concept of the Integrated Project Support Environment (IPSE), and then to Computer Assisted Software Engineering (CASE). The latter usually supports one methodology and at least one programming language.

While the CASE scene is still in a state of flux, most Ada compilers have been distributed with language-specific tools whose utility has validated the APSE concept. Each compiler developer has his set of tools, usually represented by a wheel. Language-independent additions may be made by users. There are two important moves to standardise APSEs: the Common Ada Interface Set (CAIS) and the Portable Common Tool Environment (PCTE). CAIS, based on Ada while originating in the U.S., and PCTE, based equally on Ada and 'C' while originating in Europe, share many attributes. Efforts are underway to evolve a common environment from both.

## 2.6   Isn't Ada only a military language?

Although Ada was commissioned by the U.S. Department of Defense in response to its perceived Software Crisis, the same problems of software development and maintenance prevail everywhere. There are no specifically military constructs in Ada: it is a general purpose programming language, larger than most in order to accommodate specialisms such as real-time computing and to render supersets of the language unnecessary.

Ada has therefore entered the non-military arena entirely on its own merits. There are many examples of Ada already in use in the civilian field: in banking, air traffic control, computer-aided design, the post office, chemical engineering, automatic test equipment and other areas.

The last language promoted by the DoD some thirty years ago is now considered purely commercial and many would be surprised to learn of its military origin: its name is Cobol.

## 2.7   Is Ada expensive?

Ada was the first language to be standardised before the first compiler was produced, and the technology had to advance to cope. That, and an optimistic view of what the then predominantly military market would bear, caused the first compilers in 1983 to be priced excessively.

The first few prime contractors buying these machines, often with a dedicated development machine and expensive (because scarce) Ada training, also faced familiarisation costs and (more frequently than not) the costs of moving to a newer methodology and introducing modern software engineering disciplines. Fairly or unfairly, all these costs were laid at Ada's door and (especially in the U.S.) gave the language a reputation of being costly.

Since then, the picture has changed enormously. Fully validated compilers are sold at about one per cent of the 1983 price levels, while efficiencies are such that existing development machines are used. The Ada training market is competitive. Ada-practised personnel may be transferred or recruited to bootstrap new projects. In fact, Ada has been found very successful in large-scale projects (over, say, 500K lines of code) where the compiler cost is negligible (in contrast with the 1983 situation when Ada projects were typically very small). The software engineering discipline normally imposed at the same time brings its own benefits. Against the costs can be laid the fact that better productivity and reliability can be obtained on the very first Ada project within an organisation, concomitant with the possibilities of making use of the other benefits such as portability and reusability.

## 2.8   Are the benefits of Ada lost by using a code generator?

There are an increasing number of design methods which incorporate tools for automatic generation of Ada source code. Some of the benefits of Ada are retained by use of these code generators, and some are lost. Those benefits retained are:

**Portability:** because Ada is a standard language available on many machines.

**Reliability:** advantages can be obtained because Ada is a standard, closely-defined language with a well laid-down validation procedure, which is likely to make Ada software more reliable. Because Ada is a modern language supporting software engineering principles, the software engineers writing the generators are more likely to cause reliable code to be generated.

**Efficiency:** the efficiency of Ada compilers in turning source into object code is still available. Potential users should be aware, however, that there may be some inefficiency in transforming a design representation into program source (in any language).

The benefits not obtained are:

**Readability and maintainability:** because what is maintained is some kind of design representation, not Ada code.

**Reusability:** It is the design that must be maintained, not the code. Any possible reuse should be expressed in terms of the design, not Ada constructs. While that may well be an equally good method of achieving reusability, no advantage is being taken of the features of Ada. The writers of the code generators may derive advantage if the same piece of code can be generated to perform a number of duties.

## 2.9   What is meant by Ada validation?

To ensure that Ada compilers meet a minimum standard, they have to undergo periodic validation. There are currently five validation centres: two in the U.S., and one each in the U.K., France and Germany. The U.K. centre is at the National Computing Centre in Manchester. The U.K. treaty with the AJPO differs from the French and German ones in that we can, in theory, issue our own certificates without reference to the U.S.

New validation test suites are introduced every 18 months. The current version is 1.11, in force from 1st December 1989 to 31st May 1991. There are about 4800 tests, some purely of the compiler (i.e., source code which the compiler should find fault with), and some which test the compiler, linker and runtime system. The test suite is now believed to have reached stability, with only minor changes anticipated.

Validation certificates are now valid for the duration of the relevant test suite, plus 12 months. It is permitted to validate under a forthcoming test suite up to six months ahead, so that the maximum possible validity of a certificate is 36 months. Normally, of course, a revalidation is obtained every 18 months.

Each compiler must provide the full range of Ada with no subsets or supersets. Users then get the benefits of standardisation, such as portability, reusability, supplier independence, etc.

To save on the time and trouble required to validate every combination of hardware and software that might be required to compile or run Ada, "derived" validation is available. The supplier certifies that a new hardware configuration is the same architecture as a previously validated one, or else that some minor changes have been made to the software to fix problems or improve performance. It is for a user to report to the validation centre if there is reason to believe that the derived software/hardware combination would have failed a full validation procedure. Recently the derivation procedure has been tightened up with a more searching questionnaire. The derived validation has the same validity period as the validation it was derived from.

## 2.10   Why use Ada?

Ada, in conjunction with software engineering disciplines and practices, provides the benefits mentioned above, including maintainability, improved reliability and cost containment.

Many benefits come from the highly standardised nature of Ada such as program and programmer portability. Also the writing of reusable software is made more rewarding. Reusable Ada libraries are one way of reducing the economic burden of software. They are being built up now, and many are publicly available.

It is not commonly realised that, because of Ada's precise semantic definition, an optimising Ada compiler can generate much faster code than optimising compilers in other languages. For instance, the European Space Agency recently selected Ada after Ada benchmarks outstripped those in the 'C' language.

Ada, although it has a large syntax, is quite easy to learn. It shares with that other DoD language, Cobol, the feature that a program, once compiled without syntactical and semantic errors, will stand a good chance of working first time.

It is found that the productivity of Ada programmers is better than with other languages. The design phase of projects tends to be longer, but, once the design is sorted out, the later phases are greatly reduced.

The Ada language should not be taken alone but in conjunction with software engineering principles, an APSE, and possibly a modern methodology if one is not already in place, and tremendous benefits in terms of quality and quantity of results will accrue.

# 3

# Ada UK sponsors

Sponsors of Ada UK are organisations who wish to be prominently associated with the aim of Ada UK to promote the effective use of the Ada programming language.

## 3.1 Alsys

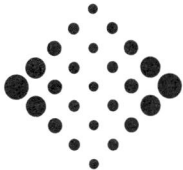 

Alsys
Partridge House
Newtown Road
Henley-on-Thames
Oxon
RG9 1EN

Contact:
Mrs Mandy Covers
Tel. +44 491 579090
Fax. +44 491 571866

Alsys is dedicated to the development and marketing of Ada products and Ada related services. As well as providing Ada development systems, Alsys also provides Ada consultancy and on site or classroom training in Ada.

The Alsys Group is a multinational company with Headquarters in Paris, subsidiaries in the United States, United Kingdom, Germany, Sweden and Japan and distributors in all the major industrialised Western nations.

Alsys Ada technology has been adopted by the major hardware manufacturers IBM, Hewlett-Packard, Unisys and Wang.

The Alsys range of Ada host compilers is available on a wide range of hardware platforms including mainframes such as DEC VAX (VMS) and the IBM 370 System (MVS, VM/CMS and AIX), UNIX workstations like the SUN 3, HP 9000, Apollo and Apple MAC and DOS systems including the IBM PS/2 and a wide range of compatibles.

Alsys also supports Ada development on a variety of RISC architectures including the Inmos transputer, SUN 4, IBM RS/6000 and MIPS.

Alsys provides a comprehensive range of tools to support the Ada programmer including a powerful symbolic debugger, AdaProbe, a text editor, cross referencer and pretty printer and more recently a program performance measuring tool known as AdaTune.

The most impressive products in the Alsys portfolio are the Ada cross development systems than can target Intel, Motorola and Inmos bare microprocessors from a range of hosts. The compilers and tools come with an array of cross assemblers and linkers and support for the popular emulators as supplied by Applied Microsystems, Tektronix, Cadre and Hewlett-Packard.

Alsys supports the longest list of Validated (ACVC) compilers on the market. A list which numbered over 40 at the last count.

## 3.2 Cray Research

Cray Research (UK) Ltd
Oldbury
Bracknell
Berkshire
RG12 4TQ
UK

Contact:
John Buchan
Tel. +44 344 485971
Fax. +44 344 426319

Originally designed to develop large, real-time embedded systems within the scientific and engineering community, Ada is now receiving a broader audience for application code development in process design and control, simulation, communications systems, expert systems, geophysical analysis, robotics, distributed applications, and management information systems.

Cray Research released its first Ada compiler in October 1988. This product provided a complete Ada capability (ANSI/MIL-STD-1815A) for customers requiring application development on Cray systems.

Today, Cray Research and Telesoft have brought a performance Ada compiler to the supercomputing community. The Cray Ada 2.0 compiler provides unsurpassed performance when combined with the fast processing speeds and large memories of Cray Research systems. Cray Ada 2.0 includes the following features which take advantage of the power of these systems:

- Automatic vectorization capabilities which provide vector performance ten or more times the performance of scalar code. Cray Ada vectorization performance now approaches that of powerful Fortran compilers, such as Cray Research's CF77 compiling system.

- Register tracking, full data flow analysis, enhanced inlining, loop invariant code motion, arithmetic strength reduction, strength reduction on loop induction variables, and common subexpression recognition all contribute to improve scalar performance by as much as 100 percent.

- Loop block, cross block and intra-block instruction scheduling capabilities which increase performance by as much as 15 percent.

- Pragma export capabilities allow routines written in Fortran, C, Pascal and the assembler to call up Ada subprograms, provided an Ada routine is the "main" subprogram.

- Capabilities allow Cray Ada users to access Fortran common blocks and C global variables using a label function.

- A support library interface package allows users to reference optimized Cray library routines such as trig functions, bit manipulations, and utility routines.

- Support is provided for calls to multitasked Fortran and C routines.

Execution performance in the Ada world is demonstrated with three benchmarks — the Dhrystone Suite, the Whetstone Suite, and Livermore Loops. Cray Ada 2.0 executes approximately 37,000 Dhrystones per second and approximately 70,000 Whetstones per second. The 14 loop version of the Livermore Loops provides a standard measure of vectorization execution performance. With this suite, Ada provides approximately 70 percent of current Cray Fortran performance and vectorizes the same number of loops.

The Department of Defense requires all contractors to use validated Ada compilers in mission-critical applications. The Ada Validation Facility publishes the Ada Compiler Validation Capability (ACVC) test suite to verify the functionality and completeness of Ada compilers. Cray Ada 2.0 conforms to the ACVC 1.11 test suite.

Future improvements to Cray Ada include enhanced scalar execution and the vectorization of additional constructs. Cray is also planning support for Ada tasks across multiple CPUs, and to provide automatic tasking similar to that available with Cray's Fortran and C compilers. Other features being considered are asynchronous I/O, real-time support, and further enhancements to library interfaces (e.g. X-Windows, POSIX, SQL, etc.) and tool and visualization improvements.

Continual enhancements to the Cray Ada compiler technology and the rich set of features available within the language will provide a powerful tool for the application developer of the 1990s.

# 3.3 DDC International

DDC International
Gl. Lundtoftevej 1B
DK-2800 Lyngby
Denmark

Contact:
Mr Palle Andersson
Tel. +45 42 87 11 44
Fax. +45 42 87 22 17
After 13 April 1991:
Tel. +45 45 87 11 44
Fax. +45 45 87 22 17

## The company

DDC International (DDC-I) is a Danish software house totally committed
to Ada software for almost 10 years now. DDC-I was the first European
company to achieve validation for an Ada compiler, the DDC-I Ada Compiler System™ (DACS™), back in 1984. This compiler system has been
ported to a large number of computers by ourselves or by our customers.

## Activities and products

DDC-I develops and markets Ada Development Systems in three product
lines:

1. DDC-I Cross Compiler Systems for Real Time Embedded Applications

2. DDC-I OEM Ada Compiler Kit

3. DDC-I Native Ada Compiler Systems

For selected target computers, DDC-I offers an optional, extremely fast
program loader utilizing the full power of Ethernet communications and a
validated Hard Deadline Scheduling (HDS) tasking kernel as an option for
time-critical applications.

**Furthermore, DDC-I offers:**

- A comprehensive range of training courses

- A comprehensive range of consultancy services

In cooperation with highly esteemed international partners DDC-I offers to undertake turn-key application development projects using Ada.

**DDC-I Ada Cross Compiler Systems:**

DDC-I and our OEM customers have developed Ada Cross Development Systems for common microprocessors such as the Intel 80x86 family, Motorola 68020, and the MIL-STD-1750A**. The DDC-I Ada Cross Compiler family has been developed and designed with the embedded systems engineer in mind, resulting in excellent code quality and unrivalled low run-time execution. The Run-Time System is a stand-alone System, designed to support the most demanding embedded real-time applications. DDC-I can supply Ada Cross Development Systems for the following host/target combinations:

| Host: | Target: |
|---|---|
| VAX™/VMS | Intel® 8086 |
| VAX™/VMS | Intel® 80186 |
| VAX™/VMS | Intel® 80286 |
| VAX™/VMS | Intel® 80386 |
| VAX™/VMS | Intel® 860 |
| VAX™/VMS | Motorola 68020 |
| VAX™/VMS | MIL-STD-1750A** |
| VAX™/VMS | Mips™R2000** |
| VAX™/VMS | Mips™R3000** |
| VAX™/VMS | Mips™R6000** |
| SUN3/SunOS® | Motorola 68020 |
| SUN3/SunOS® | Motorola 68030 |

**DDC-I OEM Ada Compiler Kit:**

The DDC-I Ada Compiler System™ is available to OEMs (computer manufacturers, large software houses) for retargeting and rehosting to their own equipment. It has been successfully ported and validated by DDC-I and OEMs, so, consequently, the portability has been proven. The DDC-I Ada Compiler System™ offers two levels of retargeting ensuring an optimum solution for any target and any requirement regarding code quality.

---

**Developed by InterACT, New York, USA.

1. For OEMs who want to port the DDC-I Ada Compiler System™, DDC-I offers various tools, and consultancy.

2. A turn-key Ada Compiler System which satisfies the customers' requirements, delivered by DDC-I.

### DDC-I Native Ada Compiler Systems:

DDC-I offers Native Ada Compiler Systems for a number of computers and systems. The compiler systems are fast and efficient Ada Development Systems. The generated code efficiency is comparable to that of existing C and Pascal Compilers, and it continues to improve under DDC-I's performance enhancement program. The Ada Compiler Systems include, but are not restricted to:

- Motorola 68020/UNIX™ based computers

- Intel$^R$ 80386/UNIX$^R$ based computers

- Sun3/SunOS$^R$ based computers

- VAX™/VMS

## Quality assurance

The DDC-I Ada Compiler Systems™ in all versions are regularly validated under the authority of the U.S. Department of Defence (Ada Joint Program Office) in accordance with MIL-STD-1815A.

---

™ DDC-I Ada Compiler Systems is a trademark of DDC International A/S and DDC-I, Inc.

™ DACS is a trademark of DDC International A/S and DDC-I, Inc.

™ VAX is a trademark of Digital Corporation.

™ UNIX is a trademark of AT&T Laboratories.

™ Mips is a trademark of MIPS Computer Systems, Inc.

$^R$ Sun3, SunOS is a registered trademark of Sun Microsystems, Inc.

$^R$ Intel is a registered trademark of Intel Corporation.

## 3.4   Encore

Encore Computer
Marlborough House
Mole Business Park
Leatherhead
Surrey
KT22 7BA
UK

Contact:
Vincent Rich
Tel. +44 372 363363
Fax. +44 372 362926

Encore Computer is the dominant supplier of high performance real-time Ada systems. Encore products include super-minicomputers, operating systems and a comprehensive Ada tool set.

Encore offers two complementary families of real-time computers; the Concept/2000 family of proprietary architecture computers and the Series 91 family of RISC based open systems. The Series 91 computers provide symmetrical multiprocessing with an aggregate performance of up to 100 MIPS through the use of four Motorola 88000 RISC CPUs, each of which can access all 272 MB of memory and all of the peripheral devices.

During the software development phase, each processor executes a single copy of Unix. This implementation, which is based on AT&T System V, is multi-threaded in order to maximize throughput by allowing each processor to concurrently execute the Unix Kernel.

Multiple copies of software tools can be executed with true concurrency. For example, multiple Ada compilers can compile different packages comprising a single Ada program with an aggregate compilation rate in excess of 7000 lines per minute. A parallel Ada "make" tool allows the compilers to operate in the most efficient manner while still observing the compilation order rules of the Ada language. Program debugging can be performed with either a contemporary Ada source level debugger or alternatively "Parasight", a windowing non-intrusive real-time monitor.

Although Unix provides a superb software development environment, it is unable to offer the absolute predictability of performance required for many real-time applications. The Encore solution to this problem is to dynamically partition the computer so that at any moment some processors are executing a real-time kernel and the remaining processors are executing Unix. This concept of multiple execution domains within the same computer allows very high performance real-time operations to be combined with the utility and open systems capabilities of the Unix operating system. Software executing in different domains can communicate via shared memory and peripheral devices such as discs.

Ada programs are developed on a processor running Unix and then linked for execution on either a Unix or real-time processor. The Ada runtime supports the ability to allow multiple processors to execute a single Ada program using the Ada task as the unit of concurrency. The Ada runtime is internally multi-threaded so that multiple Ada tasks can concurrently execute code sections within the runtime.

For real-time execution, the Ada runtime interfaces directly with the processors and peripheral devices in order to achieve the best possible performance. Incoming interrupts are vectored directly into the Ada runtime and peripheral device commands are passed directly from the Ada runtime to the device controller thereby avoiding the latency and non-determinism of the Unix Kernel.

Encore Computers and Ada related products are used in simulation, energy management, C3I systems and research applications worldwide. For further information, demonstrations and benchmarking, please contact Encore Computer in Leatherhead.

## 3.5   SD-Scicon

SD-Scicon UK Ltd
Pembroke House
Pembroke Broadway
Camberley
Surrey
GU15 3XD
UK

Contact:
Ian Pascoe
Tel. +44 276 686200
Fax. +44 276 683511

SD-Scicon is the largest independent software and systems integration company in the United Kingdom and amongst the top ten in Europe. It has over 55 offices in seven countries, employs over 4000 people worldwide, and provides a wide range of products and services into commercial, industrial, and government markets.

The four core businesses of SD-Scicon, formed by the merger in 1988 of Systems Designers plc and Scicon Ltd., are software products, facilities management, systems integration and consultancy. Operations in the UK are carried out through SD-Scicon UK Ltd. and products and services are offered in the energy, industry, commercial, government and defence communications markets.

SD-Scicon's Software Technology Centre in Camberley, Surrey, specialises in the Ada language and has a large team concentrating on Ada software development. There is particular expertise in providing development tools for embedded microprocessor applications.

SD-Scicon's overall capability in Ada technology covers a wide range of services which complement its Ada products, and this includes customisation, new targets, Run-Time System modification, emulator, simulator and multi-processor support, together with training and consultancy in methods, metrics and software management for the adoption of Ada.

Together with Digital Equipment Corporation, SD-Scicon has developed the world's leading cross-development toolset, XD Ada, which is in use on major projects in both Europe and the USA. Among these, XD Ada has been chosen as the standard Ada development cross-compiler by the four-nation Eurofighter and Eurojet consortia.

Through the close relationship with Digital, XD Ada is fully integrated with Digital's VMS operating system, VAX Ada and the Digital VAXset Case tools, which provides a unique interactive development environment. With excellent code quality through the use of powerful global optimisation techniques, XD Ada more than meets embedded systems requirements. Independently-measured performance figures show XD Ada well ahead of its competitors.

XD Ada is targeted to the Motorola M68000 family and MIL-STD-1750A microprocessors. The XD Ada Run-Time System, which provides bare target support for Ada programs, is supplied in source and object form, pre-configured for a standard target but designed to be reconfigured by the user for specific hardware. The XD Ada debugger is a re-targeted version of the VMS debugger, specially developed by Digital.

Backing SD-Scicon's Ada production and development activity is an equally highly-qualified customer support operation, with an on-line support service. Support packages are tailored to meet a customer's needs, and can include areas such as training, installation, target re-configuration and project validation.

## 3.6   VSEL

**COMBAT SYSTEMS**

VSEL
Combat Systems Division
Barrow-in-Furness
Cumbria
LA14 1AF
UK

Contact:
Peter Fitzpatrick
Tel. +44 229 873993
Fax. +44 229 873846

### Quality Software Systems

The Software Department within Combat Systems Division is committed to the delivery of high quality software systems to our customers — on time, and to budget.

Since 1984, we have been successful in winning and delivering a number of major software development contracts, ranging from real-time simulations of a submarine and its environment to the production of a Computer Aided System Engineering tool to support the specification and design of large, complex systems incorporating both people and computer based subsystems.

The 'backbone' of our success has been the commitment to:

- a Software Quality System compliant with AQAP-13 and BS 5750,

- the use of Structured Analysis and Design methods,

- the use of the Ada language,

- experience of the successful management of software contracts.

# Quality

Our software engineers are committed to incorporating quality into all our delivered software. Software Quality is a fundamental part of the software development methods used for all our projects, and, as is so often the case, is *not* added as an after-thought.

We believe that a commitment to Software Quality enables us to:

- deliver software which meets our customer's requirements,

- increase our productivity and reduce costs,

- substantially reduce our customer's maintenance costs,

- meet our customer's time-scales.

VSEL is approved to NATO standard AQAP-1 and AQAP-13, and our Software Quality System is subject to regular audit by the Directorate General of Defence Quality Assurance (DGDQA).

## Structured Analysis and Design

Combat Systems Division is committed to the use of structured Analysis and Design methods for all software development. We have a significant depth of expertise — more than 70 man years — in the use of the Yourdon (Ward/Mellor) Structured Method, and we have developed proven and efficient techniques for the development of large Ada systems from Structured Design.

The use of Structured Methods is closely integrated with our commitment to Quality, with reviews (some including the customer) being conducted at five defined points within the Analysis and Design lifecycle.

## The Ada Language

VSEL are acknowledged leaders in the field of Software Engineering with Ada, and in 1984 — only one year after the formal standardisation of the language — were awarded the first Ada contract to be placed by the Royal Navy. This software system is required for the testing and performance assessment of a large submarine system, and provides a real-time simulation of the submarine, other vessels in the ocean, and the ocean environment.

Since 1984, we have been awarded major Ada contracts, and have produced more than 1,000,000 lines of Ada software. Our use of the Ada language extends to all of the major Ada compiler technologies on host and target systems including VAX, Sun, 80x86, 680x0, and RISC technology.

## Software Management

Our commitment to Software Quality, Structured Analysis and Design methods, and the Ada language is reflected in the mechanisms used to manage software development within the department.

Our project management techniques have been closely integrated with the methods used to develop the software, with agreed milestones and deliverables being monitored closely for time-scale and risk. This monitoring provides key metrics which are used to develop and refine our methods and procedures for future projects. We pride ourselves on delivering software on time which fully meets our customer's requirements.

# 4

# Letters from Ada organisations

## 4.1 From Ada UK

Dear Reader

It is a great pleasure to write this open letter regarding the status and plans of Ada UK for 1991. Ada UK has now been in existence for over ten years and before summarizing our plans for the future it is perhaps worth putting in context where we are now. Our first ten years of activity can be subdivided into two five-year phases.

The first five years from 1980–84 was concerned very much with spreading the message among the original enthusiasts and helping them to communicate with each other in the final years of language definition and the early years of compiler writing and interpretation of the standard. Our main activities were the publication of Ada UK News and the technical conference in York.

The five years from 1985–89 were more concerned with informing and encouraging the first users. Our activities were thus aimed at a larger community. The annual prizes for students started in 1985. Ada UK News became Ada User in 1986. The realtime workshops (in cooperation with SIGAda) started in 1987 and the London based Exhibitions started in 1988.

Ada is now firmly established among its early user base and there are literally hundreds of validated compilers. So where now? A number of considerations lie in front of us. One is recognition of the fact that Ada is really a general purpose language, and although its origins lie in the needs of the embedded system sector in the USDoD, nevertheless its applicability is much wider. Indeed the USDoD has recognized this and is using Ada in much broader areas such as Management Information Systems. Another consideration is that Ada is all about Software Engineering and the value of good discipline in the development and maintenance of large programs. Object-oriented this and that has become popular and Ada is challenged by C++ — although one should note that the designer of C++ is reported to have said recently that its major benefit over C is simply encapsulation (i.e. packages which Ada has had for ten years) and the benefits of the fashionable polymorphism and inheritance are relatively minor. Be that as it may, we are being challenged, and we all have a responsibility to spread to others the benefits of Ada and to meet the challenge in a positive manner. Then there is Ada 9X, the revised version of Ada due probably in 1993 as a natural evolution in accord with the normal standardization practices of ANSI and ISO. Ada 9X should be seen as an opportunity to make Ada of broader and easier applicability and not as a feared disturbance.

We conclude that our goal in the next five years must be to help in widening the application base of Ada. We must stop preaching to the converted, and instead, take our message to a wider audience by all the means at our disposal. A broader user base will bring tremendous benefits to existing users by establishing a larger market with the corresponding economies of scale and increasing the availability of open tools and secondary standards. And indeed while extending our horizons to new areas we will continue to provide opportunities for the converted to communicate with each other.

This Ada Yearbook is a new venture of Ada UK, and we are very pleased to welcome Chapman and Hall as our publishers. The goal of the Yearbook is to provide a comprehensive central reference volume which will provide the information needed to help both existing, and more importantly, new users find their way in the world of Ada.

Chapman and Hall are now also our publishers of Ada User which has a new and revitalized style and a boarder editorial board; Ada User thus now becomes a publication which is generally available and is no longer essentially restricted to just members of Ada UK. The goal is again aimed at increasing the visibility of Ada outside the existing community. For example, there are opportunities for Ada in the restructured Europe, and we hope that Ada User will be a useful vehicle for those seeking to grasp such opportunities.

Our annual autumn conference has been restructured to include tutorials and management presentations as well as the established technical discussions. Held in Brighton in 1990 in a professional venue, we anticipate holding it in a variety of locations in the UK in future, thus bringing the message to a wider audience.

In order to assist in propagating our message, we are using the services of a professional Public Relations company, Bogard Communications. We are particularly grateful to them for increasing our liaison with the press. One direct consequence is that Ada UK now has a regular slot in Computers in

Defence which we use to communicate with the existing base of users which we must not neglect in our broader goals.

Increasing activity incurs increasing cost, and it is vital that we have a suitable income. We are thus exceedingly grateful to those organizations who have agreed to become our Sponsors. You will find them listed in all our publications, and they each have a statement regarding their activities elsewhere in this book.

We have also taken the opportunity of the stability offered by regular sponsorship to restructure our classes of membership. The old corporate membership is now replaced by a simple bulk membership discount. This has reduced our administration costs and simplified our relationship with Ada-Europe of which we are proud to be an Associate Member. All qualifying members of Ada UK are now members of Ada-Europe and thus receive the benefits of such membership.

We also recently established a mechanism for the support of Task Groups. The most active of these is concerned with Ada 9X with the goal of acting as a focus for communication between the Ada 9X project and the Ada users in the UK. The Ada 9X task group has sponsored a number of working meetings, including last year's workshop at ICL Beaumont. The Ada UK Board is keen to support other task groups with a well defined objective especially if they are aligned with the general goal of helping Ada into new areas.

I must also mention the work of the International Realtime Workshops. Initiated by Ada UK in 1987, these have been held annually in cooperation with ACM SIGAda. The first two were in Moretonhamstead, Devon, the third was in Farmingham in Pennsylvania, and the last was in Pitlochry, Perthshire. The objective of these workshops has been to get together a group of world class experts on the use of Ada in hard realtime systems in order to establish ways of improving the applicability of Ada. The last workshop focused sharply on requirements for Ada 9X. A fifth workshop is planned for 1991 in the US. Suggestions for new workshops on other topics and their organization will be gratefully received.

In order to facilitate our expanding activities we have established a number of distinct working committees to look after each area. A list of these will be found elsewhere in this book. We are always looking for help and suggestions for new initiatives. If you can think of a way of helping then please do not hesitate to contact a member of the Ada UK Board.

I do hope that you, the reader, find this first Ada Yearbook of value; it is our intent that it be a regular annual publication.

With regards
John Barnes
Chairman, Ada UK

## 4.2　From Ada in Denmark

Ada in Denmark (AiD) is the Danish national Ada organization affiliated to Ada-Europe.

AiD has eight individual members who are professionally associated with application of Ada technology, Ada education and consultancy, and with Ada compiler technology.

AiD has acted as a distribution point for information from Ada-Europe to the Danish members. There are no formal working groups within AiD, but the members have individually pursued an interest in maintaining the existing Ada standard as well as in the development of Ada 9X.

The obvious goal for AiD is to get more members — not just those who take an interest in Ada as a programming language from a technical point of view — but also those for whom the choice of Ada is an important strategic milestone.

Jergen Bundgaard
Chairman
Ada in Denmark

## 4.3　From Ada Greece

At the time of writing (October 1990) Ada Greece is in the process of being formally constituted under Hellenic Law. Individuals are working actively for the organisation and for the success of the Ada-Europe Conference, to be held in Athens, 13 – 17 May 1991. The theme of the Conference is "Ada: The Choice for '92".

Sotiris G. Samaras
Treasurer
Ada Greece

## 4.4   From Ada-France

Ada-France is the French group of Ada users. It operates as a working group of AFCET, the French Computer Society, and features about 125 members. It is a member of Ada-Europe.

Ada-France organises a yearly conference in December. The next conference will be in Toulouse, 5 – 6 December 1990.

Ada-France organises monthly meetings where Ada users can exchange experience on different topics. Recent meetings addressed visibility, management of software components, and optimisation issues for example.

A group of interested participants is active in the field of the 9X revision process and provides input to the 9X project.

A book about good Ada usage is in progress and should be issued next year.

Contact points:

AFCET
156 bd. Pereire
75017 PARIS
FRANCE
Tel: +33 1 47 66 24 19
Fax: +33 1 42 67 93 12

Chairman:
J-P. Rosen
ADALOG
115 av. du Maine
75014 PARIS
FRANCE
Tel: +33 1 43 22 44 50
Fax: +33 1 43 21 72 21

Best wishes
Jean-Pierre Rosen

## 4.5   From Ada-Ireland

Ada-Ireland is, as you know, a small organisation. However, we are pleased to look back on our successful hosting of the Ada-Europe '90 Conference in Dublin, and also, that we can report a positive response from delegates.

As a result of this events, the profile of Ada-Ireland has been raised both nationally and internationally. We now look forward to a new boost in our membership, and also to a new industrial interest in the language. In order to maintain this momentum, we plan to host a seminar on Ada in the coming months for members of the Irish Software Industry.

Ada-Ireland is, of course, fully committed to all Ada-Europe activities and in particular to the recently formed Ada Business Initiative. You are probably aware that our Chairman, Hans-Jurgen Kugler was re-elected to his position of Secretary of the Ada-Europe Board. Also our own secretary, Barry Lynch, has been invited to join the PC for next year's Conference in Athens. We look forward to passing on our newly gained experience to Ada-Greece and wish them every success for 1991.

Ada-Ireland is sorry to be loosing an active member, Avril Tobin, to the Centre for Advanced Software Design, Edinburgh. However, we look forward to maintaining a close working relationship with her as she intends to continue her role within the Ada-Europe Secretariat when she takes up her new position in early October.

Finally, the Ada-Ireland Newsletter is a quarterly publication, and anyone wishing to obtain a copy should contact Barry Lynch, Secretary Ada-Ireland, c/o Generics Software Ltd., Clonard House, Sandyford Road, Dublin 16. Hans-Jurgen Kugler (Generics Software Ltd.,) is our current Chairman and the position of Treasurer is held by Dudley Dolan (Beecom).

Kind regards
Barry Lynch
Secretary, Ada-Ireland

## 4.6 From Ada i Norge

Ada in Norway was founded on 16 February 1988, and the purpose of the association is:

- To collect and distribute information about Ada technology and its development.

- To establish contact with international, and other national, Ada bodies.

- To actively promote the use of Ada in Norway.

In order to fulfil our goals, Ada in Norway publishes a newsletter three to four times a year, and hosts Ada technical seminars twice a year.

As of 1 January 1990 the association numbered 88 personal members, 8 corporate members, and 3 supporting members.

Points of contact for Ada in Norway are:

Chairman: Anton B. Leere
Norwegian Defence Research Establishment
P.O. Box 25
N-2007 Kjeller
NORWAY
Tel: +47 6 807394
Fax: +47 6 807212
E-mail: leere%dione.ndre.uninett@nac.no

Secretary: Fridtjov Backer
Ada in Norway
FTD,
Oslo mil/Akershus
N-0015 Oslo 1
NORWAY

For the coming year we will as usual host two seminars, one in April and one in the October/November time frame. At the seminar in April, we will try to get some of the people that spoke at the Ada-Europe '90 Conference in Dublin.

Our main area of work in the coming year, will be to plan and prepare for the Ada-Europe Conference in 1993 or 1994. There has already been some contact with Ada-Europe on the matter, but no formal proposals have been filed yet.

The board of Ada in Norway feels that by hosting an Ada-Europe Conference in Norway, we will be able to get much more publicity than by our two ordinary seminars.

Another important issue will be to establish liaison with other professional computer organizations in Norway, in particular the Norwegian Data Society. This association has a large number of members, and by exposing Ada in Norway through their newsletter, we will reach a lot of computer professionals, with whom we otherwise would have difficulties contacting.

Ada in Norway will also work actively together with the academic community, in order to promote Ada in education. This is brought about by giving presentations at educational institutions, and sponsoring students to attend our seminars.

Yours
Anton B. Leere

## 4.7 From Ada-Spain

**Ada-Spain** was founded in Madrid in July 1987 by 120 people from about 30 different industrial and academic organizations throughout Spain. Founding president was Angel Alvarez from the Technical University of Madrid.

From the start **Ada-Spain** wanted to fulfil the need for an easily identifiable contact point within Spain for the international Ada community. As evidence of their desire to actively contribute to the promotion of Ada in the international sense, **Ada-Spain** hosted the 1989 Ada-Europe Conference. Around 480 participants gathered in Madrid for this event, making it the largest attended Ada-Europe Conference ever.

Currently **Ada-Spain** has 14 institutional members and some 500 individual members. A good proportion of these individual members are computer professionals who do not work in the Ada technology but would desire to do so. **Ada-Spain** aims to promote Ada related industrial and research efforts within Spain as a means to enlarge the size of the national Ada market.

The Association publishes a quarterly newsletter, **SpAda** which is distributed freely to its members, and holds an annual "massive" seminar around springtime where several prominent members from the local Ada community take turns in teaching the different parts of the language to beginners — between one and two hundred of them each year. Furthermore, other more advanced seminars are organized on a regular basis to host both international and national experts of the Ada technology. A small library of Ada related documents is also maintained for the benefit of its members.

To help spread the use and education of Ada among the Spanish academic centers, **Ada-Spain** awards an annual prize to the best academic project on Ada technology.

For any additional information regarding Ada-Spain, please contact its Secretary:

Jorge Serrano
Ada-Spain
P.O. Box 50.403
E-28080 Madrid,
SPAIN
Fax: +34-1-450 5159
E-mail: jorge@teice.es

Best regards,
Angel Alvarez

## 4.8    From Ada-Europe

Ada-Europe is an international association whose primary purpose is the promotion of the use, research, education, and knowledge of Ada, as well as the representation of the professional community in Europe in all matters relating to Ada.

Ada-Europe, in its present form, was established at the end of 1988, and is mainly formed by associate members, i.e., associations, institutions or other organizations established in Europe. Individuals who are members of these associations may become indirect members of Ada-Europe and take part in its activities. Ada-Europe has currently 11 associate members, accounting for about 1000 indirect members. The associate members are Ada in Denmark, Ada Deutschland, Ada-France, Ada Greece, Ada-Ireland, Ada Nederland, Ada i Norge, Ada Scotland, Ada-Spain, Ada in Sweden and Ada UK. Ada Switzerland is expected to join soon.

Ada-Europe has inherited some of the activities and resources of the 'old' Ada-Europe, an organization with individual membership as well as a part of the CEC Multi Annual Programme (MAP) in the Field of Data Processing, which was operative from 1979 to 1988. Perhaps the most widely known of these activities is the annual Ada-Europe Conference. This is the main wide spectrum event on Ada in Europe, and is attended every year by more than 200 participants. Other activities are usually organized during the Conference week, including an exhibition of industrial products related to Ada as well as seminars and workshops. The 1990 Conference was held in Dublin, and the 1991 Conference will be hosted by Ada Greece in Athens.

Other activities are organized through working groups or directly by the Ada-Europe Board. The workplan for 1991 includes the following activities:

**Information Dissemination** In the past the CEC has played an important role by making relevant information available to the European Ada community. Ada-Europe will take over this role so that it can be the clearinghouse for information on Ada in Europe.

**Ada 9X Working Group** It is vital that European industry is well represented during the revision process and that expert opinions are sought. The Ada 9X Working Group has given support to such activities in the past, by endorsing revision requests, promoting participation of individual members as distinguished reviewers and other roles in the Ada 9X process and organizing meetings and workshops.

**Numerics Working Group** This group has actively contributed to the development of standards and to the language revision process in the field of numeric types and computations. The topics being covered include elementary functions, floating-point manipulation primitives, real and complex types and operations, vector and matrix operations and basic linear algebra subprograms.

**Environments Working Group** The group organizes an annual workshop during the Ada-Europe Conference week, as well as other meetings. The topics covered include PCTE/CAIS, POSIX and SQL bindings, the impact of Ada 9X on environments and NSIS (the NATO Standard Interface Set).

**Reuse and Formal Methods** A Working Group has been recently set up, aiming to organize a workshop in 1992 to bring together the exponents of reuse and formal methods.

**Ada-Europe News** Ada-Europe News is a quarterly newsletter containing information about Ada-Europe activities, standardization activities, workshops, conferences and courses, new books and products and other topics of interest to the European Ada community. It is distributed to the individual members through their respective associations.

**Ada-Europe Secretariat** The Ada-Europe Secretariat provides a single contact point to all European Ada users as well as the information dissemination service. The Secretariat is currently located at the following address:

Ada-Europe Secretariat
Room 147
Centre for Advanced Software Design
219 Colinton Road
Edinburgh EH14 1DJ
Scotland.
Telephone: +44(31)444-2266

Best regards,
Juan de la Puente

## 4.9    Ada in the European Space Agency

The European Space Agency (ESA) does not in general produce software. The Agency's software is produced for a wide number of purposes ranging from highly safety critical on-board software to administrative support software by many different contractors sited throughout Europe. ESA is a reasonably large procurer of software but conversely software procurement is a relatively minor activity for the Agency when compared with the procurement of space qualified hardware and the control and monitoring of the integration activities for satellites. The procurement of software is not centralised. Each ESA directorate sorts out its own procurement with guidelines from general ESA standards and recommendations produced by the Technical Directorate and the internal ESA body responsible for software standards (The Board for Software Standardisation and Control — BSSC). This has resulted in a large variety of computers, languages and support facilities being promoted by ESA.

Since the early 1980s the ESA Technical Directorate has taken an interest in Ada. Initially this interest was confined to maintaining an awareness of developments but soon it was decided to fund studies and evaluations aimed at the use of Ada to produce Space Software. In 1987 work on two large projects, Columbus and Hermes, was started in ESA. These projects were controlled by The Space Station and Platform Directorate and The Space Transportation Directorate respectively. They both required large quantities of software and they both accepted a BSSC recommendation that the Columbus and Hermes projects should *"use Ada for all software with the exception of real-time software with critical time requirements"*. This acceptance resulted in further evaluations and studies now orientated towards specific project requirements with a view of establishing project Ada strategies.

It was appreciated by the Technical Directorate at this time that use of Ada might require different design methodologies and a contract was placed to investigate current methods and propose a design method suitable for the Agency to use with Ada. This resulted in a definition of HOOD which has aroused a lot of interest both inside and outside the space software community.

In 1988 the Columbus project revised their software requirement to *"software shall be written in Ada"* and work continued on project Ada Strategies. Ada coding standards were established, Ada compilers were evaluated, Ada training requirements were considered and Ada support tools for the project SDE's were investigated.

In 1989 a decision was made by the ISO project in the Scientific Directorate of ESA to use Ada to program its small on-board computer. This proceeded much faster than the larger space projects and currently the software produced is being tested within its sub system. It is real-time embedded software with tight memory constraints and despite its size three companies were involved in its production. So far it would appear that Ada can be used successfully for such systems although it may be necessary to ban the use of some Ada constructs (tasking), and write a special operating system to meet the constraints of on-board space software. These constraints were compensated for by the short time required for integration, the readability of the code and the speed with which software system testing was accomplished.

By 1990 it had been generally appreciated that good, effective, general solutions for using Ada were not easy to find and that if Ada was to be used efficiently not only would appropriate tools have to be supplied but education and training for software engineers was required to a far greater extent than initially anticipated. Ada was not just another language. It was a new way of thinking software and ESA would have to provide motivation to its contractors for this re-thinking. There was also a growing feeling that generic solutions to the production of project space software using Ada were too impractical and that specific solutions for specific processors and specific requirements as was done for ISO would be required to ensure the most satisfactory results.

1991 will be a decisive year for Ada in the large projects. If the "right" choices are made for computers, compiler systems, run-times and support tools, if programmers are properly trained and motivated and if the first pieces of software written in Ada are produced with few perceived problems then Ada will receive a boost and will become more securely established. The results from ISO are encouraging for small embedded real-time software. The ESA personnel monitoring and controlling the software have therefore to ensure that the unresolved decisions in the area of Ada strategy are made and that Ada is given every chance to succeed.

Current unresolved and difficult issues are choice of target and host compilers, how many different compilers do we require or can we afford, should a "safe" subset of Ada be used, and how much training support should be provided after an initial training course? All these decisions cost money which is difficult to substantiate to project managers with the vague promise of better quality software, easier maintenance and, very important to ESA, easier monitoring of the software production. The long term solution to these promises is to demonstrate "better results" by collecting metrics. This is an area in which ESA has so far been not very active and in which it is hoped an improvement can be made in 1991.

To summarise it is hoped that in 1991 practical feedback will demonstrate that Ada is a suitable language for all types of space software. Areas where technical problems may occur are: portability of Ada from host to target, reliability of Ada compilers, and performance of Ada run-times. Non-technical areas where problems may occur are: training and motivation of programmers, and cost of establishing an Ada infrastructure. As ESA is aware of these potential obstacles it is hoped that with intelligent monitoring and control of the software production and with encouraging support and decisive on-line decisions the Agency's efforts at producing software using Ada in 1991 will be shown to be successful.

Yours sincerely,
Colin Rolls

# 4.10   Ada in NATO — status and perspective

## Background

NATO has had a policy of standardisation on Ada since January 1986 for all new software developments in communications, command and control systems. The first NATO Ada systems became operational in 1990/91, and several major projects are in advanced stages of development.

## Status

In recognising the importance of a language standard, particularly in the area of containing escalating software maintenance costs, NATO has additionally acknowledged that — in the broader field of software engineering — there are several associated issues which promise further economies in both cost and resources. Amongst the most important of these are considered to be the exploitation of reusable components, employment of suitable design methods and associated tools, and — for the longer term — the adoption of an internationally agreed software environment interface standard. Hence several initiatives, both internal to the Alliance and with broad international collaboration, are being actively pursued in these areas.

## Principal activities

**Software Reuse** Through the multi-national Ada Implementation Group, a programme is underway to determine the potential application of reusable software to the NATO environment. This includes the adoption of appropriate policies and procedures — in management, technical control and economics — to best exploit the Ada language and design processes.

**Adoption of Standards** Wherever possible, it is the intention of NATO to adopt and implement appropriate internationally agreed standards for software systems. If no formally agreed standard exists in a specific area, current trends and *de facto* standards are being closely examined. Operating systems, user interfaces and DBMS interfaces are examples of this situation.

**PCIS Programme** NATO is closely involved in the portable Common Interface Standard (PCIS) programme, primarily through the 10 nation collaborative Special Working Group (SWG) on APSE which is the designated body to undertake the initial (Definition) phase of the programme. PCIS is viewed as the upwardly compatible (and common) successor to PCTE+ and CAIS-A technologies.

## Perspective

The Ada world is now well established internationally. Much of the future related software engineering development must provide a strengthened infrastructure; integrated tool support, reuse philosophy, interfacing with proprietary components (COTS), assistance for evolutionary/incremental project profiles.

G. Giannino
Chief ADASCC

# 4.11   From ECMA

ECMA is the Association of European Manufacturers. It was formed in 1960 with the following purposes:

- To study and develop, in cooperation with the appropriate national and international organisations, as a scientific endeavour and in the general interest, methods and procedures in order to facilitate and standardise the use of data processing systems.

- To promulgate various standards applicable to the functional design and use of data processing systems.

- The Association shall be a non-profit-making organisation and shall devote itself to no commercial activity whatsoever.

Many of the companies that are members of ECMA are owned by non-European companies. So companies such as DEC, IBM, Hewlett-Packard, Fujitsu and NEC are represented by their European subsidiaries.

The standards development work of ECMA is carried out by a series of Technical Committees with each TC forming Task Groups as necessary. TC27 was responsible for Ada in ECMA but, having completed its task was wound up. But a current active committee TC33 is of relevance to the Ada community.

TC33 was set up to standardise PCTE — The Portable Common Tool Environment — in 1988 under an agreement between CEC DG XIII and ECMA. PCTE was a specification developed under the CEC Esprit program. It was thought that this work would be of general value and should therefore be put into the standardisation process. ECMA was chosen as a natural home for this work as most of the companies involved in the original project were members.

The formal Scope and Programme of work of TC33 as of October 1990 is as follow:

## Title: Portable Common Tool Environment (PCTE)

**Scope:** To standardise a common tool interface, implementable on a wide range of operating environments, to ensure a suitable foundation for portable, interoperable tools and tool sets for computer-assisted systems engineering.

**Programme of Work**

1. To develop an interface standard ECMA PCTE, starting from PCTE+ Issue 3, while taking into account the requirements and specification efforts already underway as noted in item 7 below.

2. To define a Reference Model for computer-assisted systems engineering environment that will support the incremental definition and evolution of interface standards.

3. To position ECMA PCTE within that Reference Model.

4. To identify and position complementary standards and standards activities relevant to the Reference Model, and to maintain liaison with those standards organisations responsible for their maintenance.

5. To present the standard as an abstract specification with separate language bindings.

6. To maintain liaison with TC22 and with TC32-TG2.

7. To maintain liaison with the PCTE Interface Management Board (PIMB), with DGXIII of the Commission of the European Communities, with the PCTE+ programme of Technical Area 13 (TA13) of the Independent European Programme Group (IEPG), and with the German PCTE Initiative.

8. To maintain liaison with other standards organisations in order to present ECMA proposals to them and to make comments on their proposals.

The chairman of TC33 is M.W. Morron representing ICL and the vice-chairman is R. Crispin of Hewlett-Packard. There are two working Task Groups, TGRM which is the task group on the Reference Model, which is convened by R. Crispin, and TGEP which is the Task Group producing the ECMA PCTE standard. TGEP is convened by S.J. Dawes of ICL.

The current status of the work is as follows:

**ECMA PCTE Standard Status**

The output of ECMA TC33 is in the form of four documents. An ECMA Technical Report on the Reference Model for Environments, the ECMA PCTE Functional Specification Standard, the C Language Bindings Standard and the Ada Bindings Standard.

At the ECMA TC33 meeting held on 6 and 7 September 1990, after a formal vote, it was agreed unanimously that the ECMA Reference Model be endorsed by ECMA in December. It was also agreed that the ECMA PCTE Abstract Specification current draft be distributed to the ECMA membership for review, with the final draft to be distributed after a special TC33 meeting and vote to be held on 7 November 1990. The formal ECMA vote would be at the General Assembly to be held on 13 and 14 December 1990. It is planned that complete final drafts of both the C and Ada bindings be available shortly thereafter to be endorsed at the following General Assembly meeting in June 1991.

For up to date information on ECMA and the work of TC33 please contact:

The Secretary General
ECMA
114 Rue du Rhone
CH-1204 Geneva
Switzerland
Phone: +41 22 735 3634
Fax: +41 22 786 5231

Yours sincerely,
Myer Morron

# 4.12   From the Independent European Programme Group

## Technical Area 13, PCTE+ evolution

### Objectives for 1991

I have been asked to write a short letter describing the objectives for 1991 of the IEPG TA-13 PCTE+ evolution programme. It might be as well to first explain the programme.

In 1987 the eight nations who participate in the IEPG TA-13 programme sponsored a project to produce a definition of a Portable Tool Interface based upon the then existing PCTE. The new specification they named PCTE+. The primary objective of the nations then, and now, is to evolve to a specification that is acceptable for use in both military and civil applications.

A major supporting initiative is to produce the specification only after making a sequence of "open and credible" assessments based upon experience in the use of PCTE+. The nations are obtaining this experience by implementing PCTE+ on two distributed host architectures, by providing tools to work with PCTE+, by porting tools between host environments, by using PCTE+ based project support environments and by obtaining evaluations of performance and availability characteristics.

As I write, the PCTE+ specifications exist in the form of Ada and C language bindings. A Unix* (Sun) PCTE+ implementation from Belgium and France is due to be available for TA-13 use in December 1990. The design for a VMS PCTE+ environment has been completed by Spain and the UK, with software delivery to TA-13 expected in the second half of 1991. Tool design work is well underway in Turkey and the Netherlands; similar work will start shortly in Belgium, France, Italy and the UK. PCTE+ assessments have been gathered and considered; as a result there have been a few minor changes to the specification. The programme has been progressing satisfactorily.

### What of 1991?

The work described above will obviously continue and, with deliveries of PCTE+ systems, assessments will take on a more practical flavour. Tools will be provided that will cover the life-cycle spectrum from requirements capture to test and integration. About fifteen contributors from the eight nations will be associated with the programme. They will offer system

---

*Unix is a registered trademark of AT&T Laboratories.

development tools supporting SADT, JSD, HOOD, MASCOT, Ada and C, management tools to support project and configuration control and meta tools for aiding tool construction. All the nations will continue to provide PCTE+ assessments; Germany will concentrate on the areas of security and integrity.

The ambitions for 1991 are not spectacular. That year should see a steady progress of the programme towards a completion which is not due until 1992.

The IEPG TA-13 Group have not worked in isolation from similar initiatives or related bodies. Good links have been established with the US DoD (AJPO), the NATO SWG on APSE, the EC and the PCTE Interface Management Board. These links will continue. Of particular importance is the good relationship which exists between IEPG TA-13 and ECMA TC33 — who have been producing a specification for an ECMA PCTE standard based upon PCTE+. TA-13 have worked closely with TC33 and will continue to foster this relationship to ensure that ECMA PCTE will meet civil and military requirements.

PCTE+ assessment results and conclusions will be released internationally to the software engineering community as they become available. All TA-13 specifications and assessments are in the public domain.

I would like to conclude this letter by responding to a question that is often asked.

IEPG TA-13 do not themselves have plans to commercially exploit their work. However, TA-13 encourages all contractors to design and engineer their individual components to a standard that will form the basis for future marketable and maintainable items.

Thank you for the opportunity to publicize IEPG TA-13 activities. I hope that this very brief summary will whet the appetites of your readers for more information on the programme.

Ken Hayter
RSRE, Malvern

## 4.13   From the AJPO

The Ada Joint Program Office (AJPO) is responsible for managing the effort of the United States Department of Defense (DoD) to implement, introduce, and provide lifecycle support for Ada, its common high-order programming language.

In 1991, one of the most important items on the AJPO's agenda will continue to be the Ada 9X Project, which is charged with revising Ada for the 1990s. The project is proceeding on schedule and within budget. Before the end of this year, we will see the Requirements Document*, containing language capabilities that should be present in the revision. During 1991, these requirements will be mapped into language solutions and changes in the Language Reference Manual. Parallel to this effort, language changes that are being seriously considered will be implemented and demonstrated. It is going to be a busy year for the Ada 9X Project.

During 1991, I expect that international cooperation in Ada will focus on two areas: the programming support environment, and performance test packages.

In 1989 and 1990, the AJPO held a number of meetings with the Independent European Programme Group Technical Area 13 on the possible convergence of the two major tool-interface standards: in the United States, Common Ada Programming Support Environment (APSE) Interface Set, revision A (CAIS-A); and in Europe, the Portable Common Tools Environment+ (PCTE+). The result has been an agreement to work towards convergence in the form of a Portable Common Interface Set (PCIS).

It is anticipated that a specification for a new standard will be available in mid-1994. The PCIS Programme recently began the steps for selection of the PCIS Experts Team, and a workshop involving military and commercial communities is planned for April 1991, to identify the PCIS requirements baseline.

Another point of international interest is the possible merger of the two major packages for evaluating the performance of Ada compilers — the U.K. Ministry of Defence's Ada Evaluation System (AES), and the DoD's Ada Compiler Evaluation Capability (ACEC).

This is still in a very preliminary stage. One major concern to be addressed will be whether a converged package could be made available to the entire Ada community. (The ACEC is under certain limited export controls, and the AES has licensing restrictions.)

Alongside international efforts and the Ada 9X Project, the day-to-day activities of the AJPO are also important. Two of these are the validation

---

*Reproduced elsewhere in this Yearbook (ed.).

effort, and the Ada Information Clearinghouse. In the field of validation, one item to be considered is whether to "freeze" the next version of the validation test suite, the Ada Compiler Validation Capability (ACVC). The current version (1.11) expires in June 1991; and version 1.12 would expire in December 1992. Given Ada's continuing maturity, we have to investigate whether the continuing replacements are really necessary.

Using the number of validated compilers as an index of Ada's growth, things seem to bode well for 1991. In September, there were validated compilers for a total of 470 implementations — 296 base compilers (validated by witnessed testing) and 174 derived compilers (validated by registration). This was up from 292 (209 and 83) in December 1989.

The Ada Information Clearinghouse will continue to be a major source of information for the Ada community, and we welcome any comments or suggestions for change.

One particular question that affects many users is compiler support for pragmas. Some language-defined pragmas may be unsupported by a given compiler, the same language-defined pragma may be supported differently by different compilers, each compiler may provide unique implementation-defined pragmas. This has an impact on predictability for the programmer and portability for the program.

Therefore, the AJPO has tasked a survey of vendors of validated Ada compilers; we hope to determine the level of support provided for language-defined and implementation-defined pragmas within each validated compiler. This information will be available to the Ada community, and it will be forwarded to the Ada 9X Project to use in their consideration of pragmas.

John Walker
AJPO

# 4.14   From SIGAda

SIGAda is a special interest group within the Association for Computing Machinery. Its purpose is to foster the understanding and development of issues related to the introduction and use of the Ada programming language. Development process issues, tools, detailed language understanding, metrics, and related secondary standards are samples of the areas of interest within the Special Interest Group on Ada.

## Committee & Working Group Activities

We are organized into committees comprised of working groups. Each committee has a focused interest. Our current committee structure is:

- Development Methods — Emphasis upon both software and system development

- Implementation — Compiler, runtime and architecture issues

- Education — College and university currently the focus. Will be extended to secondary schools in the near term. Includes industry training.

- Policy — Procurement, government, national and international issues

- Environment — Tools, IPSEs, environment integration frameworks

- Standards — 9X, POSIX, SQL, etc.

- Formal Methods — Safety and trusted applications, formal definition of Ada

- Users — Numerics, real-time issues, commercial users, etc.

Within each committee are Working Groups too numerous to mention in a survey article. Sample subgroups include Performance Measurement, Commercial Ada Usage, Run Time Environments, and Reuse. Many 1991 activities are centered around evolving standards and pre-standards including 9X, POSIX, X Windows/PHIGS, SQL, and IPSE architecture reference models and interfaces.

# Organizational Programs

SIGAda has many types of activities:

- Sponsored Workshops

- Meetings and Conferences

- Liaison Activities

- Local Chapters

- SIGAda Lectureship Program

- Newsletter

### Sponsored Workshops

**SETA**   SIGAda and the IEEE jointly sponsor the bi-annual Symposium for Environments and Tools for Ada (SETA). This workshop is focused on specific tools, integrated environments, and meta-issues related to software and system development using Ada.

**Real-Time Ada Issues Workshops**   SIGAda sponsors the annual Real-Time Ada Workshop which focuses on real-time performance and the semantic and implementation issues involved with distributed processing.

### Meetings & Conferences

**Annual Tri-Ada Conference**   Our annual conference occurs in the fall and draws together academia, industry and government for a conference consisting of refereed papers, birds of a feather sessions, project experiences, and exhibits. The 1990 Tri-Ada will be in Baltimore, MD during the week of 4 December.

**Summer Meetings**   Our summer meetings feature a format where SIGAda's Committees and Working Groups present the results of their work, and where the Working Groups meet to work on their evolving and new work products. Future summer meetings will alternate between this 'Working Group' format and our traditional format where informal papers are presented.

**WAdaS**   ACM SIGAda cosponsored the Washington Ada Symposium (WAdaS '90) with its local Washington DC SIGAda Chapter. This cosponsorship will also occur in 1991.

## Liaison Activities

**Educational Institution Outreach**   Our 1991 goal is to increase the use and teaching of Ada and Software Engineering practices in high schools, colleges, and universities. This will be done through a targeted lectureship program at universities and secondary schools. This program will draw upon the joint resources of SIGAda, industry vendors, and the 9X and STARS programs to make both academic knowledge and practical usage commonplace in the education environment of the 1990s. Local SIGAda chapters will be coordinating activities with schools in their area.

**Organization Outreach**   The interests of SIGAda members cross the scope of many of ACM's other SIGs. One of our goals is to increase the involvement of other ACM SIGs in SIGAda activities and to increase SIGAda's involvement in the activities of other SIGs. Future plans call for non-SIGAda speakers and panels at SIGAda meetings as well as increased SIGAda membership participation at non-SIGAda events.

**Coordination with Ada Europe**   SIGAda cooperates with Ada Europe to encourage technical interchange. Each organization sends three representatives to the other's annual conference. SIGAda will send three members to Greece in 1991.

## Local SIGAda Chapters

ACM SIGAda is second only to ACM SIGGRAPH in the number of local chapters (45 with 24 new chapters forming). ACM SIGAda locals can be found throughout the U.S. and in a growing number of locations worldwide (see Ada Letters for the latest contact information). Local chapters in the most densely populated areas meet monthly, others generally meet quarterly.

## SIGAda Lectureship Program

A speakers handbook has been developed and is available to local SIGAda chapters. (SIGAda is reviewing strategies to making this handbook available to universities and colleges.) The handbook lists individuals who are willing to speak at local SIGAda chapters. Anyone interested in being listed should contact Ed Colbert or Dave Emery (see Ada Letters for contact info). Expenses for these lectures are covered by SIGAda.

## Publications: Ada Letters

Our bimonthly SIG publication is Ada Letters. It is a collection of articles, reviews, and news of interest to the Ada community. In addition to the scheduled newsletter, special issues are occasionally published. Past special issues of Ada Letters have included Proceedings of the Real-Time Ada Issues Workshop, Ada Performance Issues, and the Approved Ada Language Commentaries.

## Contact Information

For further information contact:

> Mark S. Gerhardt, SIGAda Chair
> ESL, Inc
> 495 Java Drive, ms M507
> Sunnyvale, CA 94088-3510
> Tel. +1 408 752-2459
> E-mail: gerhardt@ajpo.sei,.cmu.edu

> Ed Colbert, Vice Chair for Liaison
> Absolute Software Company, Inc.
> 4593 Orchid Drive
> Los Angeles, CA 90043-3320
> Tel. +1 213 293-0783
> E-mail: hermix!colbert@rand.org

Yours
Mark Gerhardt

# 4.15   From   the   Software   Engineering   Institute*

## SEI overview

Software has become an increasingly critical component of U.S. defence systems, and the demand for quality software produced on schedule and within budget has grown more rapidly than the ability of the defence community to supply it. The problem is not simply the creation of technology, but the transition of technology to practice.

## SEI mission

To meet this need, the U.S. Department of Defence awarded the Software Engineering Institute, a federally funded research and development center, to Carnegie Mellon University in 1984. The mission of the SEI is to improve the quality of software in mission-critical computer systems by advancing the practice of software engineering.

The SEI has a four-part mission:

1. Bring the ablest professional minds and most effective technology to bear on rapid improvement of quality of operational software

2. Accelerate reduction-to-practice of modern software engineering techniques and methods

3. Promulgate use of modern techniques and methods throughout the community

4. Establish standards of excellence for software engineering practice

## SEI objectives

To accomplish this mission, a major objective of the SEI is to promote the evolution of software engineering from an *ad hoc*, labour-intensive activity to a managed, technology-supported discipline.

The general strategy is twofold: to manage software engineering as a discipline and to provide automated support for labour-intensive activities.

In carrying out this strategy, the SEI addresses three issues of software development:

---

*Extracts from a paper given by Judy Bamberger. Printed here with permission.

**Quality** Defence systems, because of their demanding operational conditions, require software of the highest quality in terms of correctness, reliability, and performance.

**Management** Managing the software engineering process to control schedule, budget, and quality is particularly important when the software is part of a large complex MCCR system.

**Productivity** Increasing productivity helps solve two fundamental problems related to the capacity of the defence industry to produce software: the overall shortage of highly qualified software professionals and the high costs of software production.

Software quality, management, and productivity concerns must be addressed at several levels: the individual software engineer, the software development project, the organisation, and the procurement and regulatory level.

### Software Engineering Process Programme

The Process Programme is concerned with making lasting improvements in the software development process of key DoD organisations and their contractors. The overall objectives of the Process Programme are to improve the maturity of software engineering as a practice, facilitate the effective introduction of available technology, and improve the quality and productivity of software development and maintenance. A further objective is to ensure that suitable mechanisms are in place to retain these process improvements after they are achieved. These objectives directly support the mission of the SEI: to rapidly move modern software engineering technologies and methods into practice.

### Software Engineering Methods Programme

The goal of the Methods Programme is to improve the practice of software engineering by improving individual and team productivity through the identification and transition to practice of emerging software technology. The overall objectives of the Methods Programme are to: identify the specific problems that need to be solved to meet the demands for developing, supporting, and re-engineering large, complex systems; identify the software technologies with the greatest potential for addressing those problems; and understand how to best apply those technologies to relevant problems.

**Software Systems Programme**

The goal of the Software Systems Programme is to improve the way software is developed for real-time distributed systems by integrating software engineering with systems engineering and reducing the risk of adopting new technology. The overall objective of the Software Systems Programme is to pursue significant improvement in the development of real-time distributed systems by:

- establishing the SEI as a focal point for real-time computing;

- assisting the real-time systems community in reducing the risk of adopting promising new technologies;

- establishing and maintaining working relationships with government contractors and DoD programme offices in selected real-time systems domains; and

- identifying and evaluating new software systems technologies that apply across application domains.

**Education Programme**

The goal of the Education Programme is to improve software engineering education in government, industry, and academic communities. The shortage of qualified software engineering professionals results from the increased demand for software throughout society and the extended period required for the educational system to develop new academic programmes and produce large numbers of graduates from those programmes. The primary objective of the Education Programme is to increase the number of highly qualified software engineers by rapidly improving software engineering education throughout academia, government, and industry.

**Ada and STARS Support**

The Ada and STARS Support effort aims to remove technical and managerial impediments to adopting Ada and to support the DoD STARS (Software Technology for Adaptable, Reliable Systems) Programme.

The Binding of Ada and SQL Project, initiated at the request of the Ada Joint Program Office (AJPO), has investigated the problem of binding Ada with the Structured Query Language (SQL) database language. The solution to this problem was the specification of the SQL Ada Module Extensions (SAME), an interface that permits an application program written in Ada to access and manipulate data controlled by database management systems using SQL.

The Study and Analysis for Ada 9X Project is identifying and evaluating potential areas for revising the Ada standard based on the experiences of software developers and compiler implementors.

The Ada Adoption Handbook Project is to provide programme and project managers with information on how best to tap Ada's strengths and manage this new software technology. One handbook, "A Program Manager's Guide", was published in 1987; a second handbook, "Compiler Evaluation and Selection" (written by the Real-Time Embedded Systems Testbed Project), was published in April 1989.

The Software Architectures Engineering Project provides technical guidance to DoD programme offices in applying innovative, model-based software engineering solutions to the problems that characterise an application domain.

### Technology Transition Programme

The Technology Transition Programme is the focal point for SEI transition efforts. This programme works with other SEI programmes to match problems and solutions in the DoD software community. The objective of the Technology Transition Programme is to accelerate the transition and adoption of improved software engineering practices and technology by co-ordinating and managing transition efforts.

Judy Bamberger
SEI

# 4.16    From the Ada Association of Australia

The Ada Association of Australia was formed in January 1989 and has about 180 members including 15 corporate sponsors. The association was formed as a direct result of several key defence procurements using Ada and the "critical mass" of tools/programmers/quality compilers on the market. The current status of Ada usage in Australia comprises about 20 defence projects, three commercial projects and over ten studies or R & D projects. Several universities are also teaching Ada with Canberra University and Swinburne Institute of Technology advocating Ada as the best language to aid teaching software engineering.

The AAA provides its members with a quarterly magazine, a bulletin board in three major cities and a number of special events which have attracted international speakers. Quarterly meetings are also held at which there is a central theme where members contribute presentations and debate is often very lively. Past events include a visit from TRW to present their Ada Process Model, talks by Donald Firesmith from Advanced Software Technology Specialists, Colin Birmingham from Alsys, Judy Bamberger from the SEI and Major Ed Liebheart from AJPO.

The main future event which the AAA is involved in is an international Pacific Ada conference in the spring of 1992.

## Commercial Use of Ada in Australia

### Universal Defence Systems' Kernel Command Control

Universal Defence Systems Pty Limited
Suite 3, Enterprise Unit 3
Brodie Hill Drive
W.A. Technology Park
Bentley, Western Australia 6102
Tel. +61 9 470 2654
Fax. +61 9 470 26988
Telex: AA93399 INCAP

Universal Defence Systems (UDS) central software product is the Kernel Command Control (KCC), which is entirely written in Ada and consists of about 700 packages with a total of over 500,000 lines of code.

The KCC is essentially an Ada application generator, designed specifically for $C^3I$ (Command, Control, Communications and Intelligence) systems. From its inception, the KCC was designed to provide a basic core of set functions found in all command and control systems. This core is composed of a number of reusable object-oriented Ada packages. Using the pre-tested Ada objects it is possible to meet a wide range of specific application requirements at a fraction of the cost and risk of conventional approaches.

The KCC has also found some remarkable commercial applications, notably the Vessel Tracking System (VTS) and the Irrigation Monitoring System (IMS). Both of these applications are indeed C3 systems, and can therefore readily exploit the flexibility and power of the KCC.

The Vessel Tracking System can track either vessels or vehicles, and relies on satellite based technology to obtain positional information. This information is then processed by the base station software, which superimposes the incoming data onto a map of the locality. The VTS relies on the KCC database to store all the data so that multitude of functions are available to the user (e.g. track history, dead reckoning, etc.).

Perhaps surprisingly, the Irrigation Monitoring System is also a classic Command, Control and Communications application, and so can also exploit Universal Defence Systems' KCC. In this case, incoming data consists of sensor information (e.g. moisture sensors situated all over the terrain of interest) and possibly weather predictions obtained automatically from local weather stations. A complex algorithm is then used to process the data, which must take into account a myriad of factors including moisture, soil type, vegetation type, gradient, temperature, etc. to generate automatic watering programs. The benefit of the Irrigation Monitoring System is the cost savings in both water consumption (which is optimised by the system) and labour costs (as the operator can perform many maintenance tasks from the base).

Universal Defence Systems has always believed in Software Engineering, which is why it is committed to the use of Ada from the very beginning. Because of this philosophy, UDS did not have to translate code from an obsolete language, with all the inherent design risks. Instead a true object-oriented approach exploited the power of Ada to produce the enormously powerful and flexible KCC, which is a basis of the exciting commercial products above.

## Advanced Systems Research's QUIKTRAK Automatic Vehicle Location (AVL) System

Advance Systems Research Pty Limited
31 Bridge Street
Pymble NSW 2073
Australia
Tel. +61 2 488 8800
Fax. +61 2 4888 9678

QUIKTRAK is an automatic location system designed specifically to locate and track objects, such as vehicles, in an urban and suburban environment. It was developed by Advance System Research Pty Ltd in a joint venture with Lend Lease Corporation, and is presently in full commercial operation in Sydney. QUIKTRAK was developed over a period of four years and about 75% of the software was written in Ada.

Any object to be located carries an inexpensive transponder which, on demand or autonomously, briefly emits a low-power, spread-spectrum radio signal. This signal is received and processed at a number of elevated receiving sites (remote sites) and the resulting timing information is returned to a central control/processing site computer. This processor performs the calculations required to locate transponders and then forwards the position information to QUIKTRAK customers. Vehicle tracking information is presented on the customer's PC, superimposed on a background map of the coverage area.

Ada was used to develop all the software for the control/processing site and the remote sites. Details related to the control/processing site Ada development are:

| | | |
|---|---|---|
| Host | : | MicroVAX running VMS |
| Compiler | : | VAX Ada |
| Effort | : | Ten man years |

Details relating to the control/processing site Ada development are:

| | | |
|---|---|---|
| Host | : | MicroVAX running VMS |
| Target | : | 68000 |
| Compiler | : | Telesoft 68000 cross compiler |
| Effort | : | Six man years |

## Adacel's Remote Control and Maintenance System (RCMS)

Adacel Pty Ltd
875 Glenhuntly Road
Caulfield South
Victoria
Australia 3162
Tel. +61 3 528 1911
Fax. +61 3 528 2902

The RCMS has been produced for the Airways Corporation of New Zealand by Thompson Radar Australia Corporation Ltd and the role of Adacel is to develop system requirements, analyse and design the application software, integrate and support the system and provide operator training.

The system is PS2-based and remotely analyses tests and controls airways equipment such as radars, DMEs, VORs NDBs and control centres.

The system also enables maintenance of monitored equipments.

Project features include multiple protocols (Ethernet, X25, Xmodem), real-time fault analysis, Graphic user interface, Oracle database backend control. The software is being developed in Ada under DOD-STD-2167 under OS2. The project will be complete in 1991 and involves about 10 man years of effort.

Adacel is also involved in a remote control and monitoring system as part of the same contract using the generic RCMS as a kernel.

Regards
Mike Taylor
AAA European Liaison Officer

## 4.17   From Japan SIGAda

Established in the fall of 1988 with a current membership of 500, Japan SIGAda has been largely responsible for the current interest shown by potential users of Ada. Held every 3 months, Japan SIGAda is a forum for the exchange of information about Ada, such as its research subjects, software development projects, usage in the U.S. and Europe as well as specifics concerning Ada education.

Our first regular meeting in 1991 will be held on 22 January 1991 at the Tokyo Institute of Technology, where one of the topics is "OOD Experience for Telecommunication Software Development". Other regular meetings are scheduled in April, July and October.

The regular meetings are usually followed by an exhibition session to introduce Ada related products. Japan SIGAda would be happy to invite you in this session as well as for regular meetings as a speaker.

Jun Shimura
Treasurer, Japan SIGAda

# 5

# Current policy statements on Ada

## 5.1 US Department of Defense Directive

File 3405-1.HLP: text of 2 APR 87 DoD
Directive 3405.1, Computer Programming
Language Policy
(AdaIC contact, Adrian N. Walls)

April 2, 1987
NUMBER 3405.1

ASD(C)

### Subject: Computer Programming Language Policy

References:

(a) DoD Instruction 5000.31, "Interim List of DoD Approved Higher Order Programming Languages (HOL)", November 24, 1976 (hereby canceled)

(b) DoD Directive 7740.1, "DoD Information Resources Management Program", June 20, 1983

(c) DoD Directive 5000.1, "Major System Acquisitions", March 12, 1986

(d) DoD Directive 5000.29, "Management of Computer Resources in Major Defense Systems", April 26, 1976

   (e) through (j), see enclosure 1

## A. Purpose

This Directive supersedes reference (a) and supports references (b) and (c) by establishing policy for computer programming languages used for the development and support of all DoD software.

## B. Applicability and scope

This Directive:

1. Applies to the Office of the Secretary of Defense (OSD), the Military Departments (including the National Guard and Reserve), the Organization of the Joint Chiefs of Staff (OJCS), the Unified and Specified Commands, the Inspector General of the Department of Defense (IG, DoD), the Defense Agencies, and nonappropriated fund activities (hereafter referred to collectively as "DoD Components").

2. Covers all computer resources managed under reference (d) or DoD Directive 7920.1 (reference (e)).

3. Need not be applied retroactively to systems that have entered full-scale development or have passed Milestone II of references (c) and (e), and for which a documented language commitment was made in compliance with previous policy.

## C. Definitions

Special terms used in this Directive are explained in enclosure 2; otherwise, refer to the "American National Dictionary for Information Processing Systems" (reference (f)).

## D. Policy

It is DoD policy to:

1. Satisfy functional requirements, enhance mission performance, and provide operational support through the use of modern software concepts, advanced software technology, software life-cycle support tools, and standard programming languages.

2. Achieve improvements in DoD software management through the implementation of processes for control of the use of higher order languages, including specification of standards and waiver procedures.

3. Limit the number of programming languages used within the Department of Defense to facilitate achievement of the goal of transition to the use of Ada (reference (g)) for DoD software development.

   a. The Ada programming language shall be the single, common, computer programming language for Defense computer resources used in intelligence systems, for the command and control of military forces, or as an integral part of a weapon system. Programming languages other than Ada that were authorized and being used in full-scale development may continue to be used through deployment and for software maintenance, but not for major software upgrades.

   b. Ada shall be used for all other applications, except when the use of another approved higher order language is more cost-effective over the application's life-cycle, in keeping with the long-range goal of establishing Ada as the primary DoD higher order language (HOL).

   c. When Ada is not used, only the other standard higher order programming languages shown in enclosure 3 shall be used to meet custom-developed procedural language programming requirements. The use of specific HOL's shall be based on capabilities of the language to meet system requirements. Guidance in selecting the appropriate HOL to use is provided in NBS Special Publication 500-117 (reference (h)).

4. Prefer, based on an analysis of the life-cycle costs and impact, use of:

   a. Off-the-shelf application packages and advanced software technology.

   b. Ada-based software and tools.

   c. Approved standard HOL's.

5. Consider the potential impact on competition for future software and/or hardware enhancements or replacement when selecting Defense, public domain, or commercially available software packages, or advanced software technology.

6. Use life-cycle management practices, as required by DoD Directive 7920.1 (reference (e)) and DoD Directive 5000.29 (reference (d)), for the development, support, and use of software, whether custom-developed or commercially acquired.

7. Reduce software obsolescence and the cost of software maintenance through use of approved programming languages and appropriate advanced software technology during all phases of the software life-cycle.

## E. Responsibilities

1. The Assistant Secretary of Defense (Comptroller) (ASD(C)) and the Under Secretary of Defense (Acquisition) (USD(A)) shall jointly:

   a. Ensure that the policy and procedures in this Directive are implemented.

   b. Assign responsibility to a specific DoD Component to act as the DoD language-control agent for each DoD-approved standard HOL.

   c. Process nominations for changes to the list of approved HOL's.

2. The Assistant Secretary of Defense (Comptroller) shall:

   a. For automated information systems, establish programs, as appropriate, for the enhancement of the software engineering process and the transition of such technology from the marketplace and research programs to application within general purpose automated data processing systems.

   b. Define research and development requirements for automated information systems after consultation with DoD Components and provide such requirements to USD(A) for inclusion in their research and development program.

3. The Under Secretary of Defense (Acquisition) shall:

   a. Establish and support a software and information technology research and development program that is responsive to the identified needs.

   b. Manage the DoD Ada program and maintain an Ada Joint Program Office (AJPO) to oversee the maintenance of the Ada language and the insertion of Ada-related technology into the Department of Defense.

   c. Establish research programs, as appropriate, for the enhancement of software engineering technology and transferring such technology to use in intelligence systems and systems for the command and control of military forces, and to computer resources that are an integral part of a weapon system.

4. The Head of each DoD Component shall:

   a. Implement and execute internal procedures consistent with the policy and procedures in this Directive.

   b. Designate a language-control agent for each approved HOL for which the DoD Component is assigned responsibility and ensure compliance with the procedures in enclosure 4.

   c. Institute a process for granting waivers to the use of approved HOL's in accordance with section F, below.

   d. Specifically address in the Component's overall computer resources planning process:

      (1) The use of appropriate advanced software technology for developing new applications and technological upgrades of existing systems.

      (2) The current use of assembly languages, nonstandard HOL's, vendor extensions, and enhancements of standard HOL's, and actions taken to ensure that such use is minimized.

   e. Establish a program for evaluating, prototyping, and inserting advanced software technology into the development, modification, and maintenance process, and hold operational software managers accountable for investment in and migration to advanced software technology for their particular environment.

   f. Establish and maintain training, education, and career development programs that will ensure that DoD personnel are fully able to use new advanced software technologies.

# F. Waiver procedures

1. Waivers to the policy in subsection D.3, above, shall be strictly controlled and closely reviewed. Authority for issuing waivers is delegated to each DoD Component.

   a. Each proposed waiver shall contain full justification and shall, at a minimum, include a life-cycle cost analysis and a risk analysis that addresses technical performance and schedule impact. Each waiver granted by the DoD Component shall apply to only one system or subsystem.

   b. Justification for granted waivers shall be provided to USD(A) or ASD(C) within the scope of their individual responsibilities, as periodically requested for review.

2. A waiver NEED NOT be obtained for use of:

    a. Commercially available off-the-shelf applications software that is not modified or maintained by the Department of Defense.

    b. Commercially available off-the-shelf advanced software technology that is not modified or maintained by the Department of Defense.

    c. Computer programming languages required to implement vendor-provided updates to commercially supplied off-the-shelf software. Use of such languages shall be restricted to implementing the vendor updates.

3. A waiver IS REQUIRED for use of unmodified Defense or public domain software that does not conform to the language requirements of subsection D.3, above. Maintenance of the software shall be specifically addressed in the waiver request to include life-cycle maintenance costs and the availability of source codes and necessary software tools.

## G. Effective date and implementation

This Directive is effective immediately. Forward one copy of implementing documents to the Assistant Secretary of Defense (Comptroller) and one copy to the Under Secretary of Defense (Acquisition) within 120 days.

William H. Taft, IV Deputy Secretary of Defense

Enclosures — 4

1. References

2. Special Terms and Definitions

3. DoD-Approved Higher Order Programming Languages

4. Procedures for Controlling Higher Order Languages (HOL)

## References, continued — 3405.1 (Encl 1)

(e) DoD Directive 7920.1, "Life Cycle Management of Automated Information Systems (AIS)," October 17, 1978

(f) National Bureau of Standards (NBS) FIPS Publication 11-2, "American National Dictionary for Information Processing Systems," May 9, 1983

(g) ANSI/MIL-STD-1815A-1983, "Ada Programming Language," February 1983

(h) National Bureau of Standards Special Publication 500-117, "Selection and Use of General Purpose Programming Languages", October 1984

(i) DoD 4120.3-M, "Defense Standardization and Specification Program Policies Procedures and Instructions," August 1978, authorized by DoD Directive 4120.3, February 10, 1979

(j) DoD Directive 5010.19, "Configuration Management," May 1, 1979

## Special Terms and Definitions — 3405.1 (Encl 2)

1. Advanced Software Technology. Software tools, life-cycle support environments (including program support environments), nonprocedural languages, modern database management systems, and other technologies that provide improvements in productivity, usability, maintainability, portability, etc., over those capabilities commonly in use.

2. Automated Information Systems. A collection of functional user and automatic data processing personnel, procedures, and equipment (including automatic data processing equipment(ADPE)) that is designed, built, operated, and maintained to collect, record, process, store, retrieve, and display information.

3. Major Software Upgrade. Redesign or addition of more than one-third of the software.

## DoD-Approved Higher Order Programming Languages — 3405.1 (Encl 3)

| Language | Standard Number | DoD Control Agent | Industry Control Agent |
|---|---|---|---|
| Ada | ANSI/MIL-STD-1815A-1983 (FIPS 119) | Ada Joint Program Office | ANSI |
| C/ATLAS | IEEE STD 716-1985 | Navy | IEEE |
| COBOL | ANSI X3.23-1985 (FIPS 21-2) | Air Force | ANSI |
| CMS-2M | NAVSEA 0967LP-598-2210-1982 | Navy | N/A |
| CMS-2Y | NAVSEA Manual M-5049, M-5045, M-5044-1981 | Navy | N/A |
| FORTRAN | ANSI X3.9-1978 (FIPS 69-1) | Air Force | ANSI |
| JOVIAL (J73) | MIL-STD-1589C (USAF) | Air Force | N/A |
| Minimal BASIC | ANSI X3.60-1978 (FIPS 68-1) | Air Force | ANSI |
| PASCAL | ANSI/IEEE 770X3.97-1983 (FIPS 109) | Air Force | ANSI |
| SPL/1 | SPL/1 Language Reference Manual, Intermetrics Report No. 172-1 | Navy | N/A |

Note. See NBS Special Publication 500-117 (reference (h)).

## Procedures for Controlling Higher Order Languages (HOL) — 3405.1 (Encl 4)

1. All Ada compilers that are used for creation of software to be delivered to or maintained by the Government shall be formally validated in accordance with procedures and guidelines set by the AJPO.

2. Each DoD-approved HOL shall be assigned to a DoD language-control agent, as shown in enclosure 3, who shall:

   a. Have the authority and responsibility for proper support of all language-control activities needed to provide for necessary modification and improvement of the assigned HOL. The agent shall operate in accordance with DoD 4120.3-M (reference (i)).

    b. Provide configuration control for DoD HOL's in accordance with DoD Directive 5010.19 (reference (j)). For HOL's controlled under industry (e.g., Institute for Electrical and Electronic Engineers or American National Standards Institute) procedures, the agent shall represent the Department of Defense to the controlling body.

    c. Maintain a single standard definition of the assigned HOL and make this definition document available as a Federal, DoD, military, or adopted industry standard. The agent shall also gather and disseminate appropriate information regarding use of the HOL, its compilers, interpreters, and associated tools.

3. A DoD Component may nominate a language for removal from the list of approved languages by submitting a justification document, which presents the rationale for the proposed deletion and an impact analysis, to the ASD(C), who will coordinate it with USD(A).

4. A DoD Component may also nominate a language for inclusion on the list of approved languages by submitting a justification document to the ASD(C), who will coordinate it with USD(A). The justification document shall include the following:

    a. A detailed rationale for using the language, including how the candidate language meets specific DoD requirements that are not satisfied by the approved languages.

    b. A description of the language and the environment and a detailed unambiguous specification of the language.

    c. An economic analysis of the impact of the language over its expected life-cycle.

    d. A detailed plan for implementing and supporting the language, including identification of the DoD Component that will accept designation as control agent for the language.

# 5.2 Use of programming languages in the German Federal Armed Forces

## A. Preliminary Remarks

The data processing facilities utilized by the Federal Armed Forces have reached a high level in terms of quantity, diversity and complexity and are continuing to increase. The available resources, however, are limited; they require well directed and economical employment to achieve an optimum cost/benefit ratio. Standardization is a suitable approach to pursue this goal.

In the expanding field of data processing, software expenditure has increased disproportionately to that of hardware and become the predominant cost factor. Therefore, software standardization seems to be a particularly promising tool for reducing/checking life-cycle costs since

- it substantially supports portability and reusability of software,

- it is able to contribute in a special way to the reduction of expenditure for software development as well as software maintenance and modification (SWPÄ),

- it reduces the investments required for training/follow-on training as well as for development and test facilities, and

- it increases reliability to a considerable extent.

The selection and introduction of higher standard programming languages is a basic and decisive measure in this context.

Within the alliance there have been several initiatives to reduce the existing diversity of languages. US DoD and NATO have established Ada as the standard programming language.

Ada is particularly suitable for ensuring high-quality, economical software development and software maintenance and modification. It therefore seems to be advisable to establish Ada as the standard programming language to be used in the Federal Armed Forces.

Ada must be embedded in suitable programming environments in order to be able to exploit its advantages in an effective and comprehensive way.

## B. Regulation

1. Ada* is to be used as a matter of principle if software has to be newly

---

*According to ISO/8652-1987; also described in the 'Reference Manual for the Ada Programming Language', ANSI/MIL-STD-1815A-1983.

developed or existing software further developed on a broad basis. The compilers must be validated and officially approved. The use of low-level programming languages is to be minimized as far as is technically possible.

2. Projects are not affected by this regulation if another programming language has already been selected and laid down in relevant documents already adopted.

3. Conditions which may result in an exceptional authorization are listed in the Annex. The goal is to reduce the Annex item by item. Furthermore, agreement within FMOD should be ensured.

4. In all other cases, exceptional authorization is to be granted for each specific case. The most important reasons are:

   - The technical preconditions for the use of Ada cannot be provided for.
   - Interface problems resulting from the incorporation of Ada software portions into existing software cannot be resolved.
   - Agreements concerning national and international projects cannot be concluded with agencies outside the Federal Armed Forces.

   Increased costs alone are not reason enough for granting exceptional authorization.

   As a rule, the cognizant agency must document the conditions for which exceptional authorization may be granted in sufficiently technical detail in the technical concept and notify the procurement agencies via the cognizant Division/Staff in FMOD. All participants should use their influence to eliminate the reasons for waivers in each specific case.

5. The hitherto existing directives governing the use of programming languages are to be adjusted or cancelled.

6. The necessary support measures for adapting data processing training and follow-on training, exploiting available Ada technology (e.g. development of an Ada Programming Support Environment (APSE)) and adjusting the procedures and techniques of the software development cycle are to be pursued with vigor and initiated immediately.

## C. Report

After three years, a report on the experience gained must be submitted.

## Annex

List of approved conditions for which exception to para B.3 of the Regulation on the use of programming languages in the Federal Armed Forces is allowed.

1. Software (SW), the type or volume of which does not justify the employment of problem-oriented programming languages due to the technical complexity of the latter and for which these are not usually employed. If an exception to the regulation is found to be necessary, the cognizant will be notified in accordance with para B.4 of the above regulation in each specific case and this will be justified in sufficient detail.

2. Marketable software products and software included in projects which, as a matter of principle, are maintained and modified by the manufacturer only. For software specifically developed for use by the Federal Armed Forces, Ada should be prescribed even if software maintenance and modification by the Federal Armed Forces has not initially been planned.

3. Languages for database queries, database descriptions, data manipulation, knowledge-base systems and artificial intelligence applications, where Ada would be unsuitable.

4. Software for external test means should continue to be developed in the C/ATLAS technical language which has been specifically introduced and standardized for this purpose.

5. Software for purely technical/scientific applications in problems for which Ada would be unsuitable.

6. If Ada is unsuitable for meeting the real-time requirement only the directly affected functions may be developed as subroutines by using low-level programming languages (Assembler, C). The requirement is to be documented and placed on record.

# 6

# Ada 9X report*

Chris Anderson
Ada 9X Project Manager
Department of Defense
USA

The overall goal of the Ada 9X Project is to revise ANSI/MIL-STD-1815A to reflect current essential requirements with minimum negative impact and maximum positive impact to the Ada community. The Ada 9X process is a revision and not a redesign of the language and should be viewed as a natural part of the language maturation process.

A revision was undertaken because, according to the Ada Board (i.e., the US Federal Advisory Board to the Ada Joint Program Office), "some omissions, limitations, and minor errors have been discovered ... since the ANSI standard was approved. Although a major revision does not appear to be necessary to correct these problems, some revision is warranted." The Ada Board further recommended that the scope of the revision be defined in a document that captures the high level requirements to be satisfied by the revision. The Board then went on to say "The objective of the proposed revision should be to select only those changes that improve the usability of the language while minimising the disruptive effects of changing the standard."

The Ada 9X Project, initiated in October 1988, is sponsored by the Ada Joint Program Office. The Project is being conducted in a very open manner and is being accomplished in four phases: requirements, mapping, revision, and transition.

The requirements phase is almost completed. The draft Requirements Document was released for review and comment in September 1990, with the final document to be completed by December. Input to the requirements process has been gathered over the past two years from a wide variety of sources. The Ada 9X Project Office solicited revision requests from the public from October 1988 to October 1989 and received 774 requests. Language commentaries and study issues collected by ISO Working Group 9 are also being included, approximately 850 in all. The Ada 9X Project Office has held a series of special user meetings since January to discuss user needs and priorities. The following groups were included: trusted systems, safety critical, real-time embedded and information systems. Additionally, a special meeting regarding the Ada compiler validation and evaluation process was also held in July 1990.

The Requirements are being completed by a team based at the Software Engineering Institute led by John Goodenough. Analysis of the revision needs expressed in the Revision Requests and User Forums suggests that different user communities have different needs, and that changes to Ada that are important to some application domains are either unnecessary or are viewed as detrimental to other application domains. For example, support for decimal arithmetic is important if Ada is to satisfy the needs of information systems applications, but real-time and embedded system applications typically have no need for such numeric representations and would prefer that compiler vendors devote time and effort to supporting other specialized capabilities (often ones that are not critical to information systems). Educators are particularly interested in ensuring that the language can be taught easily (e.g., that there are simple rules with few exceptions) and that implementations are affordable and perform efficiently when compiling many small student programs, but these requirements are of less concern to other classes of users.

Implementers are concerned that unless the scope of the changes is small, the job of modifying compilers will be a major and expensive effort. Users are worried that if implementer resources are overextended, the Ada 9X compilers will be less efficient, less reliable, and more costly than existing compilers (at least initially). Some users are also worried that if Ada is not enhanced in some areas (for example, by providing support for distributed systems), it will fail to attract enough new users to ensure the continued improvement and availability of compilers.

Finally, a substantial minority of the revision requests submitted by the public are satisfied by some, but not all, implementations (usually in nonstandard ways permitted by the language, e.g., special pragmas or compiler switches). For such requests, the language already allows the need to be satisfied but does not ensure that it will be satisfied. Changes that lead to more implementation uniformity would be helpful here, but increased uniformity is somewhat in conflict with the diversity of user needs as previously noted.

After giving due consideration to the general nature of the requests for language changes, the Ada 9X Project has reaffirmed the essence of the Ada Board's conclusion that although improvements to Ada will be helpful in fostering its continued use, there are no fatal problems that prevent its successful use for many applications. Therefore, radical change is unjustified, and indeed, could have a significant negative impact on the ability of implementers to support user needs.

Equally important, after giving due consideration to the conflicting concerns expressed by members of the Ada community, the Ada 9X Project has established the following premise affecting the scope of the revision effort, the requirements, and the structure of the resulting standard:

> It should be possible for an Ada 9X implementation to address just the needs of a selected group of users, e.g., hard real-time applications developers, information systems developers, educators, etc.

This means the Ada 9X standard should be allowed to specify capabilities or implementation constraints that are not appropriate for every application community that therefore, need not be supported by every implementation. Such capabilities and constraints could be specified in special annexes to the standard. The idea is that these annexes are part of the standard but need not be supported by every implementation.

Allowing specialized annexes should give greater freedom to the Ada 9X Mapping/Revision Team to address the needs of specialized application areas without having to be overly concerned that a specified capability is inappropriate for some community of users (since not every implementation will have to support the required capability). This represents a change from the existing policy that all implementations support the entire language.

Since inefficient support for certain uses of language constructs is tantamount to non-support as far as some applications are concerned, it is expected that each annex will address critical performance and support issues that cannot or need not be satisfied by all implementations. For example, a hard real-time annex might specify support for "immediate" abort, while an information system annex might specify support for packed decimal arithmetic.

One advantage of this approach is that it allows for incremental transition to a full Ada 9X implementation — implementers can decide to concentrate initially on supporting just those annexes of greatest interest to their customer base. The other advantage, of course, is that it allows the specialized and critical needs of different user communities to be addressed explicitly in the standard.

Besides the Ada 9X Requirements Document, the following guidelines have also been developed to provide further direction to the Ada 9X Mapping/Revision Team during their challenging activity:

The guidelines include the following criteria:

- Implementation Ease: Changes shall be relatively easy to implement with existing compiler technology, both individually and collectively.

- Execution Efficiency: Changes shall be efficiently implementable.

- User Need: The extent of a change shall not be out of proportion with the degree of user need for the change.

- Upward Compatibility: In general, any legal Ada 83 program must also be a legal Ada 9X program and must have the same effect allowed or required by Ada 83. However, to improve the portability of Ada programs, and to satisfy other requirements, it may be necessary to eliminate some effects allowed by Ada 83 or to make some Ada 83 programs illegal. In these cases, the following guidelines shall apply:

    - No implementation-dependent behaviour allowed in Ada 83 shall be excluded in Ada 9X if that behaviour is actually supported by a significant number of implementations and is important to a significant number of users.

    - No Ada 83 program shall be illegal in Ada 9X unless it is relatively easy to correct the illegal program or it is expected that very few existing legal programs will be affected (since the programs are either pathological or erroneous).

    - Since an Ada program should not, in general, rely on the raising of pre-defined exceptions (e.g., `PROGRAM_ERROR`), Ada 83 rules requiring the raising of a pre-defined exception in a given situation can be modified without undue concern for upward compatibility.

- Reliability/Safety/Maintainability: Support for the reliability, safety, and long-term maintainability of large, complex systems shall take precedence over convenience of Ada coding. For example, this means greatly favouring statistically checkable rules over rules checked at run-time, and favouring run-time checks over uncheckable rules (erroneous behaviour).

The Mapping/Revision Team is already developing mapping issues: prospective language solutions based on the requirements. The Mapping Document should be completed in June 1991. The Mapping/Revision Team must then revise the wording in the Standard, another difficult task. The revised standard should be completed in June 1992 and ready for the six months ANSI standardization process.

Throughout the entire process, the Ada 9X Project is closely coordinating all aspects of the Project with ISO Working Group 9 in order to ensure that ISO publication of the ANSI Standard occurs as quickly after ANSI approval as possible.

The Ada 9X Project Office is currently developing the master plan for the Ada compiler validation process (i.e., the Ada 9X ACVC test suite and associated releases). The Ada 9X ACVC test suite release schedule is being developed to facilitate the gradual transition of Ada 83 to Ada 9X.

The Ada 9X Project is a challenging activity with a tremendous potential to influence software engineering in a positive fashion over the next ten years. The Project is going very well thanks to the talents of some of the world's finest software engineers.

## Acknowledgement

Excerpts of this article are from the Ada 9X Project Plan and the draft Requirements Document. Both documents can be obtained by calling one of the Ada 9X Document Distribution Centers or the Ada Information Clearinghouse Center on +1 703 685-1477.

# 7

# Papers from the Ada UK exhibition

The following papers were presented at the Ada UK Exhibition held in February 1990.

## 7.1 The practical application of Yourdon and Ada

**Peter Fitzpatrick, VSEL, Combat Systems Division**

### Abstract

This paper describes the use of the Yourdon Structured Analysis and Design method and the Ada language with the Combat Systems Division of Vickers Shipbuilding and Engineering Ltd.

An overview of both Yourdon and Ada is presented, together with a description of the mapping between design and implementation, and practical examples of the combined use of the techniques. Finally, the proven benefits of the two techniques are described.

### 7.1.1 Introduction

**VSEL Combat Systems Division**

The Combat Systems Division of VSEL has been involved in the development of electronic and software systems for some fifteen years. In 1981, the Combat Systems Division was awarded a contract to provide the first LAN-based data distribution system to be fitted in Royal Navy Submarines.

The Software Department of the Division was awarded the first Ada contract to be placed by the Ministry of Defence (Navy) in 1984, only one year after the formal definition of the Ada language was agreed, and delivered the first Ada system to the Ministry of Defence in 1988.

Since 1984 the Software Department has won contracts for the development of five major Ada systems, of which three have been completed and successfully delivered.

VSEL is committed to the use of Structured Analysis and Design methods with Ada, and this paper provides a short introduction to the analysis and design techniques used, and the interface between the design and Ada implementation.

## 7.1.2   Yourdon Structured Analysis and Design

### Tools and techniques

**General**   The variant of Yourdon used within VSEL is that defined by Paul Ward and Stephen Mellor, usually known as Ward/Mellor. This variant provides the means to describe the temporal behaviour required of the system.

The method revolves around the use of a number of tools and/or techniques. Most of the tools provide a graphical representation of the system requirements or system implementation. The complete Analysis and Design is underpinned by a comprehensive data dictionary. The following sections describe the tools and techniques.

**Data Flow Diagrams (DFDs)**   Data Flow Diagrams represent:

(a) the functional requirements of the system,

(b) the data flows within the system,

(c) the data flows between the system and the outside world,

(d) the control structure of the system.

In the example given in figure 7.1, the solid circles represent **Data Transformations**. These transformations act upon the data input to them to produce the output data.

The solid lines represent data flows. Flows with a single headed arrow are discrete flows (where the data only exists at individual points in time) and flows with double headed arrows are continuous flows (where the data exists at every instance within a time interval).

Parallel lines represent **Data Stores**. The data stored in the system or passed between data transformations is detailed in the data dictionary.

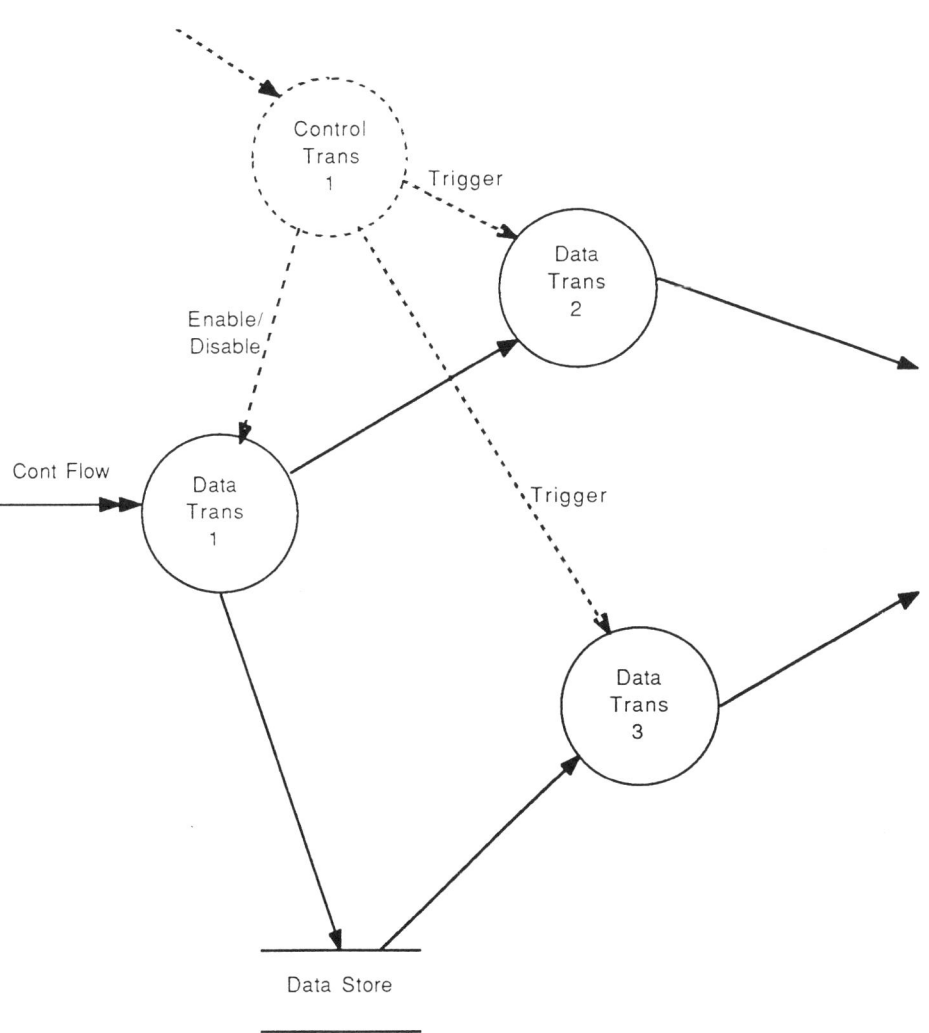

Figure 7.1. Data Flow Diagram

Broken circles represent a **Control Transform** which determines the circumstances upon which a data transformation occurs. Broken lines represent an **event**, these being the means for a control transformation to trigger, enable, or disable a data transformation or pass control information to other Control Transforms.

It is necessary to textually represent the function performed by a Data Transformation. In addition to documenting the analysis, this is useful during reviews, and can perform the function of analysis comments.

The behaviour of primitive data transforms (those which are not further decomposed) are represented by a formal notation using pre- and post-conditions in Data Transformation Specifications (DTS). Alternatively, for primitive Data Transformations, the processes performed may be defined using an algorithmic syntax or high level language.

**State Transition Diagrams (STDs)**   Each Control Transformation is supported by a State Transition Diagram.

In the example given in figure 7.2, the rectangles represent a **state**. **Transitions** between states are represented by arrows. Each arrow has an associated condition which is identified with an input event flow into the Control Transformation, and causes the state transition to occur. The condition may cause an output event flow (or flows) which is associated with an output event flow on the Control Transformation.

These event flows are shown on the DFD and provide the link between the STD and DFD.

**Entity Relationship Diagrams (ERDs)**   Entity Relationship Diagrams are the means to describe the structure of data required by the system, and the relationship(s) between one data item and another.

In the example given in figure 7.3, each **data object** is represented by a rectangle, and **relationships** between data objects as a diamond. Additional notation is used to denote subtype, numerical, and associative relationships.

Subtype relationships denote that one object 'consists of' a number of objects.

**Data Dictionary**   The Data Dictionary is the underpinning element of the method identifying and documenting all data flows within the system, and associating these flows with data transforms and data stores.

A structured syntax is used to represent data objects in a hierarchical fashion. Support is provided for standard 'logic' functions such as AND, OR, EXCLUSIVE OR, and for multiples, bounded ranges, etc.

An example of a portion of a Data Dictionary is given in figure 7.4.

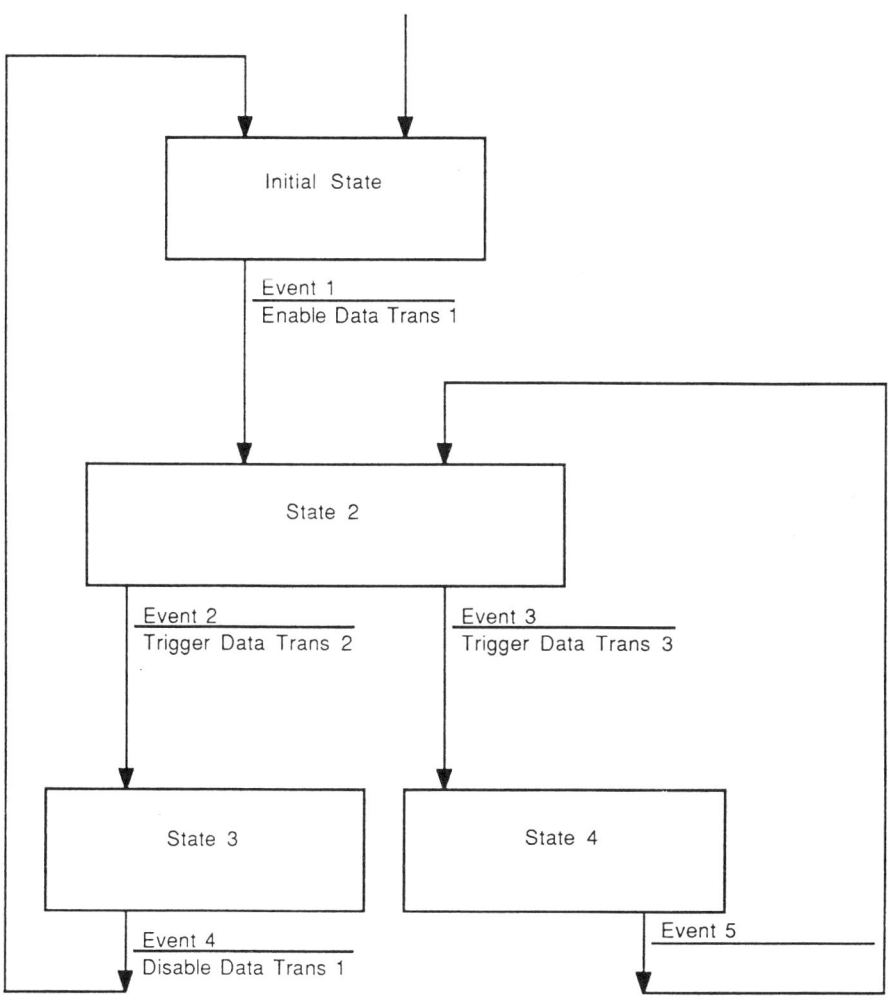

Figure 7.2. State Transition Diagram

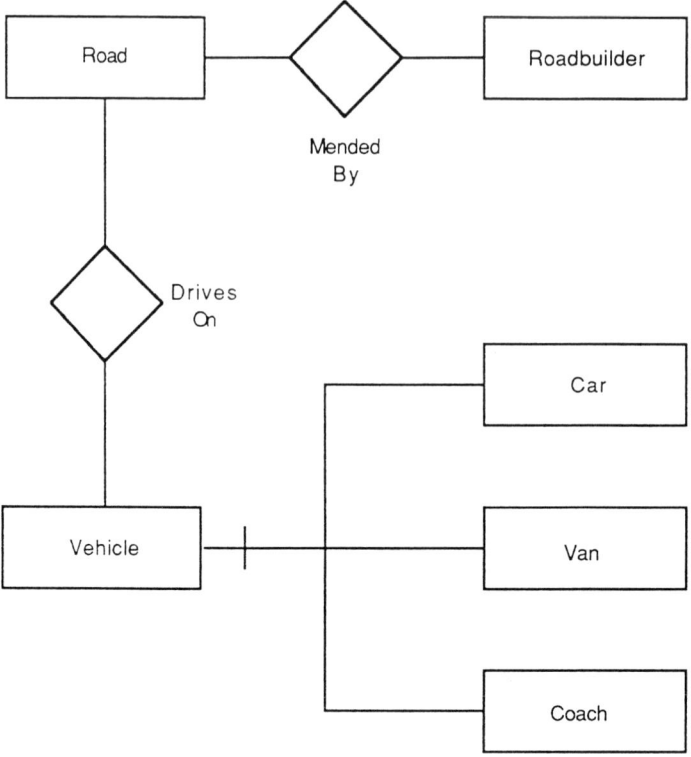

Figure 7.3. Entity Relationship Diagram

Iteration Value          =   * Number of loops to be performed *
                             **INTEGER range 0 ..   15**

No_of_Active_Entries     =   * Number of entries in the Active List *
                             **INTEGER range 1 ..   100**

Active_List              =   The list of Active Records *
                             1{Active_Record}30

Active_Record            =   * An individual data record *
                             Iteration_Value +
                             1{Active_List}No_of_Active_Entries

Figure 7.4. Data Dictionary

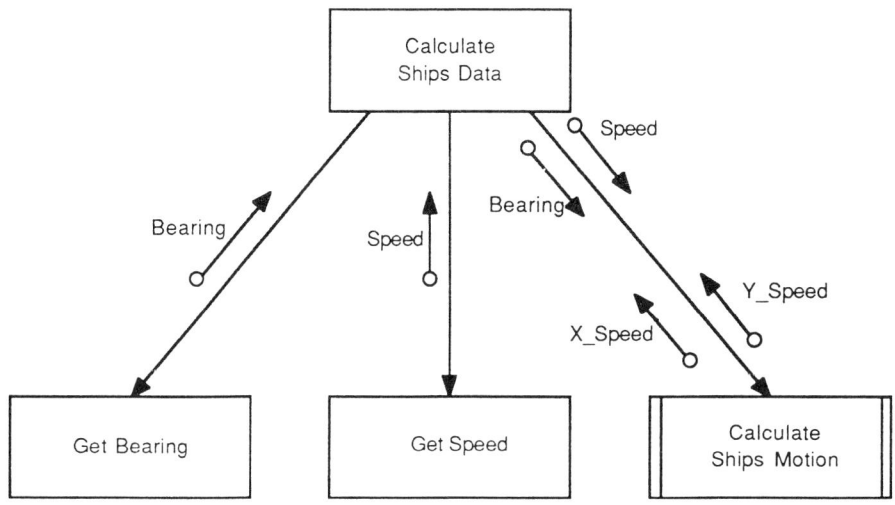

Figure 7.5. Hierarchy Diagram

**Hierarchy Diagrams** The Hierarchy Diagram represents the physical structure which will be used to implement the design. The diagram takes the form of an ordered call tree, and the syntax allows library modules, shared data areas, global data areas, and call parameters (couples) to be denoted.

In the example given in figure 7.5, the module 'Calculate Ships Data' calls the modules 'Get Bearing', 'Get Speed', and the library module 'Calculate Motion'. In each case the parameters passed and/or received are denoted as couples.

**Trace Tables** Trace Tables are used throughout the analysis and design process to ensure that all identified design elements in one stage of modelling are self-consistent, and are included in some form in the next. Such evidence of completeness and consistency are essential for Quality Assurance purposes.

Trace Tables are particularly important at a number of stages in the analysis:

(a) where the transformation from one stage to another involves partitioning,

(b) during Environment Modelling where it is important to produce a

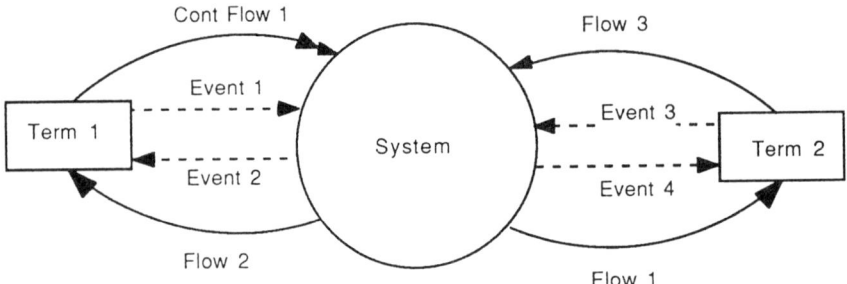

Figure 7.6. Context Diagram

consistent Event List, Data Dictionary, and Context Diagram.

**The Essential Model**

**The Environment Model**   The Yourdon technique provides for the analysis of given requirements, and not the development of those requirements from scratch.

The starting point of most analyses is a textual requirement specification. These specifications are often produced in an unstructured manner by committee. This produces requirements specifications which are self inconsistent, unnecessarily redundant, and incomplete.

The Environment Model is used to define the interfaces between the system and the 'outside world'. It consists of a **Context Diagram**, an **Event List**, a **Data Dictionary**, a **Trace Table**, and possibly an **Entity Relationship Diagram**. The Context Diagram and the Event List document the boundary of the system to be developed and the events which cross this boundary. An example of a Context Diagram is given in figure 7.6, and an Event List in figure 7.7.

The decision as to where to place the boundary of the system is not always simple. In many cases a layer of 'interface technology' may surround the system, giving the analyst many options.

The data and events passed to and from the system are initially derived from the textual requirement specification (together with additional information obtained from the customer, end user, etc.). At this stage in the analysis, particularly when defining the data passed in and out of the system, it may become apparent that parts of the requirement specification are incomplete. In a similar manner, it may also be apparent that a number of events have not been included, for example, system start-up and shut-down are often not addressed.

Ideally, a dialogue should occur between the analyst and the customer

EVENT    DESCRIPTION

Event 1    Initialisation of Term 1 complete. Determine
           setup parameters for Term 1 from maximum
           and minimum values of Cont Flow 1 sampled
           over 5 seconds.

Event 2    Flow 2 available.

Event 3    Term 2 ready for next input.

Event 4    Flow 1 available.

Figure 7.7. Event List

to rectify this situation. The Environment Model provides an easily understood graphical representation of the interface between the system and the
outside world, and documents data transfers and events to sufficient detail
to determine areas of incompleteness and inconsistency at this boundary.

**The Preliminary Data Flow Diagram**    The Environment Model has
produced an analysis of the system interface with the outside world. The
rationale behind the production of a Preliminary DFD is to model the control and data transforms required to satisfy the requirement specification.
This mapping of the required behaviour of the system allows the analyst to
determine the structure of the system.

Each requirement may be expressed as the functions required of the
systems as a response to an incoming data flow or event, or an originator
of outgoing data or events. In addition 'intermediate' data transformations
may be required to bridge the gap between incoming and outgoing data
events.

The textual requirement specification is progressively transformed into
an, often large, Data Flow Diagram, consisting of:

(a) Data Transformations representing the functions to be performed.

(b) Data Flows representing data passed into and out of the system.

(c) 'Internal' Data Flows and Data Stores between Data Transforms.

(d) Control Transformations representing the control structure of the sys-
    tem.

(e) Control Flows representing external events.

Inconsistencies, such as conflicting actions to be performed on the detection of a particular event, can be detected at this stage. Additional functions (Data Transformations) may also need to be added to enable the system to perform as required.

The Preliminary DFD and the Environment Model are the starting point for the requirement analysis. The Preliminary DFD is, however, usually extremely unwieldy and could not be used for discussions with the customer, or (since it is in itself unstructured) as a basis for a structured design and implementation.

**The Behavioural Model**   The Behavioural Model is a structured representation of the Preliminary DFD, derived from the Preliminary DFD, and presented in a 'top-down' manner from the Context Diagram.

Since the Context Diagram and the Preliminary DFD are (or should be) consistent at this stage, the production of the Behavioural Model is a process of grouping related data flows, events, and data transforms from the DFD into higher level design elements. This process is called **Upward Levelling**.

Techniques are available for the classification of events and data flows to produce optimum grouping. One of the main aims at this stage is to identify elements of the Preliminary DFD which are closely coupled, and those that are loosely coupled. This concept is referred to as **cohesion**. The grouping of closely coupled elements minimises interfaces between Transformations.

As the process of Upward Levelling proceeds, it is important to ensure that the successive levels of Data Flow Diagrams, State Transition Diagrams, and Entity Relationship Diagrams are consistent with each other and with the Data Dictionary. It is during such parts of the analysis and design life-cycle that tool support is invaluable.

The result of Behavioural Modelling is to progressively abstract the requirements towards the Context Diagram. The result is then presented as a set of levelled Data Flow Diagrams, with supporting DTS, STDs, ERDs, and Data Dictionary.

It is interesting to note that the Behavioural Model is derived 'bottom-up' and presented in a 'top-down' manner. This allows useful review of the analysis by the customer, and allows a suitable level of abstraction to be chosen for discussion and understanding.

It may be necessary to iterate the Upward Levelling and top-down presentation of the Behavioural Model to achieve the optimum grouping of related functions.

The Behavioural Model should represent the final statement of what is required of the system. It should contain only what is necessary to document the initial textual requirements in a consistent and complete manner.

A common error at this stage is to include some elements of *how* the system is to perform, rather than *what* it must perform. The inclusion of such detail may both affect the design process, and introduce an unnecessary maintenance burden.

## The Implementation Model

**The Processor Model**   The Processor Model forms the first part of the Structured Design process. Having determined what functions the system must perform, the first stage of Structured Design is to allocate the control and data transformations and data stores between a number of processors.

Many systems may not be complex enough to require more than one processor. In this case the Processor Modelling phase is omitted.

Processor Modelling may, however, be required for several reasons:

(a) the available processor may not be powerful enough to accomplish the requirement,

(b) responses to a number of external events may be required simultaneously,

(c) a distributed system may have been specified.

During Processor Modelling, the control and data transformations and data stores are assigned to a number of processors. This process should take place at the highest possible level of the Essential Model. The assignment of a Data Transformations shown at Level 1 of the Essential Model implies that all transformations contained within it at lower levels are also assigned.

This is, in effect, a partitioning of the system, and adds no more information to the functions the system will perform. Additions to the design to handle processor communication should be added where necessary at this stage.

Guidance can be offered to the analyst on the assignment of design elements to processors. For instance, it is usually the case that inter-processor communication should be reduced to the minimum by grouping closely coupled data transformations and data stores.

Processor Modelling is, however, highly reliant upon the skill and experience of the analyst. Errors made at this time can have significant effects upon the system. Costs will be increased if more processors than necessary are specified, and the risk that the software implementation will not reach the required specification is increased if too few processors are specified.

**The Task Model**   Task Modelling is, in essence, a similar process to that of Processor Modelling. Design elements which are closely coupled should be contained within a single task, and consideration should be given to the optimum number of tasks required.

During Task Modelling, the analyst should identify necessary parallelism, centralise control within tasks, and consider the input data rates to tasks. As with Processor Modelling, guidelines can be given for Task Modelling, but the process is reliant upon the experienced analyst.

Consideration should be given to the synchronous or asynchronous nature of the requirement. For instance, if the system is required to update all its output data at a fixed time period, then the nature of the system is basically synchronous, and a multiple task solution is probably inappropriate.

If a system is required to act 'immediately' on data from a number of inputs, then the nature of the system is asynchronous. In this case, one possible solution is to place the Data Transformations which handle the input data in duplicate tasks, one for each input.

Mechanisms to handle mutual exclusion and task communication should be added to the model during Task Modelling. Where clarity is increased, Data Transformations should be duplicated and denoted as such.

**The Hierarchy Model**   The Hierarchy Model represents the structure of the system implementation. A separate Hierarchy Model is produced for each task defined in the Task Model, and takes the form of a Structure Chart of the subprograms within the task, showing:

(a) subprograms, with their associated data areas,

(b) shared data areas between subprograms,

(c) parameters passed and returned,

(d) library modules.

The Hierarchy Model is derived directly from the functional description of a task as defined in the Task Model, and represents the structure of the software to be produced. The hierarchy model represents the common data areas and library modules, and defines the call structure of the task.

All subprograms identified on the Hierarchy Model are specified using a procedural language. This may be Structured English or the implementation language of the system.

## 7.1.3 The Yourdon/Ada interface

### Multi-processor issues

There is no direct Ada implementation for the Yourdon Processor Model. A number of facilities in the language, however, provide support for the passing of data between processors.

The use of (often complex) record types to define the data passed between processors allows the software engineer to use standard Ada generic packages, such as Direct_IO to implement the inter-processor interface.

Additionally, the increasing support for standard communication systems by embedded systems compilers provides the means to implement inter-processor communication using Local Area Networks such as Ethernet. The use of such packages should, however, be carefully considered, since the result may well be a loss of portability.

### Tasking

**The Finite State Machine**  The Control Transformations contained within each task defined in the Task Model may be combined into a single Control Transform. The techniques for this combination are relatively simple and are easy to implement.

It should be stressed that this is not the best means to document the control structure of a task, but simply enables the implementation to be produced in a standard manner.

This approach allows each task to be implemented in Ada as a Finite State Machine. The control logic for the state machine may be tested simply, and each Data Transform triggered by the state machine becomes a simple subprogram.

The control logic of the task is derived directly from the combined State Transition Diagram, and is expressed as a State Transition Table. This table is then executed by the Finite State Machine in the following manner.

The Finite State Machine 'reads' the State Transition Table to determine:

(a) the current state,

(b) the valid events (and therefore transitions between states) which may occur in that state,

(c) the Data Transforms which are triggered or enabled by the transitions,

(d) the resultant new state.

The Finite State Machine 'suspends itself' until an event occurs. Depending upon the event, the relevant trigger or enable is actioned by calling the appropriate subprogram(s). The resultant state is determined and the Finite State Machine again 'suspends itself' until a further valid event occurs.

This mechanism provides a simple, semi-automatic method to implement the Task Model in Ada, and has now been used successfully within VSEL on a number of projects.

**Communication between tasks**   In order to explore task communication and tasking models, a number of concepts and terms require definition:

**synchronous systems:** systems which do not employ tasking, but use an 'executive' which usually cyclically calls procedures;

**asynchronous systems:** systems which employ tasking, usually by the means of a 'scheduler' built into the language or operating system;

**mutual exclusion:** the means by which data is protected from multiple read/write operations by independent tasks;

**cross-stimulation:** the means by which control is passed between tasks.

These concepts are not peculiar to Ada, and have been used and understood in the industry for many years. In addition to the provision of a scheduler, and mechanisms for mutual exclusion and cross-stimulation, truly asynchronous systems must implement some means to divorce the production of data by one task from its consumption by another.

The mechanism employed in most systems is the queue. This allows calling tasks to place data in the queue for later consumption by the accepting task without the requirement for synchronisation. Mutual exclusion and cross-stimulation is provided by the queue, but tasks are only suspended when a queue is full (for calling tasks) or empty (for accepting tasks).

Most truly asynchronous Ada systems use queues, often implemented as Ada tasks themselves. In this case, such tasks merely provide a buffer between other tasks, decoupling the synchronisation requirements of the language.

In addition to queues, mechanisms to share data between tasks are usually provided. These are strictly not necessary, since queues may be used to pass duplicate data to tasks. This technique would appear to reduce coupling, but is unnecessarily inefficient to implement.

Queues and Shared Data must be distinguished in some manner in the Task Model, although each may be represented as data stores between tasks.

Since these design elements occur many times, a simple, reusable implementation will provide significant productivity benefits.

As discussed earlier, the provision within the Ada language for generics allows the 'customised reuse' of commonly used modules. This is ideal for the production of the generic queue.

These generic queues may take a number of forms:

**the standard queue;**

**the timeout queue:** providing the means to respond to timed events is provided in addition to the standard queue;

**the input queue:** providing the means to provide input to the system;

**the output queue:** providing the means to provide output from the system;

**the prioritised queue:** providing mechanisms for the immediate transfer of high priority information.

Each generic package requires a number of parameters to produce an instance for use within a system. These parameters are the means to 'customise' the package, and include:

(a) the record type of the data to be passed by the queue,

(b) the maximum number of data elements to be held in the queue,

(c) the physical device associated with the queue (for input and output queues).

The use of these generic packages assists the software engineer in standardising interfaces between tasks. The use of a matched pair of input and output queues (using identical parameters) can provide a mechanism for inter-processor communication.

### Libraries and type definitions

The Hierarchy Chart can be used to denote multiple instances of a subprogram. The Ada package allows these commonly called subprograms to be grouped together in generally available libraries.

Similarly, common type definitions may be identified from the Data Dictionary and grouped into type declaration packages. The Data Dictionary is the primary source of all data typing, and in many cases record definitions are simply collections of data of common types.

During the Design phase, the detail of elements held in the Data Dictionary is expressed using Ada syntax. This then provides an efficient interface between the design and implementation of data objects.

## 7.1.4   Conclusions

### Project management

The use of Yourdon and Ada has considerable effect upon project management. The 'traditional' metrics for software development are that 40% of the development time is spent in the Design phase, 30% in the Coding phase, and 30% in the Test and Integration phase.

The first impact of Yourdon is to spend considerably more time in the Analysis and Design phases (notice the addition of Analysis). The structured analysis of a system also delays the production of source code until the structure and functionality of the code has been defined, and the Coding phase is therefore shorter.

The major effect of Ada on the project is to reduce the incidence of integration errors, since all software integration aspects are checked during compilation. This reduces the Test and Integration phase.

The metrics for the use of Yourdon and Ada are that approximately 75% of the time is spent in the Analysis and Design phase, 10% in the Coding phase, and 15% in the Test and Integration phase.

The fact that the production of source code is delayed to the final 25% of a project may cause considerable concern to a project manager who measures progress in 'lines of code' produced.

Better methods of progress monitoring need to be developed. Within VSEL progress is monitored (and metrics gathered) against definable goals in the life-cycle, such as the completion of the Environment Model, Task Model, etc. The points are easily measured, since a Quality Review is always scheduled on the completion of each stage.

A somewhat extreme example of this was provided by the development of the Architecture Modelling Toolset within the IME. This system required 15 months Analysis and Design effort, followed by two months of Coding effort and three months of Test and Integration.

This represents 75% Analysis and Design, 10% Coding, and 15% Test and Integration. During the Coding phase, over 1000 Ada compilation units were produced by a five person team.

### Productivity

In addition to the relative changes in the project phases described above, the use of Yourdon and Ada provides an absolute increase in productivity.

The use of a structured approach to the complete Analysis, Design, and Implementation phases reduces the iteration and re-work required to produce a working, tested, and *debugged* system.

The productivity achieved in the development of large systems is further enhanced by the close mapping from a Yourdon Analysis and Design to an Ada Implementation. Such problems have proved costly for some companies developing large systems.

Although the metrics used within VSEL are commercially confidential, it has been estimated that the use of such techniques increases productivity by at least 20%. In addition, the use of suitable support tools can produce a further increase in productivity.

## Product quality

The use of Yourdon and Ada also increases the overall quality of the system. All aspects of the systems behaviour are documented, and since the system is developed from a structured analysis of the customer's requirements, the system is more likely to meet those requirements.

The use of the features of Ada which encourage good Software Engineering practices also increases the quality of the final system in the areas of reliability, error handling, and maintainability.

## The future

Although this paper has described the current use of Yourdon and Ada within VSEL, the development of techniques and methods should never be static.

This paper has not described the testing techniques used within the company. These techniques have been imported into our Code of Practice from knowledge of MASCOT based development, and are closely coupled with the Design phase of Yourdon.

VSEL have also incorporated object-oriented paradigms into the way in which designs are expressed using Yourdon, further increasing the capability to reuse elements at the *design* level.

There is not, nor ever will be, a *correct* way of developing software. The discipline of Software Engineering is young, and the combined use of Yourdon and Ada represents a stepping stone in the path to a mature engineering discipline.

# 7.2   Ada in nuclear energy applications

## Vincent Rich, Encore Computer Corporation

## Introduction

Over the last few years the economic and technical advantages of the Ada language have become apparent to computer scientists within the nuclear energy industry. This paper describes those features of the Ada language that make it particularly attractive to organisations developing software for nuclear energy applications.

Computers are used in the nuclear energy industry for many purposes including reactor design, monitoring and control, and operator training. A monitoring system will typically scan thousands of analog and digital inputs, converting low level voltages into engineering units (kilograms, litres, etc.), checking for alarms, displaying data on control desk display units and archiving the data. The monitoring function may be accomplished by a small number of super-minicomputers or a larger number of interconnected microprocessors.

Operator training is performed on high fidelity simulators incorporating a replica of the power station control room and computers similar to those used in the actual power station. Additional computers are used to simulate the missing components such as the reactor itself.

## System Characteristics

Both monitoring systems and simulators are characterised by very high capital costs, long life cycles (typically 20 years or more), and a substantial amount of bespoke software. Both have to operate in real-time and the reactor monitoring system must operate with a very high degree of reliability. Ada is ideally suited to these applications as it was specifically designed for large, complex real-time embedded systems with long life cycles.

Ada, through its encouragement and enforcement of good software engineering practices, enables the cost of owning software to be held at a lower level than would be possible with other languages. Prior experience has shown that Ada programs are easier to develop, more reliable, easier to comprehend and easier to modify than similar programs written in 'C' or FORTRAN.

## Management of Complexity

The comprehension of a complete reactor monitoring system is difficult due to its size. Ada allows the complexity to be managed by decomposing the system into a large number of small software packages. Each package is small enough to be easily understood in its own right and consists of a specification describing the interface to the package and a body containing the Ada statements. As the packages are integrated together, the Ada compiler will rigorously check the correctness of the interfacing between packages and expose any problems.

If the external interface of any particular package is changed then the compiler will force any other packages that interface with the modified package to be recompiled in order to verify that the interpackage interface is still valid.

## Extensive Program Checking

Ada programs exhibit higher levels of correctness and robustness than equivalent programs written in other languages due to the extensive amount of checking performed by the compiler and additional checking performed as the Ada program executes. Ada allows variables within the program to be assigned engineering unit types (kilograms, metres, etc.) and also allows the definition of operations on sets of types (for example, a divide operator that accepts operands of types volts and degrees Celsius, and returns a value of volts per degree C). The compiler completely checks the consistency of types and operators within each expression and exposes any errors. This results in design and programming errors being detected at program compilation time (when the cost of resolving the problem is small) rather than finding them at the program testing phase or worse still, not at all. Unfortunately, due to the amount of checking performed, Ada compilers are typically larger than compilers for other languages and have slower compilation rates, but this is compensated for by the significantly reduced program testing time.

If a program error is detected at execution time then the normal statement sequence is terminated at the erroneous statement and control passed to an exception handler for an orderly recovery. Error conditions can include the following: a variable exceeding its normal range of values, an attempt to address outside of the bounds of an array, an attempt to access a non-existent memory location or peripheral device, other hardware errors, etc. With FORTRAN or C programs, some of these errors would go unnoticed at the point of failure and erroneous results would then cascade through the program until a fatal error causing a program abort occurred. With the Ada exception management system, the location and type of the problem can be logged and reported to the operator, and then a recovery can be attempted or at least the system shut down in an orderly manner.

## Computer System Architecture

The computer system architecture for a reactor monitoring system can take many forms ranging from a large number of distributed microprocessors through to a single super-minicomputer. Ada lends itself well to the programming of multiprocessor systems as it is the only commonly used programming language that directly supports concurrency. From the software engineering viewpoint, the system should be constructed as a single Ada program in order to maximise the amount of checking performed by the compiler. The reason for this is that while the compiler can completely check the interfacing of all of the packages within a single program, it cannot check the correctness of communications between programs. Configuration management procedures can be adopted to ensure that each program has been compiled with the same version of the inter-program communications specification but as the number of programs grow, the possibility of a communications error increases.

Computer systems based on a number of merchant microprocessors (products of Motorola, Intel, etc.) offer substantially improved price/ performance ratios and scaleability when compared with a conventional proprietary architecture super-minicomputer. If the microprocessors are connected via a local area network, then most current Ada compilers will not allow the distribution of a single Ada program across the whole system and a multiple program strategy with its consequent loss of robustness will have to be employed.

A more attractive solution is the Symmetrical MultiProcessor (SMP) architecture comprising a number of closely coupled industry standard microprocessors where each microprocessor can access all of the memory and all of the peripheral devices. The SMP allows the entire software system to be implemented as one program and co-executed by all of the microprocessors. The Ada program contains a number of Ada tasks, each task being responsible for a particular aspect of the monitoring system. A multitask Ada program will execute correctly irrespective of the number of processors available. This allows the system to operate (with reduced performance) if one or more processors fail, or alternatively, system performance can be enhanced by simply plugging in additional processors.

The reactor monitoring system needs to operate in real-time, simultaneously reading large amounts of data, processing the data, and outputting to display devices and other systems. While the Unix operating system provides excellent support for the software development phase of the project it does not have the required real-time characteristics. This problem has been solved by using Unix for software development and initial testing, and then removing the operating system and executing the Ada program in a "bare machine mode". In this mode the program connects directly to the resources of the computer (processors, memory, peripheral devices, etc.) and Unix plays no part in the real-time operations. All of the standard features of the Ada language are available in bare machine mode, the only limitation being that the Ada programmer is unable to call operating system services (whose use is unattractive anyway as they reduce both program reliability and the portability of the program onto other systems).

## Current Ada Applications in Nuclear Energy

A nuclear reactor monitoring and control system is currently being constructed by Sema Group for a 1400 megawatt pressurised water reactor at Chooz in France. At the heart of the system are two powerful Encore super-minicomputers, one acting as the primary monitoring system and one as a hot standby. Each computer contains two processors and executes a single Ada program in a bare machine mode.

As the system runs, the status of the primary system is continuously transferred to the standby system in case a switch-over is required. The two computers are interconnected via a fibre optic link in order to avoid any electrical connections between the machines. Software development is performed by loading the Unix operating system on one of the computers and then running the CASE tools, compiler, linker, etc. Once the program preparation is complete, the computer is halted and restarted in bare mode.

In Sweden, Ada has been used on three nuclear reactor simulators. SYPRO, a Swedish systems house, has been increasing the fidelity of three existing simulators by replacing ageing Xerox computers with Encore systems programmed in Ada. In each case, the simulated control room is connected to a replica of the actual power station monitoring and control system computers and these in turn are connected via a T1 communications link to the Encore system which simulates the reactor and ancillary equipment. The Encore system contains two processors and these co-execute a single Ada program in a bare machine mode. The program contains approximately 100,000 lines of code structured as 110 Ada tasks.

## Summary

Although Ada was initially developed for large-scale embedded military projects, its characteristics closely match the requirements of the nuclear energy industry. In particular, Ada enables the construction of large and complex real-time systems for multiprocessor computers. The resulting programs are easier to understand, easier to maintain, and more robust than equivalent programs written in other languages.

## 7.3   MALPAS and Ada

### John T. Webb, RTP Software Ltd

Ada is increasingly being used in many projects, particularly those associated with the Defence arena. Other significant projects using Ada include the US space station and various air traffic control systems. Such projects often involve the production of high integrity systems with a proven and demonstrable verification process. In addition, many other systems are planned or in development which need to have the software verified to some extent. To meet this need, RTP Software have developed an Ada translator to increase their ever growing portfolio of translators for use with their MALPAS static analysis toolset.

Static analysis is a technique which provides a viable and cost-effective alternative to many dynamic testing programmes. It also overcomes many of the problems associated with dynamic testing where there is a fundamental problem of testing any item which is not of minimal complexity. Whereas dynamic testing attempts to find errors by devising as comprehensive a set of test data as possible, static analysis establishes total functionality by mathematical analysis. Hence the fundamental problem with dynamic testing of not being able to demonstrate an absence of errors is overcome.

The static analysis of an item is performed on a model, in the case of MALPAS this is expressed in an Intermediate Language (IL). Hence the task of the Ada translator is to produce an IL model of the original Ada program. This model will include details of many of the underlying semantics of a program, details of how controlling variables in loops are used for example. In some cases, the model will represent some abstraction of an Ada feature, tasking for example, which is an obvious difficulty when attempting to analyse something statically. In other cases, the level of semantic detail in the model will be under the user's control, exceptions for example. This will allow detailed information to be obtained only if it is required, thus reducing complexity in other cases.

It is a fundamental design aim of the translator that as large a subsets as possible will be handled. It is recognised that high integrity software should only be produced using a subset of Ada and various subset have been proposed. However, there does not appear to be an easily identifiable and definable 'global' subset. In any case, it is not necessarily the function of MALPAS to impose an artificially restricted subset and it may be necessary to analyse code written using full Ada. The translator restrictions are therefore small in number although plans are being considered for a later version to allow user-definable subsets. The main restrictions are the hardware department Chapter 13 features and the level of detail to which features such as tasking are modelled. Many time-dependent features can be modelled in an abstract manner which only indicates their use and not their effect. As was indicated above, exceptions will be handled to various levels of detail but will only indicate the raising of an exception and necessarily the full circumstances which led to the exception. In other words, they will merely be audited. Later releases may enable them to be monitored more effectively.

Apart from these constraints, any legal Ada program will be handled by the Ada–MALPAS system with the translator handling full Ada programs if necessary, issuing warnings where appropriate. In particular, the full Ada separate compilation system is available and it is envisaged that in later versions the program library will be used as a repository for analysis results. Generics are initially handled by analysing only the generic specification and body, each instantiation assuming that the generic has been verified. In some circumstances, it may be desirable to analyse each instantiation individually, using specific information about the generic actual parameters to provide a more refined analysis.

The translator is constructed in the classical manner of having a front end to perform syntax and semantic analysis and generating a tree-structured intermediate language which is then operated on by a back end which produces the MALPAS IL. Care is taken to ensure that the IL is recognisably derived from the original Ada source text to ensure that the MALPAS results, expressed in terms of the IL model, may be readily referred back to the original source. This aspect, combined with the problem of ensuring that the mappings result in a semantically accurate model, actually consume a large percentage of the total effort involved in the production of the translator.

Given a translator which is capable of producing a faithful model of the original Ada source, one can use the MALPAS tool set to derive a considerable amount of information about the program. The information obtainable ranges from anomalies in the control flow of the program and the use made of data to the proof of correctness against a formal specification. There are in fact six analysers and the reader. The reader assembles the internal graph as used by MALPAS from the IL produced by the translator and a 'preamble' which defines various language-dependent features. It also provides various statistics and an overall procedure call graph. The analysers are:

1. The control flow analyser which finds badly structured code.

2. The data use analyser which reveals anomalies in the use of data in general and, in the case of procedure parameters, its usage relative to its definition.

3. The information flow analyser which shows how output data is influenced by the flow of control through a program and by input data. It will also detect anomalies between actual and defined data use and ineffective statements.

4. The path assessor which counts the number of syntactically feasible paths through a program.

5. The semantic analyser which reduces a program to a black box, giving transfer functions in terms of sets of output expressions for each possible set of input conditions. The information given will cover the total input space which the program can respond to.

6. The compliance analyser which proves conformance between what a program does, as expressed by the semantic analyser, and a formal specification.

Large programs can be handled by various techniques provided as integral parts of the MALPAS system. A partial programmer allows semantic and compliance analysis to be on selected paths of complex programs. It is also possible to 'mark' nodes if it is possible to break a program into logically independent sections. In addition, the procedure specification features, which also enable package specifications to be easily handled, allow a bottom-up or top-down analysis to be carried out depending on the level of specification available. If information explosion becomes a problem, then other facilities allow complex detail to be abstracted as the analysis proceeds.

Given the tool set described, it is possible to use the Ada–MALPAS system to verify programs to the level required for putting high integrity systems into service. It will be possible to verify code retrospectively within the few restrictions outlined. However, it is far better to set up system development procedures which recognise the need to use static analysis and ensure that the maximum benefit is obtained by avoiding the use of unanalysable constructs as much as possible. Indeed, various projects have demonstrated the effectiveness of using MALPAS throughout the life-cycle, starting with the verification of a formal, mathematically based, specification and proceeding through various refinement and verification stages until a formally verified system is delivered. Work has also been done on using MALPAS with structured methods. The result of such a disciplined approach can be an overall saving in the total life-cycle costs of a system, a point worthy of consideration when planning a new project. Various regulatory bodies are also considering the merits of such an approach with the aim of ensuring greater safety in the use of high integrity systems. It is therefore expected that the Ada–MALPAS systems described will be of great value to systems developers and ultimately their customers.

# Bibliography

Webb, J.T., 'Static analysis — an introduction and example', *Proc. Intl. Workshop of Software Engineering and its applications*, Toulouse, 1988.

Webb, J.T., 'Static analysis using MALPAS, an introduction with examples', Rex, Thompson & Partners Ltd, Farnham, 1989.

Pierce, R.H. and Webb, J.T., 'Analysing Ada programs with MALPAS', *Proc. 8th Ada UK Conference*, York, 1989.

# 7.4   Ada in hard real-time: an example from flight simulation

## Georgeanne Chitwood, Harris Corporation

### Abstract

Most members of the Ada software community agree that Ada supports software engineering principles and therefore supports the development of any large-scale software system. Questions on the usability of Ada have centered on hard real-time applications. The thesis of this paper is that Ada is working now, in hard real-time, although not necessarily as the language designers intended.

The problems associated with Ada tasking are well known. The long-term solutions are embodied in the Ada language changes proposed for Ada 9X. These are being examined carefully and with full public review. Unfortunately, the value of X in Ada 9X has yet to be determined, although 3 is the number being suggested.

The development of hard real-time systems has not waited for long-range solutions. Short-term solutions have been developed by implementors. The Harris Ada Programming Support Environment is used as an example of a viable short-term solution.

Proof that Ada is being used successfully in hard real-time is given by a discussion of an application of Ada to flight simulation.

## Introduction

The importance of Ada depends on much more than its technical merit as a programming language. The growing momentum of the use of Ada is due to its acceptance as an international standard, the support and investment it receives from many government and commercial organizations, and its success on defense and non-defense projects.

In fact, the term Ada has come to represent both a programming language and the culture that has sprung up around it. Although the elders of the Ada tribe disagree vocally and at some length about technical issues, they do agree that Ada packages and strong typing support software engineering. They also generally agree that there are problems associated with the Ada tasking model. In the meantime, the hunters/warriors of the tribe have gotten on with their job, as they always do. They are implementing hard real-time systems in Ada.

The Ada Joint Program Office (AJPO) reports that their usage database contains over four hundred programs using Ada or planning to use Ada. As usage has grown, discussion of language problems has moved from theoretical to pragmatic issues involved in developing large real-time systems.

Many of the early problems attributed to the language were really implementation problems. Now that production quality compilers are available, attention has focused on the difficulties inherent in the Ada tasking model when used for real-time applications. Deficiencies have been identified that prevent the use of unrestricted Ada tasking in hard real-time systems.

The long-term solution is to solve the problems of Ada tasking in the Ada 9X language change process and to standardize on some of the ACM SIGAda Runtime Environments Working Group (ARTEWG) interface features. One short-term solution is to implement tasking models which behave differently from the Ada model. This clearly defeats any hope of transportability and violates validation. A legal short-term solution is to use the Ada tasking only when it is appropriate and construct Ada hard real-time systems using the traditional multiprogramming and executive approach.

This paper presents an example of one successful, legal short-term solution and discusses an example of its use in flight simulation.

## Real-time systems

Real-time systems [1] are defined as systems that react to external events in sufficient time to influence future events. Systems that are required to respond to events within absolute deadlines are termed "hard" real-time systems.

A hard real-time system can be thought of as a collection of cooperating processes, each responsible for handling one or more events. A system's processes may be implemented as subroutines, Ada tasks, complete programs running under an operating system, or some combination of all three. A system's processes may be independent or interdependent. Independent processes do not communicate or synchronize with other processes. Interdependent processes may communicate or synchronize with, or even initiate, other processes.

The events handled by a system's processes may be aperiodic or periodic. A process, either periodic or aperiodic, is said to meet its performance requirement if it is able to receive and react to external events within its deadline. To guarantee a given response time to periodic events, processes can be scheduled to run periodically; for example, a process that is responsible for sampling an input stream at the rate of 20 times per second is coded to sample the input stream once, then is executed at the desired 20 Hz rate.

The phrase "frequency-based scheduling", or "FBS", denotes the periodic scheduling of a system's processes. The term "deadline scheduling" has also been used to describe this scheduling technique. The executive responsible for implementing a frequency-based scheduling algorithm is referred to as a "frequency-based scheduler". This executive is sometimes referred to as a "cyclic executive".

The execution of a system composed of periodic processes proceeds as a sequence of minor cycles. A real-time system's minor cycle is the smallest unit of frequency maintained by the system's scheduler; for example, a system composed of processes running at 10 Hz, 50 Hz, and 100 Hz has a minor cycle of 100 Hz. Minor cycles are measured in terms of frequency or time: a 100 Hz minor cycle is equivalent to a 10 millisecond minor cycle. It is common practice for periodic processes to begin their execution on minor cycle boundaries and for their deadlines to occur on those same boundaries.

A system meets its schedulability requirement if no combination of external events can cause any of its processes to miss, or overrun, their deadlines. A system whose processes consistently miss their deadlines will be viewed as unresponsive. Systems whose processes overrun their deadlines during transient overload conditions will be viewed as unreliable and unpredictable. By definition, hard real-time systems cannot tolerate any deadline overruns.

Traditional methods that attempt to ensure schedulability, such as the maintenance of fifty percent spare processor capacity, do not guarantee schedulability. This method, and other such methods, can sometimes be replaced by a more rigorous analysis due to the development of real-time scheduling theory. (See Reference 3 for a discussion of real-time scheduling theory.)

## Ada tasking

The Ada mechanism for parallel processing is the task. Ada tasking can be adequate in cases where tasks are running on one processor and are synchronized by a simple rendezvous.

| Night Hawk PIWG Results | | | |
|---|---|---|---|
| T000001 | 114.6 | T000005 | 118.8 |
| T000002 | 114.6 | T000006 | 191.6 |
| T000003 | 117.2 | T000007 | 114.6 |
| T000004 | 151.0 | T000008 | 322.98 |

This table shows some results of the Association for Computing Machinery SIGAda's Performance Issues Working Group (PIWG) benchmarks for the Harris Ada compiler running with optimization and run-time checks suppressed. The computer system was a Night Hawk 3808. Results are given in microseconds.

## Priority inversion

In systems of interdependent Ada tasks, implicit priority inversions can arise through the unrestricted use of Ada rendezvous. A priority inversion occurs in a multitask application when a lower priority task blocks the execution of a higher priority task. Since low priority tasks must be allowed to execute within critical sections, priority inversions can never be completely prevented. The reliability and responsiveness of a real-time system can be significantly affected by priority inversions.

**Queuing Priority Inversion** is caused by the language's requirement that task entry calls must be queued in order of arrival, or first in first out (FIFO).

**Rendezvous Priority Inversion** happens when a high priority task is waiting to rendezvous with a low priority task which is blocked by execution of a medium priority task.

**Selective Wait Priority Inversion** may occur when two tasks of differing priorities perform entry calls to separate entries of a third task. The current definition of the language does not prevent the called task from accepting the rendezvous with the lower priority task first, although this denies service to the higher priority caller task. The Ada standard explicitly allows this inversion, for it states in LRM 9.7.1 [2] that if "...several alternatives can thus be selected, one of them is selected arbitrarily (that is, the language does not define which one)".

## Long-term solutions: proposed Ada language changes

The following list summarizes the proposed changes [3] to the Ada standard in the area of tasking:

- Augment the language with a deterministic delay construct, perhaps similar to the ARTEWG's proposed BOUNDED_DELAYS package [4].

- Remove the requirement of FIFO sorting for entry queues, and require the sorting of entry queues by task priority.

- Require the use of task priorities in choosing from the open alternatives of a selective wait statement.

- Allow a "sensible" rendezvous implementation to use the priority inheritance protocol.

- Provide a standard method of scheduling tasks in a frequency-based manner, such as the ARTEWG's synchronous scheduling package.

## Short-term solutions: real-time systems in Ada now

See [1]. The Ada tasking model was designed with the intent that one executable Ada program will execute many tasks simultaneously. In real-time however, multiple programs must be accessed repeatedly in a predetermined order, and the system must also respond immediately to external interrupts, giving full attention to tasks of higher priority. But the Ada tasking model does not allow the user to specify particular times or priorities in a program. This enforced tasking method creates a larger system overhead burden and slows down the performance of the system. Therefore, Ada compiler manufacturers now supply other methods to deal with real-time programs. They supply run-time environments which meet real-time requirements, but stay within the limits of the Ada language. Usually these environments give access to the operating system of a computer through Ada packages, constructs which define a related group of type definitions, data declarations, functions and procedures.

Essentially, real-time programming has three specific requirements that affect the use of tasking.

1. First, is a requirement for physical concurrency. Hard real-time systems have specific time constraints that are so small that multiple processors are needed, each running concurrently to gather all of the information within a specific time frame.

   Concurrency is possible but is difficult to achieve. It is necessary to provide a way for users to define the tasks to be split up on multiple processors. In order to do this, it is necessary to determine the kinds of objects each processor can access, to set up communication between processors, and to determine the data that must be accessed by each processor. This is a sophisticated and complex programming requirement (called the definition of share groups) and the Ada language was not set up for it.

   Harris provides a mechanism to share data between Ada programs, therefore relieving the user of the low level implementation that normally occurs with shared data. The package is marked with a pragma that defines the package as a sharable data pool. Subsequent accesses to objects within the package will come from the shared data pool. This allows the user to define a share group. Semaphore operations are provided allowing the user to control concurrent access to the shared data.

Harris also provides a way to map Ada data objects onto physical devices such as the external peripherals. This allows the program designer to tie the peripheral to a spot in physical memory and put data on that spot. Then, when the computer system reads memory, it reads the data put there by the device.

2. A second problem for real-time systems has to do with how tasks are scheduled and what the language says about the execution order of tasks. Real-time simulation uses a method called cyclic scheduling. Because real-time simulation is based on the concept of refresh rate, tasks are scheduled in cycles that repeat in a pre-determined manner. The Ada language defines the communication between tasks assuming a sequential execution. It does not provide methods for scheduling cyclic events.

3. Another problem is that Ada only provides a static priority model for tasks. It does not allow the user to dynamically modify priorities during execution of the application. In a cyclic model, pending some event, certain tasks may be required to have the highest priority on the system. This cannot be implemented in Ada. The cyclic model normally provides ways of defining the cycle times and frequencies. So vendors are supplying ways to dynamically modify cycle frequencies.

One solution, available from Harris, provides access to the Frequency Based Scheduler by means of an Ada package specification. As developed by Harris, Ada procedures interface with a Frequency Based Scheduler in the CX/RT real-time operating system. The scheduler runs executable Ada programs during specific required intervals. These Ada programs can share data as needed. This system can execute across multiple processors and preserves the determinism required for real-time simulation. Access to the performance monitor is also provided. In addition, an interactive data recording for the examination and modification is available. Large simulators, with hard real-time requirements, have been and are being developed using Ada with the Frequency Based Scheduler.

In addition, an Ada pragma is defined which allows the sharing of data among programs written in Ada, C and FORTRAN along with pragma interface C and FORTRAN. This gives access to the operating system facilities, and provides a convenient method for incremental conversion from those languages to Ada.

## Ada and real-time flight simulations

Harris's Ada technology has been used successfully for several years. The research and development simulation for the Stealth Bomber was done by Northrop on the Harris single-processor H-Series systems, as several other classified research projects by other developers. Some of the reports from Northrop are dated 1987. The P-3C Production Trainer was also developed on the H-Series, as requested by Quintron at the Harris Users Exchange in May, 1989. The program began in early 1988.

More recent flight simulation programs are being done on the Harris Night Hawk family of multiprocessing super-minicomputers. These programs include

- McDonnell Douglas — C-17 Aircrew Training System

- Quintron — Undergraduate Pilot Training Instrument Flight System

- Flight Safety International — Helicopter Dual Blade Element Model

- IntelliSys — 20F16

- General Dynamics, McDonnell Douglas — A-12.

## Overview of the C-17 Aircrew Training System (ATS) program

One of the largest of these programs in the C-17 ATS.

The four-engine C-17 transport, being developed by Douglas Aircraft Company, is designed to be operated by a crew of two pilots and one loadmaster. It will carry large combat equipment over intercontinental distances and land on small, austere airfields near the battle zone.

The C-17 Aircrew Training System is being developed by McDonnell Douglas Corporation. This project is sponsored by Aeronautical Systems Division (AFSC), Wright-Patterson Air Force Base, Ohio. It will provide training for C-17 pilots, loadmasters and engine run technicians. The C-17 ATS includes classroom instruction, computer-based training, training devices, simulators and maintenance support for three years, with options for up to 15 years. The product of the system is a fully qualified crew member who is guaranteed to pass an Air Force-administered evaluation.

The majority of the learning will take place on training devices. These include 12 Weapon System Trainers (WST), six of which include loadmaster training capability, a Cockpit Systems Simulator, and cargo trainers.

The Weapon System Trainers will be FAA Phase II flight simulators with six axis motion and a 225 degree horizontal field of view. They will have daylight, dusk and night-time visual presentation.

The six WST loadmaster stations will be three-dimensional representations of C-17 loadmaster stations. They can be used for independent loadmaster training or to provide the three-person crew with capability to carry out a full mission in the WST.

The Cockpit Systems Simulator will be a duplicate of the Weapon System Trainers, but without the visual and motion capability.

Harris Corporation's Night Hawk computer is the computational system for the Weapon System Trainers. The WST software is being developed in Ada by McDonnell Douglas Training Systems, McDonnell Douglas Corporation, in St. Louis, Missouri. FlightSafety International will build the simulators using the McDonnell Douglas Multiview visual display systems.

## Overview of the Rotor Wing Blade Element Simulation Program

The program [5] that I have chosen to discuss at some length as an example of how well Ada is working in hard real-time is unique among all the other flight simulations being done on Harris Night Hawk systems. It is a *commercial application of Ada!*

There was no requirement for FlightSafety International to use Ada on this or any other commercial program. They chose to use Ada on its merits as a language which supports Software Engineering. They also expect the design methodology and much of the code developed for this program to be used for their military applications.

In the Rotor Wing Blade Element Simulation Program, a single Phase-II flight simulator will be developed for the Bell 212 and the Bell 412 helicopters by the Simulation Systems Division of FlightSafety International (FSI).

The main goal of this research and development project is to gain experience in the use of Ada and Software Engineering techniques in the development of simulator software. Subsidiary goals are to develop expertise in the following areas:

1. use of an Ada-based Program Design Language (PDL),

2. development of software to U.S. military standards,

3. application of Software Engineering techniques,

4. use of an UNIX-based software development environment.

Although the goal of this project is to investigate the use of Ada on a production simulator with stringent real-time processing requirements, this is not a feasibility study. The completed simulator will be installed at FlightSafety's Training Center in Fort Worth, Texas, where it will be used for initial and recurrent pilot/co-pilot training.

Object Oriented Design techniques were used to develop the architectural model for the simulator software. The model was validated through rapid-prototyping of the most time-critical section of the software design and is being used as the basis for the design of the software for the full simulator.

The software is computationally intensive and includes a 200 Hz finite-element rotor-blade simulation. All of the software is being written in Ada, although the systems architect anticipates that a small amount of C may be required for I/O drivers. It is being developed on a dual-processor Harris Night Hawk computer system. The same Night Hawk system will be used in the simulator.

The software will consist of approximately 40,000 Ada statements (terminal semicolons) or about 120,000 lines of Ada code. As of the end of January, 1990, approximately 16,000 Ada statements have been written.

As well as development of a software architecture and production of the prototype, the five and one half month design phase included time spent to become familiar with the Unix system, the features and utilities of the Harris real-time Unix operating system and the Ada environment. In addition, time was spent on structuring the Ada libraries. This phase was carried out by the system architect.

The flight group began data analysis in June and July, 1989. The full ten member design team was completed in November, 1989. All team members have extensive experience in flight simulator development. Hardware/Software Integration is scheduled for the third week of June, 1990.

## Design issues for the Rotor Wing Blade Element Simulation Program

FlightSafety International (FSI) is experienced in the development of real-time simulators in FORTRAN. They recognized that an optimum design of an Ada system is, or should be, quite different from that of a FORTRAN system. They chose a software system architect who was experienced with Ada software engineering and real-time simulators and charged him with developing a design approach embodied in an architecture for Ada-based flight simulators.

The software under design is described by Mike Caffey, the system architect as follows: "The rotor-blade dynamics software for the 212/412 performs a finite-element analysis of the forces acting on each blade of the rotor. In this model, each blade is divided into several segments and the force components acting on each segment of each blade are calculated independently and summed to determine the total force acting on the rotor. Due to the speed of rotation of the blade this model must execute at 200 Hz." [5]

Object Oriented Design (OOD) techniques were identified as the most suitable approach for software that is to be implemented in Ada. It was not found to be useful for requirements analysis. Although OOD was used in the middle phases of design, there were considerable differences from classical OOD.

The key issues affecting the design had to do with real-time requirements. The most significant issue is the stringent 200 Hz processing requirements of the rotor-blade dynamics software. A second issue was a need to provide a design mechanism to address using more than one CPU. FlightSafety wanted to run the 200 Hz software on one processor and run the remaining software on the other CPU. There must also be a design mechanism to allow communication between independent processes on one or both CPUs. OOD does not consider such issues.

Another consideration in design was FSI's decision to use the Frequency Based Scheduler (FBS) which is available on the Harris Night Hawk systems. The FBS, described earlier in this paper, schedules multiple operating system processes at fixed frequencies across multiple CPUs. This eliminated the necessity for FSI to write and debug a real-time executive. Although they saw the FBS as giving a great deal of flexibility to the software, they spent considerable time ensuring that the design was not so tied to the FBS, that migration would be difficult.

Finally, the designers considered how to make data available to a real-time monitor without using large Ada packages in common areas as had been previously done for FORTRAN.

## Software architecture

Rapid prototyping was used to validate a design approach for the whole system. Several approaches were examined by development of a slice of the simulator. This allowed FlightSafety to evolve a software architecture that is appropriate to Ada and satisfies the real-time requirements of flight simulation. By the time full development started, most of the design issues had been solved and there was Ada code available that served as examples for the full team.

The following description of the software is extracted from Reference 5. Changes were made to distinguish between use of the term task in Ada and in simulation. Simulation usage has been replaced by the more general term process. The software for the Bell 212/412 is divided into several subsystems such as engines, navigation, rotor dynamics, fuel, etc. Each of these subsystems is implemented as a separate operating system process that is scheduled at a fixed frequency by the Harris Frequency Based Scheduler.

Communication between each of the simulation processes is accomplished through a shared memory region. The shared memory region is comprised of several Ada packages referred to as "state packages". There is one state package for each operating system process. The process that owns the state package broadcasts data that is required by other processes to the state package. The other processes import (with) the state package and read the required data. Each state package contains only information that is required by other subsystems. [5]

When contrasted with the traditional (FORTRAN) approach, where one monolithic process was assigned to each CPU, the advantages of the multiple process approach are that there is increased modularity, flexible configuration management, better fault tolerance and increased protection of common data.

The process that is used to implement each subsystem is composed of several parts: a main program, a subsystem package, and numerous object packages. The main program for each subsystem performs all of the interface to the Frequency Based Scheduler, thus isolating the machine dependent part of the code.

The code used to implement each subsystem is contained in the subsystem package imported by the main program. This package calls its subprograms each time the main program is triggered by the Frequency Based Scheduler. The subprograms can broadcast data only to the subsystem state package for their subsystem, although they can read data from any subsystem package.

The "object packages" implement components of the subsystem as private types. The object packages are imported by the main subsystem package and are used extensively in the software to promote modularity and reuse. To a large extent, programs in subsystem packages simply put together programs contained in the object packages. [5]

### Prototype

The high frequency portion of the rotor blade simulation was developed using this design approach. In the initial tests, no optimization of any kind was used.

Then various options were used to optimize the execution of the prototype. Since using an Objected Oriented approach tends to produce code that makes a large number of subprogram calls, pragma INLINE was used extensively. Note that this pragma is not supported by all compilers. Another optimization was accomplished by using the HAPSE compiler option that specifies the bodies of generic units are not to be shared. Pragma SUPPRESS was used to reduce the amount of run-time checking. Finally, the highest (Fourth) level of optimization available on the Harris compiler was used.

"In total, the time required for executing the prototype model was reduced almost fifty percent from the initial run, which used no compiler optimization and no Ada pragmas for optimization, to the final run which used the highest level of optimization available on the Harris compiler and used Ada pragmas extensively to in-line subroutine calls and suppress run-time checks". [5]

After optimization, "the execution time of the prototype was at a very acceptable level". [5]

After the completion of the design phase described in Reference 5, FSI had a methodology and a prototype of 1000 Ada statements which was very fast — 180 Hz with thirty percent spare time on one CPU. With the development of an additional 15,000 Ada statements, they report that full optimization now reduces the execution time of their unoptimized code by over sixty percent. They also report that their Ada source code is smaller than comparable FORTRAN source code due to the fact that this level of optimization makes coding techniques used to speed up FORTRAN unnecessary.

**The Rotor Wing Blade Element Simulation Program: summary**

Through the rapid prototyping effort for the Rotor Wing Blade Element Simulation Program, FlightSafety International has developed a design model that can be used for flight simulation software written in Ada. The model is based on Object Oriented Design, but takes into account requirements for designing real-world, hard real-time systems. The success of this development highlights the need for a team leader who thoroughly understands Ada, Software Engineering and the applications area. This program allowed time for a great deal of effort to be put into the design phase. Problems were solved in prototyping, before the main design team began to work. "A major lesson learned in the prototyping effort was that a clear understanding of design method and good software design practices is essential to take full advantage of the capabilities of the Ada language". [5]

## Summary

Ada is now being used successfully in many applications, including hard real-time flight simulations. Although Ada tasking is not being used extensively in these applications, the Software Engineering features are.

## Acknowledgement

I would like to thank Michael Caffey of FlightSafety International for the time he spent discussing the Rotor Wing Blade Element Simulation Program with me and for his permission to use material from his paper in my talk.

## References

1. Chitwood, G. and Jones, B.E., 'Ada the Real-Time World', *5. Deutscher Ada Anwenderkongress*, January, 1990.

2. United States Department of Defense 'Reference Manual of the Ada Programming Language', ANSI/MIL-STD-1815A-1983, February, 1983.

3. Jones, B.E., 'Ada in a Hard Real-Time Environment', American Institute of Aeronautics and Astronautics, Inc, 1989.

4. ACM SigAda Runtime Environments Working Group 'A Catalog of Interface Features and Options for the Ada Runtime Environment', *ARTEWG*, December 1987, pp. 3–24.

5. Caffey, M.E., 'Software Architectures for Ada-Based Flight Simulators', *Interservice/Industry Training Systems Conference*, November, 1989.

# 8

# Ada Follies*

## 8.1   Introduction

The Ada Follies is a musical review which is staged by Ada people at the major conferences each year, particularly Tri-Ada and Ada-Europe. It is masterminded by Judy Bamberger and has played to packed houses and a very appreciative "in" audience.

The backbone of the Follies is a song book of traditional melodies reworked on an Ada theme, and often reflecting local colour. For example, at Ada-Europe in Madrid in 1989, Follies exploited Bizet's Carmen by adapting "The Habanera" thus:

> My name's Ada: and I'm the one.
> ANSI and ISO think I'm so much fun.
> I am Ada: you must try me.
> See what I do for productivity.

and the famous "Toreador" chorus:

> Buy my compiler: it's the one for you.
> Don't look at theirs; mine's best it's true!
> When performance is all you need,
>     Try mine and check out the speed!
> The code is fast and small,
>     And that's not all;
> Dynamic memory is freed!

One of the all-time favourite songs, though, is the following, based on "I am the very model of a Modern Major-General" from the Gilbert and Sullivan operetta, HMS Pinafore.

---

*The songs are taken from the "Ada Follies Songbook", copyright © 1990 Ada Follies. Reprinted with permission.

## 8.2   It is the very model of a modern Reference Manual

by Norman Cohen, after Gilbert and Sullivan, from HMS Pinafore

It is the very model of a modern Reference Manual.
That's why it is the standard of the General and the Admiral.
It tells the rules of Ada, the compile-time and the run-time too,
And even gives some others whose enforcement is left up to you.
Six point four treats Procedure Calls, the Named and the Positional,
And nine point seven, Entry Calls, the Timed and the Conditional.
For Multi-tasking programs Section Nine has got a lot o' news
With many cheerful facts about Selective Waits and Rendezvous.

If Statements are to Execute, Expressions to Evaluate,
Then what are Declarations for? The book says to Elaborate.
In short, for writing programs for the General and the Admiral
It is the very model of a modern Reference Manual.

Section one point six explains the Ada forms felonious:
Illegal and Exceptional and — worst of all — Erroneous.
And if your program has a nasty pathologic tendency,
Then on some order it may have an Incorrect Dependency.
Eleven six will tell you all the ways that you may optimise
And give you an example where the outcome is a rude surprise.
The pragma INTERFACE of section thirteen nine is there, what's more,
To link your Ada code to that infernal nonsense FORTRAN IV.

Four point five point seven talks of properties numerical,
While various cross-references take care of matters clerical.
In short, for writing programs for the General or Admiral,
It is the very model of a modern Reference Manual.

In fact, when you know what is meant by Real, Composite, and
Discrete,
When you can tell at sight a Terminated Task from one Com-
plete,
When at such affairs as Overloading you are more astute,
And when you know precisely what is meant by Static Attribute,
When you have learned what progress can be made at low pri-
ority,
And when you've memorised Appendix C in its entirety,
In short, when your compiler's made it through the Validation
Suite,
You'll say a better Reference Manual has never hit the street.

As an Ada definition, though, it's cryptic and ambiguous;
The effort to interpret it, ongoing and continuous;
But since it is the standard of the General and Admiral,
It is the very model of a modern Reference Manual.

# Part Two

# Reference material

# 9

# Validated Ada compilers

## 9.1 An introduction to the validation process[*]

An "Ada implementation" is an Ada compiler, linker and any other necessary software with both its host computer (on which the compiler is run) and the target computer (on which the generated code will be run).

The purpose of validation is to encourage conformity of Ada implementations with the standard — the Ada Programming Language; also referred to as ANSI/MIL-STD-1815A (1983). However, users are cautioned that the yardstick of conformity testing is the collection of test programs contained in the Ada Compiler Validation Capability (ACVC). Thus, compliance is measured only within the limits of these tests.

Also, characteristics not specified by the standard, such as performance or suitability for a particular application, are outside the scope of Ada validation.

The validation process is carried out by the Ada certification body; this consists of: the Ada Joint Program Office (AJPO) for overall direction; the Ada Validation Organization (AVO) and the ACVC Maintenance Organization (AMO) for technical support; and the Ada Validation Facilities (AVFs) for performing validations.

There are two ways of obtaining validated status: validation by AVF testing; and for "derived" compilers only, validation by registration.

---

[*]Extracted from the file containing the list of validated Ada compilers.

### Ada Compiler Validation Capability (ACVC):

As indicated above, the Ada Compiler Validation Capability (ACVC) is a suite of programs (and support software) that are designed to test whether an Ada implementation complies with the Ada programming language.

Before a new version of the ACVC test suite is used for validation, it is released for a public review period of six months. During this period, a compiler implementor (developer/vendor) or any interested party may submit comments to the ACVC Maintenance Organization. At the end of six months, the new version of the ACVC is released for validation use for a period of 18 months. Effective October 1988, a compiler's validation certificate expires one year after the expiration date of the ACVC version used for the validation.

### Validation by AVF testing:

In order to obtain a validation certificate, there are six steps that must be completed by a customer and the Ada certification body. These steps are:

1. A formal validation agreement between the customer and an AVF — this is required in order to obtain validation services.

2. Prevalidation — this consists of customer testing, submission of results to the AVF, and resolution of any test issues that may arise (for instance, a missing or incomplete result to a test).

3. Validation testing performed by an AVF at the customer's site.

4. A Declaration of Conformance — this is completed and signed by the customer not later than at validation testing. A validation certificate will not be issued until a Declaration of Conformance has been completed.

5. A Validation Summary Report (VSR) — this is prepared by the AVF to document the validation by testing.

6. A Validation Certificate — this is issued by authority of the AJPO for a successfully tested Ada implementation.

For each certificate issued, the AJPO makes an entry in the list of validated Ada compilers. This entry will be removed when the certificate expires.

### Validation of a derived compiler (validation by registration):

An Ada implementation may be "derived" from one that has been validated by testing (a base implementation). The implementor of a derived compiler may request that it be validated by registration, rather than by AVF testing.

For an implementation to be derived, four conditions must be true:

1. the validation certificate for the base implementation has an expiration date at least three months beyond the time of derivation;

2. the host and target computer systems of both the base and derived Ada implementations have compatible instruction sets and operating systems;

3. the derived Ada implementation contains an Ada compiler that was obtained from the Ada compiler of the base implementation by changes that are within the scope of accepted software maintenance practices; and

4. the "result profile" for the Ada implementation is either the same as the base implementation or, if there are minor differences, these differences are justified as being within the scope of accepted software maintenance practices.

Two Ada implementations which pass a given ACVC version have the same "result profile" when:

(a) they use the same customized test suite;

(b) inapplicable test programs in the customized test suite are the same for both implementations;

(c) inapplicable test programs are inapplicable for the same reasons; and

(d) any implementation dependent characteristics tested for by the customized test suite are the same for both implementations.

The AVF will review registration requests for completeness and plausibility of information. A derived compiler that is accepted by the AVF and the AVO will be forwarded to the AJPO to be added to the public list of validated Ada compilers.

**For further information:**

For further information, see "Ada Compiler Validation Procedures, Version 2.0, May 1989". Copies are available through the Defense Technical Information Center (DTIC) and the National Technical Information Service (NTIS). The accession number is ADA 210 406.

## NTIS

National Technical Information Service
U.S. Department of Commerce
5285 Port Royal Road
Springfield, Virginia 22161
Tel. +1 703 487-4650

The National Technical Information Service sells documents to the public.

## DTIC

Defense Technical Information Center
Cameron Station
Alexandria, Virginia 22314
Tel. +1 703 274-7633 AV 284-763

The Defense Technical Information Center distributes documents only to Military, government, or defense contractors who are registered users of DTIC.

## Ada validation facility managers

Mr. Bobby Evans
Ada Validation Facility
Language Control Facility ASD/SCEL
Building 676, Room 135
Wright-Patterson Air Force Base
Ohio 45433-6503
Tel. +1 513 255-4472

Ms. Jane Pink
Mr. Mike Ryan
The National Computing Centre, Ltd.
Oxford Road
Manchester
England, M1 7ED
Tel. +44 61 228 6333

Mr. Fabrice Garnier de Labareyre
AFNOR
Tour Europe, Cedex 7
F-92080 Paris la Defence
France
Tel. +33 1 42 91 5960

Dr. William Dashiell
National Institute of Standards and Technology
National Computer Systems Laboratory
Building 255, Room A266
Gaithersburg, MD 20899
Tel. +1 301 975-2490

Mr. Michael Tonndorf
IABG, Dept ITE
Einsteinstrasse 20
D-8012 Ottobrunn
Germany
Tel. +49 89 6088 2477

# 9.2   Introduction to the list

The data were extracted from:

> File VAL-COMP: List of Validated Ada
> Compilers for October 1990 (10/3/90)
> (Form G10-1090, V10-1090;
> AdaIC point of contact: Michele Kee)

The following are Ada compilers that have been validated by the Ada Joint
Program Office (AJPO). Compilers are listed in order of vendor. The list is
updated monthly, and presently includes 296 base compilers and 200 compilers
derived from base implementations. For the most current information on
validated Ada compilers, please contact the Ada Information Clearinghouse on
+1 703 685-1477.

The entries are shown in the following format:

## Vendor and compiler
> host machine
> *target machine, if different from the host*
> (certificate number)

The vendor and compiler details are not repeated if they are identical to the
previous entry. Some long lists of machine numbers have been abbreviated.

The certificate number has the following form:

(#YYMMDDFX.XXNNN): YYMMDD is the date on-site testing was
completed; F is the Ada Validation Facility; X.XX is the ACVC Version; NNN
is a unique sequence number that is assigned by the AVO.

For example, the certificate number #890113W1.10024 means the compiler
completed on-site testing January 13, 1989, at Wright-Patterson AFB under
ACVC 1.10.

"BASE" indicates Validated through Registration of the base system listed
elsewhere.

NOTE: All Ada Validation Certificates issued for validations completed with
ACVC Version 1.10 expire on December 1, 1990. All Ada Validation
Certificates issued for validations completed with ACVC Version 1.11 will
expire on June 1, 1992.

## 9.3   Alphabetical list

### AETECH IntegrAda, Version 4.1.0
Compaq Deskpro 286 (under MS DOS 3.1)
(#890113W1.10024)
KayPro 386 (under MS DOS 3.21)
(#890113W1.10025)
Compaq Deskpro 386/25 (under MS DOS 3.31)
(#890113W1.10026)

### AETECH, INC. IntegrAda 4.2.0
Zenith Z-248 Model ZFX-0248-50 (under MS-DOS 3.30)
(#900125N1.10253)
Unisys 386 (under SCO Unix 3.2.0)
(#900125N1.10257)

### AETECH, INC. IntegrAda, Version 3.2
Zenith Z-386/25 (under Interactive Unix 2.1)
(#890919W1.10163)

### AETECH, INC. IntegrAda, Version 4.2
Unisys 386 (under MS DOS 3.3)
(#890919W1.10160)
IBM PS/2 Model 70 (under MS DOS 3.3)
(#890919W1.10162)
Zenith Z-386/25 (under MS DOS 3.3)
(#890919W1.10164)
Zenith Z-3727-ET (under Interactive Unix 2.1)
(#890919W1.10165)
Zenith Z-3727-ET (under MS DOS 3.3)
(#890919W1.10166)
Zenith ZCV-2322 (under MS DOS 3.3)
(#890919W1.10167)

### AETECH, INC. IntegrAda, Version 5.2
IBM PS/2 Model 80 (under SCO Xenix 2.2.2)
(#890919W1.10161)

### Alliant Computer Systems Corporation Alliant FX/Ada Compiler, Version 2.2
Alliant FX/80 (under Concentrix, Release 5.0)
(#890605W1.10083)
FX/80, FX/40, FX/8, FX/4, FX/1, FX/82, VFX/80, VFX/40, VFX/4
& VFX/82 (under Concentrix, Release 5.0)
(BASE #890605W1.10083)

## Alsys AlsyCOMP_002, Version 4.3
HP 9000 S 350 (under HP-UX, Version 6.2)
(#890314A1.10038)

## Alsys AlsyCOMP_003, Version 4.1
Zenith Z-248 (under MS/DOS version 3.2)
(#881121A1.10003)
IBM PS/2 Model 60 (under MS/DOS version 3.2)
(#881121A1.10004)

## Alsys AlsyCOMP_003, Version 4.2
PC/AT, Vectra 286 (ES/12) & Compaq 386 (under MS-DOS v3.2)
(BASE #881121A1.10003)
Sperry IT (under MS-DOS v3.2)
(BASE #881121A1.10003)
PS/2 Model 80 (under MS-DOS v3.3)
(BASE #881121A1.10004)

## Alsys AlsyCOMP_003, Version 4.3
Compaq 386, HP Vectra 286 (ES/12), Sperry IT & IBM PC/AT (under
MS/DOS v3.2)
(BASE #881121A1.10003)
IBM PS/2 Models 60 & 80 (under MS/DOS v3.2 & v3.3, resp.)
(BASE #881121A1.10004)

## Alsys AlsyCOMP_003, v4.2
Zenith Z-248 (all models) (under MS-DOS v3.2)
(BASE #881121A1.10003)

## Alsys AlsyCOMP_004, Version 4.31
APOLLO DN 4000 (under Domain/OS SR 10.0)
(#890314A1.10036)

## Alsys AlsyCOMP_005, Version 4.3
SUN 3/260 (under SunOS release 3.2)
(#890314A1.10037)

## Alsys AlsyCOMP_006, Version 4.1
IBM 9370 Model 90 (under VM/IS CMS release 5.1)
(#881216N1.10012)
IBM 9370 Model 90 (under VM/IS CMS release 5.1)
*IBM 370 3984Q (under MVS 3.2)*
(#881216N1.10015)

## Alsys AlsyCOMP_010, Version 4.32
MicroVAX II (under ULTRIX 32, Version 3.0)
(#891208A1.10229)

## Alsys AlsyCOMP_011, Version 5.1

VAX 6210 (under VMS 5.0-2)
*Motorola MVME133A-20 (68020/68881), with ARTK Version 5.1 (bare machine)*
(#891129A1.10227)

## Alsys AlsyCOMP_012, Version 5.1

HP 9000 S 370 (under HP-UX, Version 6.5)
*Motorola MVME121 (68010), with ARTK Version 5.1 (bare machine)*
(#891102A1.10195)

## Alsys AlsyCOMP_013, Version 4.1

IBM PC/AT (under PC-DOS 3.1)
*IBM 370 3084Q (under MVS 3.2)*
(#881216N1.10013)
IBM PC/AT (under PC-DOS 3.1)
*IBM 9370 Model 90 (under VM/IS CMS release 5.1)*
(#881216N1.10014)

## Alsys AlsyCOMP_015, Version 5.1

Sun-3/260 (under SunOS release 3.2)
*Motorola MVME130COF (68020/68881), with ARTK Version 5.1 (bare machine)*
(#891102A1.10196)

## Alsys AlsyCOMP_016, Version 4.1

WANG PC 386 (under MS/DOS with Pharlap Extender version 3.2)
(#881121A1.10005)
IBM PS/2 Model 80 (under MS/DOS with Pharlap Extender v3.2)
(#881121A1.10006)

## Alsys AlsyCOMP_016, Version 4.2

Compaq 386 (under MS-DOS with Pharlap Extender Version 3.1)
(BASE #881121A1.10005)

## Alsys AlsyCOMP_016, v4.3

CompuAdd 316, 320 & 325 (under MS/DOS v3.3 Phar Lap DOS Extender)
(BASE #881121A1.10005)

## Alsys AlsyCOMP_017, V4.3

MicroVAX II (under MicroVMS 4.7)
*INMOS T222 transputer implemented on a B416 TRAM (bare), using an IBM PC/AT under MS-DOS 3.1 running INMOS Iserver V1.41 for file-server support via a CAPLIN QT0 board link*
(#891124N1.10202)

## Alsys AlsyCOMP_017, Version 4.0

MicroVAX II (under MicroVMS V4.7)
*INMOS T425 transputer implemented on a B403 TRAM, using the
Host running INMOS Iserver V1.30 for file-server support via a
CAPLIN QT0 board link (bare machine)*
(#890531N1.10087)
MicroVAX II (under MicroVMS V4.7)
*INMOS T800 transputer implemented on a B403 TRAM, using the
Host running INMOS Iserver V1.30 for file-server support via a
CAPLIN QT0 board link (bare machine)*
(#890531N1.10088)

## Alsys AlsyCOMP_018, Version 4.32

VAX 6210 (under VMS 5.0-2)
(#891208A1.10228)

## Alsys AlsyCOMP_019, Version 4.1

Zenith Z-248 Model 50 (under MS/DOS, Version 3.2)
*Intel iSBC 286/12 single board computer (bare machine)*
(#890119A1.10032)

## Alsys AlsyCOMP_019, Version 4.2

Zenith Z-248 Model 50 (under MS-DOS v3.2)
*Intel iSBC 86/35, iSBC 186/03 & iSBC 286/12*
(BASE #890119A1.10032)

## Alsys AlsyCOMP_023, Version 4.2

IBM 370 3084Q (under MVS 3.2)
(#890720N1.10124)

## Alsys AlsyCOMP_027, Version 4.3

APPLE MACINTOSH II (under A/UX release 1.1 Beta 1)
(#890314A1.10039)

## Alsys AlsyCOMP_028, Version 4.33

Compaq 386/20 (under Compaq DOS 3.31)
*Motorola MVME130COF (68020/68881) with ARTK v4.33 (bare
machine)*
(#890926A1.10173)

## Alsys AlsyCOMP_029, v4.2

ALTEC ZIP-386 (under MS-DOS 3.3)
*Intel iSBC386/31, with ARTK v4.2 (bare machine)*
(BASE #890119A1.10032)

## Alsys AlsyCOMP_030, Version 4.2
VAX 6210 (under VMS 5.0)
*Intel iSBC 386/31 with ARTK v4.2 (bare machine)*
(#890927A1.10172)

## Alsys AlsyCOMP_031, Version 4.2
SUN 3/260 (under SunOS release 3.2)
*Intel iSBC 286/12 with ARTK v4.2 (bare machine)*
(#890927A1.10171)
Sun-3/140 (under MS/DOS v3.3 Phar Lap DOS Extender)
*Intel iSBC 186/03A, with ARTK v4.2 (bare machine)*
(BASE #890927A1.10171)

## Alsys AlsyCOMP_032, Version 4.1
COMPAQ DESKPRO 386 (under OS/2 version 1.0)
(#881121A1.10007)
IBM PS/2 Model 60 (under OS/2 version 1.0)
(#881121A1.10008)

## Alsys AlsyCOMP_033, v4.2
Sun-3/140 (under SunOS v4.1)
*Intel iSBC 386/116 (bare machine)*
(BASE #890927A1.10171)

## Alsys AlsyCOMP_034, Version 4.1 & 4.2
MULTITECH 1100 (under INTERACTIVE 386/ix release 1.04); Sun
386i (under SunOS v4.0); Prime EXL 320 (under System V Release 3.0
PRIME EXL)
(BASE #881121A1.10009)

## Alsys AlsyCOMP_034, Version 4.1
MULTITECH 1100 (under Interactive 386/ix release 1.04 (Unix V.3))
(#881121A1.10009)

## Alsys AlsyCOMP_034, Version 4.2.1
Compaq 386/20e (under Interactive 386/ix v2.01)
(BASE #881121A1.10009)

## Alsys AlsyCOMP_035, Version 4.3
CETIA UNIGRAPH 6000 (under Unigraph/X release 3.0.1)
(#890314A1.10040)

## Alsys AlsyCOMP_036, Version 5.1
Apollo DN3000 (under DOMAIN/OS SR 10.1)
*Motorola MVME101 (68000), with ARTK Version 5.1 (bare machine)*
(#891121A1.10197)

## Alsys AlsyCOMP_037, V4.0

INMOS T800 transputer on a B405 TRAM (bare) with an INMOS B008
communications link implemented in an IBM PC/AT (under
MS-DOS 3.1 and INMOS Iserver V1.30)
*INMOS T800 transputer implemented on a B405 TRAM (bare),
using an IBM PC/AT under MS-DOS 3.1 running INMOS Iserver
V1.30 for file-server support via an INMOS B008 board link*
(#890623N1.10107)
INMOS T800 transputer on a B405 TRAM (bare) with an INMOS B008
communications link implemented in an IBM PC/AT (under
MS-DOS 3.1 and INMOS Iserver V1.30)
*INMOS T425 transputer implemented on a B403 TRAM (bare),
using an IBM PC/AT under MS-DOS 3.1 running INMOS Iserver
V1.30 for file-server support via an INMOS B008 board link*
(#890623N1.10108)

## Alsys AlsyCOMP_037, V4.3

INMOS T800 transputer on a B405 TRAM (bare) with an INMOS B008
communications link implemented in an IBM PC/AT (under
MS-DOS 3.1 and INMOS Iserver V1.41)
*INMOS T222 transputer implemented on a B416 TRAM (bare),
using an IBM PC/AT under MS-DOS 3.1 running INMOS Iserver
V1.41 for file-server support via an INMOS B008 board link*
(#891213N1.10201)

## Alsys AlsyCOMP_038, Version 4.2

IBM PC AT (under IBM Secure Xenix version 1.1)
(BASE #881121A1.10009)
Wang PC380 (under SCO Xenix System V release 2.2.3)
(BASE #881121A1.10009)
Zenith Z-248, all models (under IBM Secure Xenix version 1.1)
(BASE #881121A1.10009)

## Alsys AlsyCOMP_040, Version 4.3

IBM PC/AT (under MS/DOS, Version 3.2)
*TACCS AN/TYQ-33(V) (BTOS, Version 7.0)*
(#900115A1.10241)

## Alsys AlsyCOMP_042, Version 5.3

IBM 9370 Model 90 (under AIX/370 Version 1.2)
(#900627N1.11013)

## Alsys AlsyCOMP_043, Version 4.4

Apple Macintosh IIcx (under System 6.0.3)
(#900115A1.10240)

## Alsys AlsyComp_003, v4.2
IBM PS/2 Model 60 (under MS-DOS version 3.2)
(BASE #881121A1.10004)

## Alsys AlsyComp_016, v4.2
Wang PC 386 (under MS-DOS with Pharlap Extender, version 3.2)
(BASE #881121A1.10005)
IBM PS/2 Model 80 (under MS-DOS with Pharlap Extender, v3.2)
(BASE #881121A1.10006)

## Alsys AlsyComp_020, v4.2
MicroVAX 3400 (under VMS 5.0)
*Intel iSBC 86/35, 186/03A & 286/12, with ARTK v4.2 (bare machines)*
(BASE #890927A1.10172)

## Alsys AlsyComp_031, v4.2
Sun-3/140 (under SunOS v4.0.3)
*Intel iSBC 86/35, with ARTK v4.2 (bare machine)*
(BASE #890927A1.10171)

## Alsys AlsyComp_032, v4.2
Compaq DeskPro 386 (under OS/2 version 1.0)
(BASE #881121A1.10007)
IBM PS/2 Model 60 (under OS/2 version 1.0)
(BASE #881121A1.10008)

## Alsys AlsysCOMP_003, Version 4.3
Zenith Z-248 (all models) (under MS/DOS v3.2)
(BASE #881121A1.10003)

## Alsys AlsysCOMP_016, Version 4.3
Compaq 386 (under MS/DOS v3.1 with Pharlap Extender)
(BASE #881121A1.10005)
GRiDCASE 386 1500 Series (under MS/DOS v3.3 with Pharlap
Extender)
(BASE #881121A1.10005)
Hewlett Packard Vectra RS/25C & RS/20 (under MS/DOS v3.3 with
Pharlap Extender)
(BASE #881121A1.10005)
Wang PC 386 (under MS/DOS v3.2 with Pharlap Extender)
(BASE #881121A1.10005)
IBM PS/2 Models 70 & 80 (under MS/DOS v3.2 with Pharlap
Extender)
(BASE #881121A1.10006)

## Alsys AlsysCOMP_032, Versions 4.2 & 4.3

IBM PC/AT (under IBM OS/2 v1.0)
(BASE #881121A1.10007)
IBM PS/2 Models 70 & 80 (under IBM OS/2 v1.0)
(BASE #881121A1.10008)

## Alsys AlsysCOMP_034, Version 4.2

IBM PS/2 Models 80 (under IBM AIX version 1.1)
(BASE #881121A1.10009)

## Apollo Computer, Inc. Domain/ADA V3.0.mbx

DN4000 (under Domain/OS SR10.2)
*Motorola MVME133A-20 (68020/68881) (bare machine)*
(#891128S1.10234)

## Apollo Computer, Inc. Domain/Ada, V3.0m

DN3500 (under Domain/OS, SR10.1.0.2)
(#890719W1.10125)

## BBN ADVANCED COMPUTERS, INC. TC2000 pSOS Ada, Version 4.0

BBN TC2000 (under nX 1.0)
*BBN TC2000 (under TC2000 pSOS 0.8.2)*
(#900131I1.10268)

## BBN Advanced Computers, Inc. TC2000 Ada, Version 4.0

BBN TC2000 (under nX 1.0)
(#891123I1.10218)

## BBN Advanced Computers, Inc. TC2000 Ada, Version 4.00.02d

BBN TC2000 (under nX 2.0)
(BASE #891123I1.10218)

## BBN Advanced Computers, Inc. TC2000 pSOS Ada, Version 4.00.02d

BBN TC2000 (under nX 2.0)
*BBN TC2000 (under TC2000 pSOS 1.0.0)*
(BASE #900131I1.10268)

## BiiN BiiN Ada, V2.00

BiiN 60 (under BiiN/OS, V1.02)
(#881208W1.10010)

## BiiN BiiN Ada, V2.01

BiiN 60 (under BiiN/OS V2)
(BASE #881208W1.10010)

## Bull HN Information Systems Inc. GCOS 8 Ada Compilation System, Version 2.3

DPS 9000 (under GCOS 8 SR 4000)
(#890831S1.10146)
DPS 8000 (under GCOS 8 SR 3000)
(#890924S1.10231)
DPS 8000 & 90 (under GCOS 8 SR 4000)
(BASE #890831S1.10146)
DPS 8/70 (under GCOS 8 SR 3000)
(BASE #890924S1.10231)

## CONVEX Computer Corporation CONVEX Ada, Version 1.1

CONVEX C210 (under CONVEX Unix, Version 7.1)
(#890508W1.10077)
CONVEX C201, C202, C120, C210, C220, C230, C240, C210i, C220i &
C230i (under CONVEX Unix, Version 7.1 or ConvexOS, Version 8.0)
(BASE #890508W1.10077)

## Computer Sciences Corporation MC Ada V1.2.beta/Concurr ent Computer Corporation

Concurrent/Masscomp 5600 (under UNIX; Masscomp RTU V4.1)
*Concurrent/Masscomp 5600 (Dual 68020 processor configuration),*
*with CSC-developed Ada Real-Time Operating System (ARTOS)*
*V1.0 for bare machine environments (bare machine)*
(#900121S1.10251)

## Concurrent Computer Corporation C3 Ada, Version R00-00

Concurrent Computer Corporation 5600 (under RTU Version 4.0A)
(#891103I1.10199)
Concurrent Computer Corporation Series 6000 (MC68030/68882) and
Series 5000 (MC68020/68881) (all models) (under RTU Versions 4.0,
4.1A, 4.1 & 5.0)
(BASE #891103I1.10199)

## Concurrent Computer Corporation C3 Ada, Version R02-02

Concurrent Computer Corporation Series 3200; Micro3 & Micro5 (under
OS/32, Version R08-02.03)
(BASE #890711W1.10109)

## Concurrent Computer Corporation C3 Ada, Version R02-02.00

Concurrent 3280 MPS (under OS/32, Version R08-02.03)
(#890711W1.10109)

## Concurrent Computer Corporation C3 Ada, Version R02-03

Concurrent Computer Corporation Series 3200; Micro3 & Micro5 (under OS/32, Versions R08-02.03 & R08-03)
(BASE #890711W1.10109)
Concurrent Computer Corporation Series 3200; Micro3 & Micro5 (under OS/32, Version R08-03.1)
(BASE #890711W1.10109)

## Concurrent Computer Corporation C3Ada, Version 0.5

Concurrent Computer Corporation 8400 (MIPS R3000/3010) (under RTU Version 5.1)
(#90042711.11008)
Concurrent Computer Corporation 8500 (MIPS R3000/R3010) (under RTU Version 5.1)
(BASE #90042711.11008)

## Concurrent Computer Corporation C3Ada, Version 1.0

Concurrent Computer Corporation Series 6000, 5000 (under RTU Versions 4.0A, 4.0, 4.1A, 4.1 & 5.0)
(BASE #89110311.10199)

## Concurrent Computer Corporation MC-Ada, Version 1.2

Concurrent 6600 (MC68030) w/MC68882 Floating Point (under RTU Version 5.0)
(#890818S1.10130)
Concurrent 6600 (MC68030) w/Lightning Floating Point (under RTU Version 5.0)
(#890818S1.10131)
Concurrent 5000 series (MC68020) w/MC68881 Floating Point (under RTU Version 5.0)
(BASE #890818S1.10130)
Concurrent 6000 series (MC68030) w/MC68882 Floating Point (under RTU Version 5.0)
(BASE #890818S1.10130)
Concurrent 5000 series (MC68020) w/Lightning Floating Point (under RTU Version 5.0)
(BASE #890818S1.10131)

Concurrent 6000 series (MC68030) w/Lightning Floating Point (under RTU Version 5.0)
(BASE #890818S1.10131)

## Control Data Corporation ADA/VE, Version 1.3
CYBER 932 (under NOS/VE level 727)
(#890901S1.10147)
CYBER 180 Series, all models (under NOS/VE Level 727)
(BASE #890901S1.10147)

## Cray Research, Inc. Cray Ada Compiler, Version 1.1
CRAY X-MP (under UNICOS Release 5.0)
(#890523W1.10080)
CRAY-2 (under UNICOS Release 5.0)
(#890523W1.10081)
CRAY X-MP (under UNICOS Release 4.0)
(BASE #890523W1.10080)
CRAY-2 (under UNICOS Release 4.0)
(BASE #890523W1.10081)

## DDC International A/S DACS for Sun-3 -> Lynwood/LynX, Version 4.4 (1.1)
Sun-3/50 (SunOS UNIX, Version 4.2, Release 4.0_Export)
*Lynwood j430 (under LynX, Version 1.4F)*
(#891027S1.10184)

## DDC International A/S DACS for Sun-3/SunOS, Version 4.4 (1.1)
Sun-3/60 (under SunOS UNIX, Version 4.2, Release 4.0_Export)
(#891027S1.10183)

## DDC International A/S DACS-386/UNIX, Version 4.4
ICL DRS300 (under DRS/NX, Version 3, Level 1)
(#891027S1.10185)
RC900 (under UNIX V, Release 1.0.4)
(#891027S1.10186)

## DDC International A/S DDC-I Ada Compiler System, Version 4.3
VAX 8530 (under VMS 4.5)
(#881212W1.10011)

## DDC-I, Inc. DACS-386/UNIX 4.4.1
Compaq Deskpro 386 (all models) (under 386/ix Release 2.0.2)
(BASE #891027S1.10185)
Compaq Deskpro 386—all models (under 386/ix Release 1.0.6)
(BASE #891027S1.10185)

Intel System 302–all models (under UNIX System V/386 Release 3.2) (BASE #891027S1.10185)

## DDC-I, Inc. DACS-80186 with Hard Deadline Scheduling RTS, Version 4.3

Complete DEC family of VAX, VAXstation, and MicroVAX computers (under VMS 4.6, MicroVMS 4.6 & VMS 5.0)
*Intel iSBC 186/03A (80186) (bare machine)*
(BASE #890324S1.10067)

## DDC-I, Inc. DACS-80186, Version 4.3

MicroVAX II (under MicroVMS 4.6)
*Intel 80186 iSBC 186/03A (bare machine)*
(#890324S1.10067)
DEC family of VAX, VAXstation & MicroVAX computers (under MicroVMS 4.6 and VAX/VMS 4.6 & 5.0)
*Intel 80186 iSBC 186/03A (bare machine)*
(BASE #890324S1.10067)

## DDC-I, Inc. DACS-80286 Protected Mode with Hard Deadline Scheduling RTS, Version 4.3

Complete DEC family of VAX, VAXstation, and MicroVAX computers (under VMS 4.6, MicroVMS 4.6 & VMS 5.0)
*Intel iSBC 286/12 (80286) in Protected Mode (bare machine)*
(BASE #890324S1.10067)

## DDC-I, Inc. DACS-80286 with Hard Deadline Scheduling RTS, Version 4.3

Complete DEC family of VAX, VAXstation, and MicroVAX computers (under VMS 4.6, MicroVMS 4.6 & VMS 5.0)
*Intel iSBC 286/12 (80286) (bare machine)*
(BASE #890324S1.10067)

## DDC-I, Inc. DACS-80286, Version 4.3

DEC family of VAX, VAXstation & MicroVAX computers (under MicroVMS 4.6 and VAX/VMS 4.6 & 5.0)
*Intel 80286 iSBC 286/12 (bare machine)*
(BASE #890324S1.10067)

## DDC-I, Inc. DACS-80386 Protected Mode with Hard Deadline Scheduling RTS, Version 4.3

Complete DEC family of VAX, VAXstation, and MicroVAX computers (under VMS 4.6, MicroVMS 4.6 & VMS 5.0)
*Intel Multibus I iSBC 386/21 (80386) (bare machine)*
(BASE #890324S1.10068)

## DDC-I, Inc. DACS-80386 Protected Mode, Version 4.3

MicroVAX II (under MicroVMS 4.6)
*Intel Multibus I 80386 iSBC 386/21 (bare machine)*
(#890324S1.10068)
DEC family of VAX, VAXstation & MicroVAX computers (under
MicroVMS 4.6 and VAX/VMS 4.6 & 5.0)
*Intel Multibus I 80386 isBC 386/21 & Intel Multibus II 80386 iSBC
386/116 (bare machine)*
(BASE #890324S1.10068)

## DDC-I, Inc. DACS-80386 with Hard Deadline Scheduling RTS, Version 4.3

Complete DEC family of VAX, VAXstation, and MicroVAX computers
(under VMS 4.6, MicroVMS 4.6 & VMS 5.0)
*Intel Multibus II iSBC 386/116 (80386) (bare machine)*
(BASE #890324S1.10068)

## DDC-I, Inc. DACS-8086 with Hard Deadline Scheduling RTS, Version 4.3

Complete DEC family of VAX, VAXstation, and MicroVAX computers
(under VMS 4.6, MicroVMS 4.6 & VMS 5.0)
*Intel iSBC 86/05A (8086) (bare machine)*
(BASE #890324S1.10067)

## DDC-I, Inc. DACS-8086, Version 4.3

DEC family of VAX, VAXstation & MicroVAX computers (under
MicroVMS 4.6 and VAX/VMS 4.6 & 5.0)
*Intel 8086 iSBC 86/05A (bare machine)*
(BASE #890324S1.10067)

## DDC-I, Inc. DACS-AIX/PS2, Version 4.4

IBM PS/2 Models 70 & 80 (under AIX 1.1)
(BASE #891027S1.10185)

## Data General Corporation ADE Revision 3.01

MV 15000 & MV 10000 (under AOS/VS 7.60 & AOS/VS II 1.00, resp.)
(#890615S1.10126)
MV family of computers (under AOS/VS 7.60 & AOS/VS II 1.00)
(BASE #890615S1.10126)

## Digital Equipment Corporation VAX Ada Version 2.1

DEC family of VAX, MicroVAX II, VAXstation II (under VMS Versions
5.2 & 5.3)
(BASE #890127S1.10033)

## Digital Equipment Corporation VAX Ada Version 2.1

DEC family of VAX, MicroVAX II, VAXstation II (under VMS 5.2 & 5.3)
*DEC family of VAX (under VAXELN Version 4.1, with VAXELN*
*Ada Version 2.0 (rts))*
(BASE #890127S1.10034)

## Digital Equipment Corporation VAX Ada, Version 2.0

VAX 8800 (under VMS, Version 5.0)
(#890127S1.10033)
VAX 8800 (under VMS, Version 5.0)
*MicroVAX II (under VAXELN Toolkit Version 3.2, in combination*
*with VAXELN Ada Version 2.0)*
(#890127S1.10034)
MicroVAX, VAXstation, VAX (under VMS, Version 5.0)
*MicroVAX (under VAXELN Toolkit Version 3.2, in combination*
*with VAXELN Ada Version 2.0)*
(BASE #890127S1.10034)
MicroVAX, VAXstation, VAX (under VMS, Version 5.0)
(BASE #890127S1.10033)

## Elxsi Elxsi VADS Version 5.6

Elxsi 6400 (under ENIX 4.3 BSD 12.1)
(#890712W1.10115)
Elxsi 6400 (under ENIX SYSTEM V 12.1)
(#890712W1.10116)

## Encore Computer Corporation APLEX Ada Compiler Revision 2.2

Gould/Encore CONCEPT/32 series 67xx, 97xx & 98xx (under MPX-32
Revision 3.4U03)
(BASE #890418W1.10072)

## Encore Computer Corporation APLEX Ada Compiler Revision 2.3

Gould/Encore CONCEPT/32 series 67xx, 97xx & 98xx (under MPX-32
Revisions 3.4U02, 3.4U03 & 3.5)
(BASE #890418W1.10072)

## Encore Computer Corporation Encore Verdix Ada Development System, Version 5.5

Encore Multimax 320 (under Umax 4.2, Version R3.3)
(#890727S1.10127)
Encore Multimax 320 (under Mach, Version 0.5 Beta)
(#890727S1.10128)

Encore Multimax 320 (under Umax V, Version R2.2)
(#890727S1.10129)

## Evans & Sutherland MIPS Ada version 2.10

ESV series 3, 5, 10, 20, 30, 40, 50 Workstations (under ES/os 1.2)
(BASE #890614W1.10098)

## Gould/Computer Systems Inc. APLEX Ada Compiler Revision 2.2

Gould/Encore PowerNode Models 90xx, 60xx, and Gould/Encore
CONCEPT/32 Models 67xx (under UTX/32 Revision 2.1)
(BASE #890418W1.10069)
Gould/Encore PowerNode Models 90xx & 60xx, and Gould/Encore
CONCEPT/32 Models 67xx (under UTX/32 Revision 2.1)
*Gould/Encore PowerNode Models 90xx & 60xx, and Gould/Encore*
*CONCEPT/32 Models 97xx & 67xx (bare machine, with Ada Real*
*Time Executive)*
(BASE #890418W1.10070)
Gould/Encore NP1 Models 40xx (under UTX/32 Revision 3.1)
(BASE #890418W1.10071)
Gould/Encore CONCEPT/32 Models 97xx, 67xx & 98xx (under
MPX-32 Revision 3.4U02)
(BASE #890418W1.10072)
Gould/Encore PowerNode Model 9080 (under UTX/32 Revision 2.1)
(#890418W1.10069)
Gould/Encore PowerNode Model 9080 (under UTX/32 Revision 2.1)
*Gould/Encore CONCEPT/32 Model 6744 (bare machine, with Ada*
*Real Time Executive)*
(#890418W1.10070)
Gould/Encore NP1 Model 4050 (under UTX/32 Revision 3.1)
(#890418W1.10071)
Gould/Encore CONCEPT/32 Model 9780 (under MPX-32 Revision
3.4U02)
(#890418W1.10072)

## Harris Corp. Harris Ada, Version 5.0

Harris NH-3800 (under CX/UX 4.0)
(#890118W1.10016)
Harris HCX-9 (under CX/UX 4.0)
*Harris NH-3800 (under CX/UX 4.0)*
(#890118W1.10017)
Harris NH-3800, NH-3400 & NH-1200 (under CX/UX 4.0, CX/RT 4.0)
(BASE #890118W1.10016)

Harris HCX-2300, HCX-2500, HCX-2550, HCX-2900, HCX-7100, HCX-7201, HCX-7202; Harris NH-7100 & NH-7200 (under CX/UX 4.0, CX/RT 4.0)
*Harris NH-3800, NH-3400, NH-1200 (under CX/UX 4.0, CX/RT 4.0)*
(BASE #890118W1.10017)

### Harris Corp. Harris Ada, Version 5.0.1

Harris NH-1200, NH-3400 & NH-3800 (under CX/UX 4.1, CX/RT 4.1)
(BASE #890118W1.10016)
Harris HCX-2300, 2500, 2550 & 2900 (under CX/UX 4.1, CX/RT 4.1)
*Harris NH-1200, NH-3400 & NH-3800 (under CX/UX 4.1, CX/RT 4.1)*
(BASE #890118W1.10017)

### Harris Corporation, Computer Systems Division Harris Ada, Version 5.0

Harris H1000 (under VOS 8.1)
(#890627W1.10103)
Harris HCX-2900 (under CX/UX 4.1)
(#890627W1.10104)
Harris H60, H700, H800, H900, H1000, H1100, H1200, H1500 & H1600 (under VOS 8.1)
(BASE #890627W1.10103)

### Harris Corporation, Computer Systems Division Harris Ada, Versions 5.0 & 5.0.1

Harris HCX-2300, HCX-2500, HCX-2550 & HCX-2900 (under CX/UX 4.1, CX/RT 4.1)
(BASE #890627W1.10104)

### Hewlett Packard Company HP 9000 Series 300 Ada Compiler, Version 4.35

HP 9000 Series 300 Model 350 (under HP-UX, Version 6.5)
(#890504W1.10078)
HP 9000 Series 300 Model 370 (under HP-UX, Versin 6.5)
(#890504W1.10079)

### Hewlett Packard Company HP 9000 Series 300 Ada Compiler, Version 4.35

HP 9000 Series 300 Models 350, 332, 330 & 320 (under HP-UX, Version 7.0)
(BASE #890504W1.10078)

HP 9000 Series 300 Models 345, 370, 375, 360 & 340 (under HP-UX, Version 7.0)
(BASE #890504W1.10079)
HP 9000 Series 800 Model 850 (under HP-UX, A.B3.10 (release 3.1))
(#891019W1.10178)
HP 9000 Series 800 Models 808, 832, 834, 845 & 870; and Series 600 Models 635 & 645 (under HP-UX, Version A.B7.00 (release 7.0))
(BASE #891019W1.10178)
HP 9000 Series 800 Models 815, 825, 835, 840, 850 & 855 (under HP-UX, Version A.B7.00 (release 7.00))
(BASE #891019W1.10178)

## INTEL Corporation Ada386 Version 3.23
VAX 8350 (under VMS 5.0-2)
*Intel 386-120 (80386/387) board (bare machine)*
(#890602I1.10136)

## Intel Corporation iPSC/2 Ada, Release 1.1
iPSC/2 Parallel Supercomputer, System Resource Manager (under Unix System V, Release 3.2)
*iPSC/2 Parallel Supercomputer, CX-1 nodes (under NX/2)*
(#891116W1.10191)

## InterACT Corporation InterACT Ada 1750A Compiler System Release 3.3
VAX-11/785 (under VMS 4.5)
*Fairchild 9450/1750A in a Hewlett Packard 64000 (bare machine)*
(#891116S1.10232)

## InterACT Corporation InterACT Ada 1750A Compiler System Release 3.4
VAX (under VMS 4.5)
*Fairchild 9450/1750A in a Hewlett Packard 64000 (bare machine)*
(BASE #891116S1.10232)
VAX-11/785 (under VMS 4.5)
*Fairchild 9450/1750A in an Hewlett Packard 64000 (bare machine)*
(BASE #891116S1.10232)

## InterACT Corporation InterACT Ada MIPS Cross-Compiler System Release 1.0
MicroVAX 3100 Cluster (under VMS 5.2)
*MIPS R2000 on an Integrated Solutions, Inc., Advantedge 2000 board (bare machine)*
(#891116S1.10233)

### InterACT Corporation InterACT Ada Mips Cross-Compiler System Release 1.1
MicroVAX 3100 Cluster (under VMS 5.2)
*MIPS R2000 in an Integrated Solutions Inc. Advantedge 2000 board (bare machine)*
(BASE #891116S1.10233)
VAX, VAXstation, MicroVAX (under VMS 5.2)
*MIPS R2000 in an Integrated Solutions, Inc. Advantedge 2000 board (bare machine)*
(BASE #891116S1.10233)

### InterACT Corporation InterACT Ada Mips Cross-Compiler System Release 1.1-2
MicroVAX 3100 (under VMS 5.2)
*Westinghouse Guidance Instruction Set Architecture (GISA) board (bare machine)*
(BASE #891116S1.10233)

### International Business Machines Corporation IBM AIX Ada/6000, Version 1.1.0
IBM RISC System 6000 Model 7013-530 (under AIX 3.1)
(BASE #891129W1.10198)

### International Business Machines Corporation IBM Development System for the Ada Language AIX/RT Follow-on, Version 1.1
IBM RT Follow-on (under AIX 3.1)
(#891129W1.10198)

### International Business Machines Corporation IBM Development System for the Ada Language, AIX/RT Ada Compiler, Version 1.1.1
IBM RT PC 6150-125 (under AIX, Release 2.2)
(#890420W1.10066)

### International Business Machines Corporation IBM Development System for the Ada Language, AIX/RT Ada Compiler, Version 1.1.2
IBM RT 6150-125 (under AIX Release 2.2)
(BASE #890420W1.10066)

### International Business Machines Corporation IBM Development System for the Ada Language, AIX/RT Ada Compiler, Version 1.2
IBM RT PC 6150-125 (under AIX, Release 2.2)
(BASE #890420W1.10066)

## International Business Machines Corporation IBM Development System for the Ada Language, CMS/MVS Ada Cross Compiler, Version 2.1.1

IBM 3083 (under VM/HPO Release 4.2)

*IBM 4381 (under MVS/XA Release 2.7)*

(#890420W1.10075)

## International Business Machines Corporation IBM Development System for the Ada Language, MVS Ada Compiler, Version 2.1.1

IBM 4381 (under MVS/XA Release 2.7)

(#890420W1.10074)

## International Business Machines Corporation IBM Development System for the Ada Language, VM/CMS Ada Compiler, Version 2.1.1

IBM 3083 (under VM/HPO Release 4.2)

(#890420W1.10073)

## Irvine Compiler Corporation ICC Ada Release 6.0.0

HP 9000 Model 350 (under HP-UX Release 6.2)

*HP 64000 UX with 68020 Emulation Pod (bare machine)*

(#891212W1.10203)

MicroVAX 2000 (under MicroVMS 4.7)

*ICC Simulator for Intel i80960MC, executing on the Host (bare machine)*

(#891212W1.10204)

HP 9000 Model 350 (under HP-UX Release 6.2)

(#891212W1.10205)

HP 9000 Model 825 (under HP-UX Release 2.1)

(#891212W1.10206)

Sun 3/50 (under SunOS Release 4.0)

(#891212W1.10207)

ISI Optimum V VME-68K30 (under 4.3 BSD UNIX Release 5.0.3)

(#891212W1.10208)

## KRUPP ATLAS ELEKTRONIK GMBH KRUPP ATLAS ELEKTRONIK Ada Compiler VVME 1.81

VAX 6310 (under VMS 5.1)

*KRUPP ATLAS ELEKTRONIK GMBH MPR 2300 (under EOS 2300 Version 1.4)*

(#891124I1.10235)

## Loral/Rolm Mil-Spec Computers ADE Revision 3.01
Data General MV 10000 (under AOS/VS 7.64)
*HAWK/32 (under AOS/VS 7.64)*
(#890804S1.10141)
Data General MV 10000 (under AOS/VS 7.64)
*HAWK/32 (under ARTS/32 Revision 2.71)*
(#890804S1.10142)

## MIPS Computer Systems MIPS ADA, Version 2.10
MIPS M/120 (under RISC/os 4.0)
(#890614W1.10098)
MIPS M/500, M/800, M/1000, M/2000, RC2030 & RS2030 (under RISC/os 4.0)
(BASE #890614W1.10098)

## MIPS Computer Systems MIPS ASAPP 3.0
MIPS M/2000 (under RISC/os 4.50)
*R3200-6 CPU board (bare machine)*
(#900619W1.11010)

## MIPS Computer Systems MIPS ASAPP, Version 2.10
MIPS M/120 (under RISC/os 4.0)
*R3200-6 CPU board (bare machine)*
(#890614W1.10099)
MIPS M/120, M/500, M/800, M/1000, M/2000, RC2030 & RS2030 (under RISC/os 4.0)
*R3200-6, R3200-8, R2600 (2601), R2800 (2801) CPU boards (bare machines)*
(BASE #890614W1.10099)

## MIPS Computer Systems MIPS Ada 3.0
MIPS M/2000 (under RISC/os 4.50)
(#900619W1.11011)

## MODCOMP MODCOMP TeleGen2 Ada Host Compilation System 1.4A
MODCOMP Model 9730 (under MODCOMP REAL/IX A.1)
(#900131I1.10269)
MODCOMP 9720, 9735 & 9740 series (under MODCOMP REAL/IX A.1)
(BASE #900131I1.10269)

## Meridian Software Systems, Inc. AdaGraduate, Version 3.0

IBM PS/2 Model 60 (with Floating-Point Co-Processor) (under IBM PC-DOS 3.30)
(BASE #890405W1.10050)

## Meridian Software Systems, Inc. AdaVantage Version 3.0

Ardent Titan P2 (under Ardent/Unix, Version 2.1)
(#890719W1.10117)
Multiflow Trace 300 (under Trace/Unix, Version 4.1.5)
(#890719W1.10118)
Apple Macintosh II (with Floating Point Co-Processor) (under System 6.0.3)
(#890719W1.10119)
Apple Macintosh SE 30 (under System 6.0.3)
(#890719W1.10121)
DECstation 3100 (under Ultrix, Version 3.0)
(#890719W1.10122)
IBM PS/2 Model 70 (under XENIX, Version 2.3.2)
(#890719W1.10123)

## Meridian Software Systems, Inc. AdaVantage Version 4.0

IBM PS/2 Model 80 (with Floating Point Co-Processor) (under IBM PC-DOS 3.30)
(BASE #890405W1.10049)
IBM PS/2 Model 60 (with Floating Point Co-Processor) (under IBM PC-DOS 3.30)
(BASE #890405W1.10050)
IBM PS/2 Model 30 (with Floating Point Co-Processor) (under IBM PC-DOS 3.30)
(BASE #890405W1.10051)
ITT XTRA/286 (with Floating Point Co-Processor) (under IBM MS-DOS 3.20)
(BASE #890405W1.10052)
SCI 303 (with Floating Point Co-Processor) (under IX 1.0.6)
(BASE #890405W1.10055)
Sun 3/60 (under SunOS Version 4.1)
(BASE #890405W1.10056)
Sun 3/260 (under SunOS Version 4.1)
(BASE #890405W1.10057)
Zenith Z-248 Model ZW-248-82 (with Floating Point Co-Processor) (under IBM MS-DOS 3.10)
(BASE #890405W1.10058)

DECstation 3100 (under Ultrix, Version 3.0)
(BASE #890719W1.10122)

## Meridian Software Systems, Inc. AdaVantage, Version 3.0
IBM PS/2 Model 80 (with Floating Point Co-Processor) (under IBM
PC-DOS 3.30)
(#890405W1.10049)
IBM PS/2 Model 60 (with Floating Point Co-Processor) (under IBM
PC-DOS 3.30)
(#890405W1.10050)
IBM PS/2 Model 30 (with Floating Point Co-Processor) (under IBM
PC-DOS 3.30)
(#890405W1.10051)
ITT XTRA/286 (with Floating Point Co-Processor) (under MS-DOS
3.20)
(#890405W1.10052)
SCI 302 (with Floating Point Co-Processor) (under MS-DOS 3.30)
(#890405W1.10053)
SCI 302 (with Floating Point Co-Processor) (under IX 1.0.6)
(#890405W1.10054)
SCI 303 (with Floating Point Co-Processor) (under IX 1.0.6)
(#890405W1.10055)
Sun 3/60 (under SunOS Version 4.1)
(#890405W1.10056)
Sun 3/260 (under SunOS Version 4.1)
(#890405W1.10057)
Zenith Z-248 Model ZW-248-82 (with Floating Point Co-Processor)
(under MS-DOS 3.10)
(#890405W1.10058)
IBM PS/2 Model 80 (with Floating-Point Co-Processor) (under XENIX,
Version 2.3.2)
(BASE #890719W1.10123)

## Meridian Software Systems, Inc. AdaVantage, Version 4.0
Apple Macintosh II (with Floating Point Co-Processor) (under
System 6.0.3)
(#900130W1.10237)
Apple Macintosh SE 30 (under System 6.0.3)
(#900130W1.10238)
DECstation 2100 & 5000 (under Ultrix, Version 3.0)
(BASE #890719W1.10122)

## Meridian Software Systems, Inc. AdaVantage, Version 4.0.1

IBM PS/2 Model 80 (with Floating Point Co-Processor) (under IBM
PC-DOS 3.30)
(BASE #890405W1.10049)
IBM PS/2 Model 60 (with Floating Point Co-Processor) (under IBM
PC-DOS 3.30)
(BASE #890405W1.10050)
IBM PS/2 Model 30 (with Floating Point Co-Processor) (under IBM
PC-DOS 3.30)
(BASE #890405W1.10051)
ITT XTRA/286 (with Floating Point Co-Processor) (under
MS-DOS 3.20)
(BASE #890405W1.10052)
Zenith Z-248 Model ZW-248-82 (with Floating Point Co-Processor)
(under MS-DOS 3.10)
(BASE #890405W1.10058)
Apple Macintosh II (with Floating Point Co-Processor) (under
System 6.0.3)
(BASE #900130W1.10237)
Apple Macintosh SE 30 (under System 6.0.3)
(BASE #900130W1.10238)

## Motorola, Inc. Motorola VME Delta Series TeleGen2 Ada Compilation System, Version 1.4

Motorola Delta Series (under Motorola SYSTEM V/68 Version V3.5)
(BASE #890829W1.10144)

## Motorola, Inc. Motorola VME Delta Series TeleGen2 Ada Compilation System, Version 4.0

Motorola Delta Model 8608 (MVME180 (MC88000)) (under Motorola
UNIX SYSTEM V/88, Release 3)
(#891125I1.10219)

## Motorola, Inc. Motorola VME Delta Series TeleGen2 Ada Cross Compilation System, Version 4.0

Motorola Delta Model 2616 (MVME132xt, 68020/68881) (under
Motorola SYSTEM V/68 Version V3.5)
*Motorola MVME181 (MC88100) (bare machine)*
(#891206I1.10265)

## Motorola, Inc. Motorola VME Delta Series TeleGen2 Ada Development System, Version 1.4a

Motorola Delta 1000, 2000 & 3000 Series (under Motorola SYSTEM V/68, Version V3.5)

*Motorola VME133\*, MVME135\*, MVME136\* (68020 board families); Motorola MVME141\* & MVME147\* (68030 board families) (bare machines)*

(BASE #890829W1.10145)

## Motorola, Inc. Motorola VME Delta Series TeleGen2 Compilation System Version 1.4

Motorola Delta Model 2616 (MVME132XT, 68020/68881) (under Motorola SYSTEM V/68 Version V3.5)

(#890829W1.10144)

Motorola Delta Model 2616 (MVME132XT, 68020/68881) (under Motorola SYSTEM V/68 Version V3.5)

*Motorola MVME133A-20 (MC68020) (bare machine)*

(#890829W1.10145)

## NEC Corporation NEC Ada Compilation System for EWS-UX/V, Version 1.1(4.4)

EWS4800 Series models 2, 4, 10, 20, 50 & 60 (under EWS-UX/V, R7.1)

(BASE #891027S1.10183)

## NIPPON TELEGRAPH and TELEPHONE CORPORATION AdaDIPS, Version 1.0

NTT DIPS V20 (under DIPS-UX (V0))

(#890901S1.10132)

## New York University NYU Ada/Ed, Version 1.10

Sun-3/60 (under Sun UNIX 4.2 Rel 3.4)

(#890523W1.10085)

VAX-8600 (under VMS version 4.7)

(#890523W1.10086)

## PYRAMID TECHNOLOGY CORPORATION Pyramid Ada, Version 5.0

Pyramid 9000 (under Pyramid OSX 5.0)

(#890926W1.10174)

Pyramid MIServer (under Pyramid OSX 5.0b)

(#890926W1.10175)

## Proprietary Software Systems, Inc. PSS Ada Compiler VAX/VMS, Version TV-01.000

VAX 8350 (under VMS Version 4.7)

(#890710I1.10120)

## Proprietary Software Systems, Inc. PSS VAX/1750A Ada Compiler, Version TX-01.00

VAX 8350 (under VMS 5.1)
*MIL-STD-1750A/PSS AdaRAID Version MD-08.11, executing on the Host (bare machine simulation)*
(#89121811.10259)

## R.R. Software, Inc. IntegrAda 4.2.0 DOS

Any Computer System comprising: cpu: any that executes the Intel 8086/8088 instruction set; fpu: optional; memory: 640 KByte RAM or greater; disk: 10 MByte hard drive (under MS-DOS 2.00 or newer)
(BASE #900125N1.10253)

## R.R. Software, Inc. IntegrAda 4.2.0 Unix

Any Computer System comprising: cpu: Intel 80386; fpu: optional; memory: 1.5 MByte RAM or greater; disk: 40 MByte hard drive (under SCO Unix 3.2 and Interactive Unix 3.2)
(BASE #900125N1.10257)

## R.R. Software, Inc. IntegrAda 4.2.0 Xenix

Any Computer System comprising: cpu: Intel 80386; fpu: optional; memory: 1.5 MByte RAM or greater; disk: 40 MByte hard drive (under SCO Xenix 2.2 or newer)
(BASE #900125N1.10257)

## R.R. Software, Inc. JANUS/Ada Version 2.1.3

IBM PS/2 Model 70 (under MS DOS 3.3/Phar Lap)
(#890919W1.10152)
Unisys 386 (under SCO Xenix 2.3.2)
(#890919W1.10153)
IBM PS/2 Model 80 (under SCO Xenix 2.2.2)
(#890919W1.10154)
Zenith ZFX-0248-50 (under MS DOS 3.3)
(#890919W1.10155)
Zenith Z-386/25 (under Interactive Unix 2.1)
(#890919W1.10156)
PC's Limited 386-80386 (under MS DOS 3.1/Phar Lap)
*PC's Limited 386-8086 (under MS DOS 3.1)*
(#890919W1.10157)
IBM PS/2 Model 70-80386 (under MS DOS 3.3/Phar Lap)
*IBM PS/2 Model 70-8086 (under MS DOS 3.3)*
(#890919W1.10158)
Northgate 386 (under MS DOS 4.01)
(#890919W1.10159)

Northgate 386 (under SCO Unix 3.2)
(#890919W1.10168)
Hewlett Packard Vectra RS/20C (under SCO Xenix 2.3.2)
(#890919W1.10169)

## R.R. Software, Inc. JANUS/Ada, Version 2.1.1

IBM PC XT (under MS DOS 3.3)
(#890113W1.10018)
Compaq Deskpro 286 (under MS DOS 3.1)
(#890113W1.10019)
Compaq Deskpro 386/25 (under MS DOS 3.31)
(#890113W1.10020)
PC's Limited 386 (under MS DOS 3.1)
(#890113W1.10021)
Compaq Deskpro 386/25 (under MS DOS 3.31/Phar Lap)
(#890113W1.10022)
PC's Limited 386 (under MS DOS 3.1/Phar Lap)
(#890113W1.10023)

## R.R. Software, Inc. Janus/Ada 2.1.3 386 to DOS

Bell 386 (under MS-DOS 4)
(#900125N1.10258)
Any Computer System comprising: cpu: any that executes the Intel
80386/80486 instruction set; fpu: optional; memory: 1.5 MByte RAM
or greater; disk: 20 MByte hard drive (under MS-DOS 3.30 or newer)
*Telxon PTC-710 & PTC-730 (under MS-DOS 3.21)*
(BASE #900125N1.10255)
Any Computer System comprising: cpu: any that executes the Intel
80386 or 80486 Instruction set; fpu: optional; memory: 1.5 MByte RAM
or greater; disk: 20 MByte hard drive (under MS-DOS 3.30 or newer)
(BASE #900125N1.10256)
Any Computer System comprising: cpu: any that executes the Intel
80386/80486 instruction set; fpu: optional; memory: 1.5 MByte RAM
or greater; disk: 20 MByte hard drive (under MS-DOS 3.30 or newer)
*Any Computer System comprising: cpu: any that executes the Intel
8086/8088 instruction set; fpu: optional; memory: 640 KByte RAM
or greater; disk: 10 MByte hard drive (under MS-DOS 2.00 or
newer)*
(BASE #900125N1.10258)

## R.R. Software, Inc. Janus/Ada 2.1.3 DOS

Bell 286 (under MS-DOS 4)
(#900125N1.10254)

Bell 286 (under MS-DOS 4)
*Telxon PTC-730 (under MS-DOS 3.21)*
(#900125N1.10255)
Any Computer System comprising: cpu: any that executes the Intel
8086/8088 instruction set; fpu: optional; memory: 640 KByte RAM or
greater; disk: 10 MByte hard drive (under MS-DOS 2.00 or newer)
(BASE #900125N1.10254)
Any Computer System comprising: cpu: any that executes the Intel
8086/8088 instruction set; fpu: optional; memory: 640 KByte RAM or
greater; disk: 10 MByte hard drive (under MS-DOS 2.01 or newer)
*Telxon PTC-710 & PTC-730 (under MS-DOS 3.21)*
(BASE #900125N1.10255)

## R.R. Software, Inc. Janus/Ada 2.1.3 Unix

Unisys 386 (under SCO Unix 3.2.0)
(#900125N1.10256)
Any Computer System comprising: cpu: Intel 80386; fpu: optional;
memory: 1.5 MByte RAM or greater; disk: 40 MByte hard drive (under
Interactive Unix 3.2.2)
(BASE #900125N1.10256)
Any Computer System comprising: cpu: Intel 80386; fpu: optional;
memory: 1.5 MByte RAM or greater; disk: 40 MByte hard drive (under
SCO Unix 3.2)
(BASE #900125N1.10256)

## R.R. Software, Inc. Janus/Ada 2.1.3 Xenix

Any Computer System comprising: cpu: Intel 80386; fpu: optional;
memory: 1.5 MByte RAM or greater; disk: 40 MByte hard drive (under
SCO Xenix 3.2)
(BASE #900125N1.10256)

## Rational MC68020 Family Cross Development Facility, Version 5

R1000 Series 200 Model 20 (under Rational Environment D_11_0_8)
*Motorola MVME135 (MC68020) (bare machine)*
(#890712W1.10112)

## Rational MC68020/OS-2000 Cross Development Facility, Version 5

R1000 Series 200 Model 20 (under Rational Environment D_11_0_8)
*Motorola 68020 in Philips PG2100 (under OS-2000 Version 2.2)*
(#890712W1.10113)

### Rational MIL-STD-1750A Cross Development Facility, Version 5
R1000 Series 200 Model 20 (under Rational Environment D_11_0_8)
*Mikros MKS 1750A/SO (bare machine)*
(#890712W1.10111)

### Rational Rational Environment, Version D_12_0_0
R1000 Series 200 Model 10 (under Rational Environment D_12_0_0)
(#890601W1.10084)

### Rational VAX/VMS Cross Development Facility, Version 5
R1000 Series 200 Model 20 (under Rational Environment D_11__0_8)
*DEC VAXstation II (under VMS 4.7)*
(#890712W1.10114)

### Ready Systems RTAda Comprehensive Development System, Version 2.05
Sun-3, all models (under Sun UNIX Version 4.2 Release 3.5)
*Motorola MVME133A-20 (MC68020) (bare machine)*
(BASE #890409W1.10044)
MicroVAX, VAXstation, VAX (under VAX/VMS Version 5.0)
*Motorola MVME133A-20 (MC68020)*
(BASE #890409W1.10064)

### Rockwell International Corporation DDC-Based Ada/CAPS Compiler System Version 4.3
MicroVAX, VAXstation, VAX (under VMS 5.2)
*CAPS/AAMP1 (bare machine)*
(BASE #891101W1.10181)
MicroVAX, VAXstation, VAX (under VMS 5.2)
*CAPS/AAMP2 (bare machine)*
(BASE #891101W1.10182)

### Rockwell International Corporation DDC-Based Ada/CAPS Compiler System, Version 4.1
VAX 8700 (under VMS 5.2)
*CAPS/AAMP1 (bare machine)*
(#891101W1.10181)
VAXstation 3100 Model 30 (under VMS 5.2)
*CAPS/AAMP2 (bare machine)*
(#891101W1.10182)

## Rockwell International Corporation DDC-Based Ada/CAPS Compiler System, Version 4.4
MicroVAX, VAXstation, VAX (under VMS 5.2)
*CAPS/AAMP2 (bare machine)*
(BASE #891101W1.10182)

## Rockwell International Corporation DDC-Based Ada/CAPS Compiler System, Version 5.0
MicroVAX, VAXstation, VAX (under VMS 5.3-1)
*CAPS/AAMP2 (bare machine)*
(BASE #891101W1.10182)

## SD_Scicon plc XD Ada 1750A, Version 1.0
VAX Cluster (comprising a VAX 8600 & 7 MicroVAX IIs) (under VMS 5.1)
*Fairchild F9450 on the SBC-50 board (MIL-STD-1750A) (bare machine)*
(BASE #890920N1.10170)

## SD_Scicon plc XD Ada MC68000 V1.0-09
VAX Cluster (comprising VAX 8600 & 7 MicroVAX IIs) (under VMS 5.1)
*MC68000 processor on an MVME117-3FP MPU VME module using an MC68881 floating-point peripheral (bare machine)*
(#900204N1.10252)

## SD_Scicon plc XD Ada MC68000, Version S1.0-10
VAX Cluster (comprising 1 VAX 8600 & 7 MicroVAX IIs) (under VMS 5.1)
*MC68000 processor on an MVME117-3FP MPU VME module using an MC68881 floating-point peripheral (bare machine)*
(BASE #900204N1.10252)

## SD_Scicon plc XD Ada MC68020 T1.0-02V
VAX Cluster (comprising a VAX 8600 and 7 MicroVAX IIs) (under VMS 5.0)
*MC68020 on the MVME 133 XT board (bare machine)*
(#890321N1.10041)

## SD_Scicon plc XD Ada MC68020 Version 1.0
VAX Cluster, comprising a VAX 8600 & 7 MicroVAX IIs (under VMS 5.0)
*Motorola MVME133XT (MC68020)*
(BASE #890321N1.10041)

### SD_Scicon plc XD Ada MC68020 Version 1.1

VAX Cluster, comprising a VAX 8600 & 7 MicroVAX II computers
(under VMS 5.0)
*Motorola MVME133XT (bare machine)*
(BASE #890321N1.10041)

### SD_Scicon plc XD Ada MC68020/MVME135, Version 1.1

VAX Cluster (comprising a VAXserver 3600, 2 MicroVAX 2000s & 1
MicroVAX II) (under VMS 5.0)
*Motorola MVME135-1 (MC68020) (bare machine)*
(BASE #890321N1.10041)

### SD_Scicon plc XD Ada MIL-STD-1750A T1.0-05A

VAX Cluster (comprising a VAX 8600 & 7 MicroVAX IIs) (under
VMS 5.1)
*Fairchild F9450 on a SBC-50 board (MIL-STD-1750A) (bare
machine)*
(#890920N1.10170)

### SD_Scicon plc XD Ada MIL-STD-1750A, Version V1.0A-07

Local Area VAX Cluster (comprising VAXserver 3600, 2 MicroVAX
2000s & 1 MicroVAX II) (under VMS 5.0)
*Fairchild F9450 on the SBC-50 board (MIL-STD-1750A) (bare
machine)*
(BASE #890920N1.10170)

### STERIA Ent_Alsy_01, Version 4.2

CETIA UNIGRAPH 6000 (under Unigraph/X release 3.0.4)
*Motorola MC68020 in PMF, with ARTK Version 4.2 (bare machine)*
(#900109A1.10239)

### SYSTEAM KG SYSTEAM Ada Compiler CADMUS/MUNIX Version 1.81

Cadmus 9921/4 (under Munix, Version V.3-3.1)
(#890825I1.10189)

### SYSTEAM KG SYSTEAM Ada Compiler S.7000/BS2000 Version 1.81

Siemens 7.530-B (under BS2000, Version 7.5A)
(#890831I1.10188)

### SYSTEAM KG SYSTEAM Ada Compiler SUN/SUNOS, Version 1.81

Sun 3/60 (under SunOS, Version 4.0.3)
(#891102I1.10200)

## SYSTEAM KG SYSTEAM Ada Compiler VAX/VMS x MC68020/OS-9, Version 1.81

VAX 8350 (under VMS 4.7)
*KWS EB68020 (under OS-9/68020 Version 2.1)*
(#89032911.10076)

## SYSTEAM KG SYSTEAM Ada Compiler VAX/VMS x MC68020/BARE

VAX 8530 (under VMS, Version 4.7)
*Motorola MVME133XT (MC68020/68882) (bare machine)*
(#89082511.10176)

## SYSTEAM KG SYSTEAM Ada Compiler VAX/VMS x MC68020/OS-9 Version 1.81

VAX 8530 (under VMS, Version 5.1)
*Motorola MVME147 (68030) (OS-9/68030, Version 2.3)*
(BASE #89032911.10076)

## SYSTEAM KG SYSTEAM Ada Compiler VAX/VMS, Version 1.82

VAX 8530 (under VMS, Version 5.1)
(#90050911.11009)

## SYSTEAM KG SYSTEAM Ada Compiler VAX/VMS, Version V1.81

VAX 8530 (under VMS 4.6)
(#89013111.10035)

## Siemens AG Siemens BS 2000 Ada Compiler V2.0

Siemens 7.590G (under BS2000/V9.0)
(#89030611.10059)
Siemens Series (under BS2000/V7.5, /V7.6, /V8.0, /V8.5, /V9.0, /V9.2 & /V9.5)
(BASE #89030611.10059)

## Silicon Graphics Computer Systems 4D ADA 3.0

Iris-4D/380 (under IRIX Release 4D-3.3)
(#900703W1.11014)
Iris-4D/220S (under IRIX Release 4D-3.3)
(#900703W1.11015)
Iris-4D/25 (under IRIX Release 4D-3.3)
(#900703W1.11016)

## Silicon Graphics Computer Systems 4D Ada, Version 2.0

Iris-4D/210 (under IRIX Release 4D-3.2)
(#890613W1.10100)

Iris-4D/70 (under IRIX Release 4D-3.2)
(#890613W1.10101)
Iris-4D/20 (under IRIX Release 4D-3.2)
(#890613W1.10102)
Iris-4D/240, /220 & /120 (under IRIX Release 4D-3.2)
(BASE #890613W1.10100)
Iris-4D/50 & /80 (under IRIX Release 4D-3.2)
(BASE #890613W1.10101)

## Software Leverage, Inc. Parallel-Leverage d Ada, Version S5.5.2

Sequent Symmetry S81 (under Dynix 3.0.12)
(#890628W1.10106)
Prime EXL 1200 Series; and UNISYS 6000/70 & /80 (under Dynix
3.0.12)
(BASE #890628W1.10106)
Sequent Symmetry S27 (under Dynix 3.0.12)
(BASE #890628W1.10106)

## TELESOFT SysV 386 Ada Cross Compilation System, Version 3.23

Intel 520 (under UNIX System V.3)
*Intel 386-120 (80386/387) board (bare machine)*
(#890911I1.10187)

## TELESOFT TeleGen2 Ada Development System for 386 UNIX V.3, Version 3.23

Intel 320 (80386) system (under Multibus I UNIX system V.3.0)
(BASE #890602I1.10137)

## TELESOFT TeleGen2 Ada Development System for VAX to E68K Version 3.23

DEC MicroVAX, VAXstation, VAXserver, VAX-11, VAX 8xxx & VAX
6xxx series (under VMS 5.0, 5.1 & 5.2, as supported)
*Motorola (MC68020) families; and Motorola (MC68030) families;
and Force CPU-30 (MC68030/MC68882) (bare machines)*
(BASE #890409W1.10064)
VAXserver 3602 (under VAX/VMS Version 5.0)
*Motorola MVME101 (MC68000) (bare machine)*
(#890409W1.10062)
VAXserver 3602 (under VAX/VMS Version 5.0)
*Motorola MVME117 (MC68010) (bare machine)*
(#890409W1.10063)

VAXserver 3602 (under VAX/VMS Version 5.0)
*Motorola MVME133A-20 (MC68020) (bare machine)*
(#890409W1.10064)

## TELESOFT TeleGen2 Ada Development System for VAX/VMS Version 3.23
All MicroVAX, VAXstation, VAX (under VAX/VMS 5.0, 5.1 & 5.2)
(BASE #890409W1.10042)
VAXserver 3602 (under VAX/VMS Version 5.0)
(#890409W1.10042)

## TELESOFT TeleGen2 Ada Development System for the 1750A, Version 2.1.0
IBM 4381 P3 (under MVS/XA, Version 3.8)
*MIL-STD-1750A ECSPO RAID Simulator Version 4.0, executing on a MicroVAX II (under VMS, Version 5.2) (bare machine)*
(#891030W1.10179)
IBM 3083 JX (under VM/HPO, Version 4.2)
*MIL-STD-1750A ECSPO RAID Simulator Version 4.0, executing on a MicroVAX II (under VMS, Version 5.2) (bare machine)*
(#891030W1.10180)

## TELESOFT TeleGen2 Ada Development System, Version 1.4
Sun-3/280 (under Sun UNIX Version 4.2 Release 3.5)
(#890409W1.10043)
Sun-3/280 (under Sun UNIX Version 4.2 Release 3.5)
*Motorola MVME133A-20 (MC68020) (bare machine)*
(#890409W1.10044)
Sun-3/280 (under Sun UNIX Version 4.2 Release 3.5)
*Motorola MVME101 (MC68020) (bare machine)*
(#890409W1.10060)
Sun-3/280 (under Sun UNIX Version 4.2 Release 3.5)
*Motorola MVME117 (MC68010) (bare machine)*
(#890409W1.10061)
Hewlett Packard 9000/370 (under HP/UX 6.5)
(#891126I1.10217)
Hewlett Packard 9000/340 (under HP/UX 6.5)
*Motorola MVME133A-20 (MC68020) (bare machine)*
(#891126I1.10221)
Sun-4/260 (SPARC Processor) (under Sun UNIX 4.2, Release 4.0)
*Motorola MVME133A-20 (MC68020) (bare machine)*
(#891126I1.10222)

SUN-3/80 (under SunOS Version 4.0.3)
*FORCE CPU-30, CPU-31, CPU-32 & CPU-37*
*(MC68030/MC68882) (bare machine)*
(BASE #890409W1.10044)
All Hewlett-Packard 9000/340, /360 & /370 machines (under
HP/UX 6.5)
(BASE #8911261I.10217)

## TELESOFT TeleGen2 Ada Development System, Version 1.4A

Sun-3, all models (under SunOS 3.5, 4.0 & 4.1)
(BASE #890409W1.10043)
C3 Navy Desktop Tactical Computer (DTC-2) (under C3 Realtime
SunOS 1.0)
(BASE #890801W1.10134)
Sun SPARCsystems, Sun-4/100, /200 & /300 series–all models (under
Sun UNIX 4.2, Releases 4.0.3 & 4.1)
(BASE #890801W1.10134)
Unisys 80386-Based Personal Workstation 2 Series 800 Systems (under
SCO UNIX System V.3.2)
(BASE #900131I1.10267)
Sun-3, all models (under SunOS 3.5, 4.0 & 4.1)
*Motorola VME 133\*, MVME135\*, MVME136\* (68020 board*
*families); Motorola MVME141\* & MVME147\* (68030 board*
*families) (bare machines)*
(BASE #890409W1.10044)

## TELESOFT TeleGen2 Ada Development System, Version 4.0

Data General AViiON 5120 Server (under DG/UX Release 4.20)
(#891124I1.10220)
Tektronix XD88/30 (under Utek V Release 3.2b Version 3)
(#891124I1.10266)
VAX 3800 (under VAX/VMS 5.2)
*Motorola MVME181 (MC88100) (bare machine)*
(#891127I1.10224)

## TELESOFT TeleGen2 Ada for 386 DOS Version 3.23

Zenith ZBF-3340-EK (under MS-DOS Version 3.21)
(#890630I1.10140)

## TELESOFT TeleGen2 Ada for 386 UNIX V.3 Version 3.23

Nimbus VX (80386) system (under Interactive UNIX sys V.3.2)
(#890602I1.10139)

Intel 520 (80386) system with Multibus II (under Intel UNIX sys V.3.0)
(#8906021I.10137)

## TELESOFT TeleGen2 Ada for SCO Unix V.3, Version 1.4A

ALR 386/216 (under SCO Unix System V.3.2)
(#9001311I.10267)

## TELESOFT TeleGen2 Ada for SUN-386i Version 1.4

SUN-386i (under SunOS, version 4.0.1)
(#8906021I.10138)

## TELESOFT TeleGen2 Macintosh Ada Development System Version 1.4

Apple Macintosh IIx (under Apple A/UX release 1.1)
(#890801W1.10133)

## TELESOFT TeleGen2 Macintosh Ada Development System, Version 1.4b

Apple Macintosh II & IIx (under Apple A/UX Release 1.1)
(BASE #890801W1.10133)

## TELESOFT TeleGen2 Sun-3 Ada Development System Version 4.0

Sun-3/280 (under Sun UNIX 4.2 Release 3.5)
(#890829W1.10143)
Sun-3/280 (under Sun UNIX 4.2 Release 3.5)
*Motorola MVME181 (MC88100) (bare machine)*
(#8912021I.10223)

## TELESOFT TeleGen2 Sun-4 Ada Development System Version 1.4

Sun-4/280 (SPARC Processor) (under Sun UNIX 4.2, Release 4.0.3)
(#890801W1.10134)

## TELESOFT TeleGen2+ Ada Development System for VAX to E68K, Version 3.23

DEC MicroVAX, VAXstation, VAXserver, VAX-11, VAX 8xxx & VAX
6xxx series (under VMS 5.0, 5.1 & 5.2, as supported)
*Motorola MVME133*, MVME135*, MVME136* (68020 board
families); Motorola MVME141* & MVME147* (68030 board
families) (bare machines)*
(BASE #890409W1.10064)

## TELESOFT TeleGen2+ Ada Development System, Version 1.4

Sun-3/280 (under Sun UNIX 4.2 Release 3.5)
*Motorola MVME133A-20 (MC68020) (bare machine)*
(#89112711.10226)
Motorola Delta 1000, 2000 & 3000 Series (under Motorola SYSTEM
V/68, Version V3.5)
*Motorola VME133\*, MVME135\*, MVME136\* (68020 board
families); Motorola MVME141\* & MVME147\* (68030 board
families) (bare machines)*
(BASE #890829W1.10145)

## TELESOFT TeleGen2+ Ada Development System, Version 3.23

VAX 3800 (under VAX/VMS 5.2)
*Motorola MVME133A-20 (MC68020) (bare machine)*
(#89112611.10225)

## THOMSON-CSF, DIVISION CIMSA SINTRA AlsyCOMP_039, Version 4.23

CETIA UNIGRAPH 2000 (under Unigraph/X release 3.0.6)
*THOMSON MLX32/20T (under MOP MLX Version 1, with ARTK
Version 4.23)*
(#891212A1.10230)

## THOMSON-CSF, DIVISION CIMSA SINTRA AlsyCOMP_041, Version 4.23

VAX 3300 (under Ultrix-32, Version 3.1B)
*THOMSON MLX32/20T (68020/68881) (under MOP MLX Version
1, with ARTK Version 4.23)*
(#900208A1.10242)

## THOMSON-CSF, DIVISION CIMSA SINTRA AlsyCOMP_041, Version 4.23

VAX 3300 (under Ultrix-32, Version 3.1B)
*THOMSON CM68 (68020/68881) (under CHRONOS, Version 5,
with ARTK Version 4.23)*
(#900208A1.10243)

## TLD Systems, Ltd. TLD HP/MIL-STD-1750A Ada Compiler System, Version 2.1.3

HP 9000/350 (under HP-UX, Version 4.0)
*HP64000 with Tasco MDC281 Emulator (with TLDspk Single
Program Kernel, Version 2.1.3) (bare machine)*
(#900212W1.10247)

## TLD Systems, Ltd. TLD MV/MIL-STD-1750A Ada Compiler System, Version 2.1.3

Data General MV/32 20000-2 (under AOS/VS, Version 7.65)
*TLDsim MIL-STD-1750A Instruction Set Simulator, executing on the Host (with TLDspk Single Program Kernel, Version 2.1.3) (bare machine simulation)*
(#900212W1.10245)

## TLD Systems, Ltd. TLD MV/MV Ada Compiler System, Version 2.1.3

Data General MV/32 20000-2 (under AOS/VS, Version 7.65)
(#900212W1.10249)

## TLD Systems, Ltd. TLD Sun/MIL-STD-1750A Ada Compiler System, Version 2.1.3

Sun 3/160 (under SunOS, Version 4.0)
*HP64000 with Tasco MDC281 Emulator (with TLDspk Single Program Kernel, Version 2.1.3) (bare machine)*
(#900212W1.10245)

## TLD Systems, Ltd. TLD VAX/HAWK Ada Cross Compiler System, Version 2.1.3

MicroVAX 3500 (under VMS 5.1)
*LRMSC-HAWK/32 (under AOS/VS, Version 7.57)*
(#900212W1.10248)

## TLD Systems, Ltd. TLD VAX/MIL-STD-1750A Ada Compiler System, Version 1.4.0

MicroVAX 3500 (under VMS 5.1)
*Tektronix 8540/PACE MIL-STD-1750A Emulator (with TLDspk Single Program Kernel, Version 1.4.0) (bare machine)*
(#900212W1.10244)

## TLD Systems, Ltd. TLD VAX/MIL-STD-1750A Ada Compiler System, Version 2.1.3

MicroVAX 3500 (under VMS 5.1)
*TLDsim MIL-STD-1750A Instruction Set Simulator, executing on the Host (with TLDspk Single Program Kernel, Version 2.1.3) (bare machine simulation)*
(#900212W1.10246)

## Tandem Computers Incorporated Tandem Ada, Version T9270C30

Tandem NonStop VLX (under GUARDIAN 90, Version C20)
(#890621W1.10105)

Tandem NonStop VLX, TXP, II & CLX (under GUARDIAN 90, C20)
(BASE #890621W1.10105)

## Tartan Laboratories Incorporated SUN Ada960MC Compiler V2.0
SUN 3/50 (under SunOS 3.5)
*Intel 80960MC on an Intel EXV80960MC board (bare machine)*
(#890621I1.10151)

## Tartan Laboratories Incorporated Tartan Ada Sun/C30, Version 2.2
Sun 3/60 (under SunOS 3.5)
*320C30 on TI Application Board (bare machine)*
(#891205I1.10263)

## Tartan Laboratories Incorporated Tartan Ada Sun/Sun, Version 2.1
Sun 3/60 (under SunOS Version 3.5)
(#890412I1.10082)

## Tartan Laboratories Incorporated Tartan Ada Sun/Sun, Version 3.02
Sun-3/60 (under SunOS 4.0)
(BASE #890412I1.10082)

## Tartan Laboratories Incorporated Tartan Ada ULTRIX, Version 3.02
VAXstation 3100 (under ULTRIX V3.0)
(BASE #891207I1.10261)

## Tartan Laboratories Incorporated Tartan Ada ULTRIX, Version INT-3
VAXstation 3100 (under ULTRIX V3.0)
(#891207I1.10261)

## Tartan Laboratories Incorporated Tartan Ada ULTRIX/68K, Version 3.02
MicroVAX II (under ULTRIX V2.2)
*Tektronix 8541 Emulator for 68020 using TekDB V5.04 emulation software (bare machine simulation)*
(BASE #891207I1.10262)

## Tartan Laboratories Incorporated Tartan Ada ULTRIX/68K, Version INT-2
VAXstation 3100 (under ULTRIX V3.0)
*Tektronix 8541 Emulator for 68020 using TekDB V5.04 emulation software (bare machine simulation)*
(#891207I1.10262)

## Tartan Laboratories Incorporated Tartan Ada VMS, Version V11.008024031

VAX 8350 (under VMS 4.7)
(#89092811.10264)

## Tartan Laboratories Incorporated Tartan Ada VMS/1750A Version 2.11

All members of the VAX family of computers (under MicroVMS 4.7,
VMS 4.7 & VMS 5.0)
*Fairchild F9450 (MIL-STD-1750A)*
(BASE #89062111.10148)
VAXstation 3200 (under MicroVMS 4.7)
*Fairchild F9450 (MIL-STD-1750A) (bare machine)*
(#89062111.10148)

## Tartan Laboratories Incorporated Tartan Ada VMS/1750A, Version 3.1

DEC MicroVAX, VAXstation, VAXserver, VAX-11, VAX 8xxx & VAX
6xxx series (under MicroVMS 4.7, and VMS 5.0 & 5.1, as supported)
*Fairchild F9450 (MIL-STD-1750A)*
(BASE #89062111.10148)

## Tartan Laboratories Incorporated Tartan Ada VMS/68K Version 2.1

All members of the VAX family of computers (under MicroVMS 4.7,
VMS 4.7 & VMS 5.0)
*Motorola MVME134 (68020/68881) (bare machine)*
(BASE #89062111.10149)
VAXstation 3200 (under MicroVMS 4.7)
*Motorola MVME134 (68020/68881) (bare machine)*
(#89062111.10149)

## Tartan Laboratories Incorporated Tartan Ada VMS/C30, Version 2.2

VAXstation 3100 (under VMS 5.1B)
*320C30 on TI Application Board (bare machine)*
(#89120511.10260)
All VAX family computers (under MicroVMS V4.7 & V5.0, VMS V4.7 &
V5.0, as supported)
*320C30 on PC/M DSP-2A Processor Board (bare machine)*
(BASE #89120511.10260)

## Tartan Laboratories Incorporated VMS Ada960MC Compiler R1.0

VAXstation 3200 (under MicroVMS 4.7)

*Intel 80960MC on an Intel EXV80960MC board (bare machine)*
(#8906211I.10150)

All members of the VAX family of computers (under MicroVMS 4.7, VMS 4.7 & VMS 5.0)

*Intel 80960MC on an Intel EXV80960MC board (bare machine)*
(BASE #8906211I.10150)

## Tartan Laboratories Incorporated VMSAda960MC Compiler R1.02

All members of the VAX family of computers (under MicroVMS 4.7, VMS 4.7 & VMS 5.0)

*Intel 80960MC on Intel EXV80960MC board (bare machine)*
(BASE #8906211I.10150)

## TeleSoft TeleGen2 Ada Development System for AIX PS/2, Version 1.0

IBM PS/2 Model 80 (under AIX, Release 1.1)
(#8909111I.10177)

## TeleSoft TeleGen2 Ada Development System for VAX to E68K, Version 4.0

VAXserver 3800 (under VAX/VMS Version 5.2)
*Motorola MVME133A-20 (MC68020) (bare machine)*
(#9001311I.10270)

## TeleSoft TeleGen2 Sun-3 Ada Development System, Version 4.01

Sun-3/280 (under Sun UNIX 4.2, Release 4.0.3)
(#9005251I.11012)

## TeleSoft TeleGen2 VAX/1750a Cross Compilation System, Version 3.23

MicroVAX II (under VMS 5.1)
*MIL-STD-1750a ECSPO ITS Simulator, Version 4.0 executing on the Host (bare machine)*
(#890710W1.10110)

## Tolerant Systems Tolerant Ada Development System, Version 2.3

Tolerant Eternity (under TX, Release 5.4.0)
(#890911W1.10135)

## U.S. NAVY Ada/L, Version 2.0 (/NO_OPTIMIZE Option)
VAX 8550 and VAX 11/785 (under VMS, Version 5.1)
*AN/UYK-43 (bare machine)*
(#891201S1.10211)

## U.S. NAVY Ada/L, Version 2.0 (/OPTIMIZE Option)
VAX 8550 and VAX 11/785 (under VMS, Version 5.1)
*AN/UYK-43 (bare machine)*
(#891201S1.10212)

## U.S. NAVY Ada/M, Version 2.0 (/NO_OPTIMIZE Option)
VAX 8550 and VAX 11/785 (under VMS, Version 5.1)
*AN/AYK-14 (bare machine)*
(#891130S1.10215)
VAX 8550 and VAX 11/785 (under VMS, Version 5.1)
*AN/AYK-14 (bare machine)*
(#891130S1.10216)
VAX 8550 and VAX 11/785 (under VMS, Version 5.1)
*AN/UYK-44 (bare machine)*
(#891201S1.10213)

## U.S. NAVY Ada/M, Version 2.0 (/OPTIMIZE Option)
VAX 8550 and VAX 11/785 (under VMS, Version 5.1)
*AN/UYK-44 (bare machine)*
(#891201S1.10214)

## U.S. NAVY AdaVAX, Version 3.0 (/NO_OPTIMIZE Option)
VAX 8350 and VAX 11/785 (under VMS, Version 5.1)
(#891130S1.10209)

## U.S. NAVY AdaVAX, Version 3.0 (/OPTIMIZE Option)
VAX 8600 and VAX 11/785 (under VMS, Version 5.1)
(#891130S1.10210)

## UNISYS Unisys TeleGen2 Ada Compiler Version 3.22
UNISYS 5000/80 (MC68020), /85 (MC68020), /90 (MC68020) & /95 (MC68020) (under UNISYS System V, Release 5.0)
(BASE #890409W1.10065)

## UNISYS Unisys U Series Ada Development System, Version 3.23
Unisys 5000/95 (MC68020) (under UNISYS System V, Release 5.0)
(#890409W1.10065)

## Verdix Corporation Sun4->Sun3, Version 5.7
Sun 4/260 (under SunOS 4.0)
*Sun 3/280 (under SunOS 4.0)*
(#890331W1.10046)

## Verdix Corporation VADS DEC-RISK=>68k, Ultrix 3.1, VAda-110-61125, Version 6.0
DECstation 3100 (under Ultrix 3.1)
*Motorola MVME147 (MC68030) (bare machine)*
(#900726W1.11024)

## Verdix Corporation VADS HP 9000/300, HP-UX 7.0, VAda-110-1515, Version 6.0
HP 9000/350 (under HP-UX 7.0)
(#900726W1.11018)

## Verdix Corporation VADS IBM PS/2 AIX => 68K, VAda-110-35125, Version 6.0
IBM PS/2 Model 80 (under AIX 1.1)
*Motorola MVME133A-20 (MC68020) (bare machine)*
(#900510W1.11005)

## Verdix Corporation VADS IBM PS/2 AIX => Intel 80386, VAda-110-35315, Version 6.0
IBM PS/2 Model 80 (under AIX 1.1)
*Intel iSBC 386/12 (bare machine)*
(#900510W1.11004)

## Verdix Corporation VADS IBM PS/2, Version 6.0
IBM PS/2 Model 80 (under AIX 1.1)
(#891116W1.10190)

## Verdix Corporation VADS IBM RISC System/6000, AIX 3.1, VAda-110-7171, Version 6.0
IBM RISC System/6000 Model 530 (under AIX 3.1)
(#900726W1.11017)

## Verdix Corporation VADS IBM RISC System/6000=>386, AIX 3.1, VAda-110-71315, Version 6.0
IBM RISC System/6000 Model 530 (under AIX 3.1)
*Intel iSBC 386/116 (bare machine)*
(#900726W1.11026)

## Verdix Corporation VADS IBM RISC System/6000=>68k, AIX 3.1, VAda-110-71125, Version 6.0
IBM RISC System/6000 Model 530 (under AIX 3.1)
*Motorola MVME147 (MC68030) (bare machine)*
(#900726W1.11025)

## Verdix Corporation VADS IBM RT, Version 6.0
IBM 6150 Model 135 (under AIX 2.2.1)
(#891116W1.10192)

## Verdix Corporation VADS ISI Self, Version 5.7
IS68K (Integrated Solutions) (under UNIX 4.3 BSD)
(#890331W1.10048)

## Verdix Corporation VADS Prime EXL/320, UNIX System V/386 3.2, VAda-110-3232, Version 6.0
Prime EXL/320 (under UNIX System V/386 3.2)
(#900726W1.11019)

## Verdix Corporation VADS SUN4/UNIX->68K (68020), Version 6.0
Sun 4/260 (under SunOS 4.0)
*Motorola MVME147 (68030/68882)*
(#891116W1.10193)

## Verdix Corporation VADS Sun-4 SunOS, VAda-110-4040, Version 6.0
Sun 4/280 (under SunOS 4.0)
(#900510W1.11006)

## Verdix Corporation VADS Sun3 SunOS => 68K, VAda-110-13125, Version 6.0
Sun 3/280 (under SunOS 4.0)
*Motorola MVME147 (MC68030) (bare machine)*
(#900510W1.11007)

## Verdix Corporation VADS Sun3 SunOS, VAda-110-1313, Version 6.0
Sun 3/280 (under SunOS 4.0)
(#900510W1.11003)

## Verdix Corporation VADS Sun3 SunOS, VAda-110-1313, Version 6.0
Sun-3/50, /60, /80, /150, /160, /260, /280, /470 & /480 (under SunOS 4.0)
(BASE #900510W1.11003)

## Verdix Corporation VADS Sun3 UNIX, Version 5.7
Sun3/280 (under SunOS 3.5)
(#890610W1.10091)

## Verdix Corporation VADS Sun3 UNIX, Version 6.0

Sun-3 family (Sun-3/52, /75, /110, /160, /180, /260 & /280) (under SunOS 3.5 & 4.0)
(BASE #890610W1.10091)

## Verdix Corporation VADS Sun3/UNIX -> 68K (68020), Version 5.7

Sun3/280 (under SunOS 3.5)
*Motorola MVME133A-20 (bare machine)*
(#890610W1.10092)

## Verdix Corporation VADS VAX UNIX, Version 5.5

VAX-11/750 (under UNIX 4.3 BSD)
(#890610W1.10093)

## Verdix Corporation VADS VAX UNIX->68K, Version 5.7

VAX 11-750 (under UNIX 4.3 BSD)
*Tektronix 8541 emulator (MV68020 Support System), using TEKDB 5.01 emulation software (bare machine)*
(#890331W1.10045)

## Verdix Corporation VADS VAX VMS -> 68K (68000), Version 5.7

MicroVAX 3600 (under VMS 5.0)
*Microbar GPC68000 (bare machine)*
(#890610W1.10094)

## Verdix Corporation VADS VAX VMS -> Intel 80386, Version 5.7

MicroVAX 3600 (under VMS 5.0)
*Intel iSBC 386/20P (bare machine)*
(#890610W1.10090)

## Verdix Corporation VADS VAX VMS, Version 6.0

MicroVAX II (under VMS 5.0)
(#890610W1.10089)

## Verdix Corporation VADS VAX VMS->68K, Version 5.7

MicroVAX 3600 (under VMS 5.0)
*MVME 133A-20 (MC68020) (bare machine)*
(#890331W1.10047)

## Verdix Corporation VADS VAX/Ultrix=>68k, Ultrix 3.1, VAda-110-02125, Version 6.0

MicroVAX 3100 (under Ultrix 3.1)
*Tektronix MV System, MV 68020 Support System, using TekDB Version 5.0.2 emulation software (bare machine simulation)*
(#900726W1.11023)

## Verdix Corporation VADS VAX/VMS 5.2, VAda-110-0303, Version 6.0

MicroVAX 3100 (under VAX/VMS V5.2)
(#900726W1.11020)

## Verdix Corporation VADS VAX/VMS=>68k, VMS 5.2, VAda-110-03125, Version 6.0

MicroVAX 3100 (under VAX/VMS V5.2)
*Motorola MVME147 (MC68030) (bare machine)*
(#900726W1.11021)

## Verdix Corporation VADS VAX/VMS=>Intel 386, VMS 5.2, VAda-110-03315, Version 6.0

MicroVAX 3100 (under VAX/VMS V5.2)
*Intel iSBC 386/32 (bare machine)*
(#900726W1.11022)

## Verdix Corporation VADS VMS -> MIL-STD-1750A, Version 6.0, MP

DEC MicroVAX III (under VMS 5.0)
*Tektronix 1750A Emulator (Ethernet Download), v1.00-00 with VADS EXEC v6.0 (bare machine)*
(#891116W1.10194)

## Verdix Corporation VAda-110-01125, Version 6.0

VAX-11/750 (under UNIX 4.3 BSD)
*Tektronix 8541 emulator (MV68020 Support System), using TEKDB 5.01 emulation software (bare machine)*
(BASE #890331W1.10045)

## Verdix Corporation VAda-110-0202, Version 6.0

VAXsystem 3100 (under ULTRIX 3.1)
(#900228W1.11002)

## Verdix Corporation VAda-110-0303 Version 6.0

MicroVAX, VAXserver, VAXstation, VAX (under VMS 5.0)
(BASE #890610W1.10089)

## Verdix Corporation VAda-110-03315 Version 6.0

MicroVAX 3600 (under VMS 5.0)
*Intel iSBC 386/20P*
(BASE #890610W1.10090)

## Verdix Corporation VAda-110-1313 Version 6.0

Sun-3/50, /60, /80, /150, /160, /260, /280, /470 & /480 (under SunOS 4.0)
(BASE #890610W1.10091)

## Verdix Corporation VAda-110-15125 Version 6.0
HP 9000 Series: Models 300, 310, 320, 330, 340, 350, 360 & 370
(under HP-UX 6.2)
*Motorola Series (MC68030), Series (MC68020); and Sun*
*Microsystems 3E board set (bare machines)*
(BASE #890216W1.10031)

## Verdix Corporation VAda-110-15125, Version 5.7
HP 9000 Series 300 Model 350 (under HP-UX 6.2B)
*Motorola MVME-147 (MC68030/68882)*
(BASE #890216W1.10031)

## Verdix Corporation VAda-110-15125-1, Version 5.7
HP 9000 Series 300 Model 350 (under HP-UX, Release 6.2B)
*MVME-133A-20 (MC68020) (bare machine)*
(#890216W1.10031)

## Verdix Corporation VAda-110-1515, V5.7
Hewlett Packard 9000/350 (under HP-UX 6.2 Version B)
(#881118W1.10001)

## Verdix Corporation VAda-110-1515, Version 6.0
HP 9000 Series 300: Models 300, 310, 320, 330,.340, 350, 360 & 370
(under HP-UX 6.2)
(BASE #881118W1.10001)

## Verdix Corporation VAda-110-1616 Version 6.0
Integrated Solutions IS68K (under UNIX 4.3 BSD)
(BASE #890331W1.10048)

## Verdix Corporation VAda-110-2323, Version 5.5
Sequent Balance 8000 (under Sequent Dynix, Release 3.0.4)
(#890216W1.10029)

## Verdix Corporation VAda-110-3333, Version 5.7
Prime EXL (under Unix System V / 386, Release 3.0)
(#890216W1.10027)

## Verdix Corporation VAda-110-3333, Version 6.0
Prime EXL (under Unix System V / 386, Release 3.0)
(BASE #890216W1.10027)

## Verdix Corporation VAda-110-3434, V5.7
SUN 386i (under SunOS Release 4.0)
(#881118W1.10002)

## Verdix Corporation VAda-110-3434, Version 6.0
Sun-386i/150 & Sun-386i/250 (under SunOS 4.0)
(BASE #881118W1.10002)

## Verdix Corporation VAda-110-40125 Version 6.0

Sun-4/110, /150, /260 & /280; SparcServer 330, 370 & 390; and
SparcStation I, 330 & 370 (under SunOS 4.0)
*Motorola Series (MC68030), Series (MC68020); and Sun
Microsystems 3E board set (bare machines)*
(BASE #891116W1.10193)

## Verdix Corporation VAda-110-4013 Version 6.0

Sun-4/110, /150, /260 & /280; SparcServer 330, 370 & 390; and
SparcStation I, 330 & 370 (under SunOS 4.0)
*Sun-3/50, /60, /80, /150, /160, /260, /280, /470 & /480 (under
SunOS 4.0)*
(BASE #890331W1.10046)

## Verdix Corporation VAda-110-4040 Version 6.0

Sun-4/110, /150, /260 & /280; SparcServer 330, 370 & 390; and
SparcStation I, 330 & 370 (under SunOS 4.0)
(BASE #890216W1.10030)
Sun-4/260 (under SunOS, Release 4.0)
(#890216W1.10030)

## Verdix Corporation VAda-110-5151, Version 5.7

AT&T 3B15 (under Unix System V, Release 3.1.1)
(#890216W1.10028)

## Verdix Corporation VAda-110-5151, Versions 5.7 & 6.0

AT&T 3B15, 3B2/400, /500, /522, /600, /600G, /700, /800,
/1000-60, /1000-70 & /1000-80 (under UNIX System V releases 3.1,
3.1.1, 3.2, 3.2.1 & 3.2.2, as supported)
(BASE #890216W1.10028)

## Verdix Corporation VAda-110-6161, Version 6.0.2

DECstation 3100 (under ULTRIX 3.1)
(#900228W1.11001)
DECstation 2100, 5000; DECsystem 5400, 5810, 5820, 5830, 5840
(under ULTRIX 3.1)
(BASE #900228W1.11001)

## Verdix Corporation VAda-110-7070, Version 6.0

IBM 6150 Model 125 (under AIX 2.2.1)
(BASE #891116W1.10192)

## Verdix Corporation VAda-115-40800, Version 1.3

Sun-4/110, /150, /260 & /280; SparcServer 310, 330, 370, 390 & 490;
and SparcStation I, 310, 330 & 370 (under SunOS 4.0)
*Motorola Series (MC68030), Series (MC68020); and Sun
Microsystems 3E board set (bare machines (using Integrated*

*VADSWorks 1.3 run-time kernal))*
(BASE #891116W1.10193)

## Wang Laboratories, Inc Wang VS Ada, Version 4.01.01
Wang VS 7010, 7110, 7120, 7150 & 7130; 8220, 8230, 8260, 8430, 8460, 8470 & 8480; and 10050, 10075 & 10100 (under Wang VS OS 7.29.xx & 7.30.02)
(BASE #900116W1.10236)

## Wang Laboratories, Inc. Wang VS Ada, Version 4.1
Wang VS 8480 (under Wang VS OS 7.29.23)
(#900116W1.10236)

## York Software Engineering Limited York Ada Compiler Environment (ACE) Release 4
DuPont Pixel Systems bRISC (under UNIX System V.3)
(#890531N1.10095)
High Level Hardware Orion 1/05 (under Berkeley UNIX Release 4.2)
(#890531N1.10096)
Intergraph Inter Pro 340 (under UNIX System V.3)
(#890531N1.10097)
InterAct 220, 3050, 6040, 6080, 6240 & 6280 (under UNIX System V.3)
(BASE #890531N1.10097)
InterPro 125, 225, 340, 360, 3050, 3070, 6040, 6240, 6080 & 6280 (under UNIX System V.3)
(BASE #890531N1.10097)
InterServe 200, 300, 3000, 4200, 5200, 6000, 6105 & 6505 (under UNIX System V.3)
(BASE #890531N1.10097)
InterView 220 & 3050 (under UNIX System V.3)
(BASE #890531N1.10097)
Mobile GIS/C2 (under UNIX System V.3)
(BASE #890531N1.10097)

# 10

# Ada suppliers

Compiled by John Hole
Racal Communications Ltd

This is primarily a list of Ada suppliers in the UK.

## Advanced System Architecture Ltd

North Block
Bentley Hall
Bentley
ALTON
Hants GU3 4PU
UK

Tel. +44 420 23815
Fax. +44 420 23741

Products/Services:
    Development Tools

## AdaTraining Ltd

Astra Centre
Edinburgh Way
HARLOW
Essex CM20 2BE
UK

Tel. +44 279 450000

Products/Services:
    Training

## Alsys

Alsys Ltd
Partridge House
Newtown Road
HENLEY-ON-THAMES
Oxon RG9 1EN
UK

Tel. +44 491 579090
Fax. +44 491 571866

Alsys SA
29 Avenue de Versailles
La Chatiaqueraie
78170 La Celle Saint-Cloud
FRANCE

Tel. +33 1 39 18 12 44
Fax. +33 1 39 18 26 80

Alsys Gmbh
Am Ruepperner Schloss 7
D-7500 Karlsruhe 51
GERMANY

Tel. +49 721 883025

Products/Services:
    Compilers
    Development Tools
    Training
    Consultancy

## Applied Learning

1 Hogarth Business Park
Burlington Lane
Chiswick
LONDON W4
UK

Tel. +44 1-994 4404

Products/Services:
    Training Packages

## Concurrent Computer Corporation

227 Bath Road
SLOUGH
Berks
UK

Tel. +44 753 77777
Fax. +44 753 24657

Products/Services:
    Compilers
    Development Tools

## Computer Operational Requirements Analysts Ltd

CORAL House
274a High Street
ALDERSHOT
Hants GU12 4LZ
UK

Tel. +44 252 333777

Products/Services:
    Consultancy

## Datel Technology Ltd

323 Clifton Drive
LYTHAM ST ANNES
Lancs FY8 1HN
UK

Tel. +44 253 713311

Products/Services:
    Training

## DDC International

Lundtoftevej 1B
DK-2800 Lyngby
DENMARK

Tel. +45 42871144
Fax. +45 42872217

Products/Services:
    Compilers

## Digital Equipment Company

PO Box 115
Worton Grange
Imperial Way
READING
Berks RG2 0TL
UK

Tel. +44 734 868711

Products/Services:
    Compilers
    Development Tools
    Training Packages

## Encore Computer (UK) Ltd

Marlborough House
Mole Business Park
Randalls Road
LEATHERHEAD
Surrey KT22 7BA
UK

Tel. +44 372 363363
Fax. +44 372 362926

Products/Services:
    Compilers
    Development Tools

## EVB Software Engineering Inc

5320 Spectrum Drive
Frederick
MD 21701

Tel. +1 301 695 6960

Products/Services:
    Development Tools
    Reusable Components

## Ferranti International

Western Road
BRACKNELL
Berks RG12 1RA
UK

Tel. +44 344 483232

Products/Services:
    Training

## Harris Systems Ltd

Computer Systems Division
Eskdale Road
Winnersh
WOKINGHAM
Berks RG11 5TR
UK

Tel. +44 734 698787
Fax. +44 734 695805

Products/Services:
    Compilers
    Development Tools

## GEC Marconi Software Systems

Elstree Way
BOREHAMWOOD
Herts WD6 1RX
UK

Tel. +44 1-906 6788

Products/Services:
    Compilers
    Development Tools
    Training

## Generics Software Ltd

Clonard House
Sandyford Road
Dublin 16
EIRE

Tel. +353 1 954012

Products/Services:
    Development Tools
    Training

## GSE Software Engineering GmbH

Pixisstr. 2
8000 Munich
WEST GERMANY

Tel. +49 89 92100819
Fax. +49 89 92100811

Products/Services:
    Compilers
    Development Tools

## Hatfield Polytechnic

Computer Science Business Services
School of Information Sciences
Hatfield Polytechnic
College Lane
HATFIELD
Herts AL10 9AB
UK

Tel. +44 7072 79318

Products/Services:
    Training

## Hewlett-Packard Ltd

Cain Road
BRACKNELL
Berks RG12 1HN
UK

Tel. +44 344 360000
Fax. +44 344 361240

Products/Services:
    Development Tools

## High Integrity Systems

Astra Centre
Edinburgh Way
HARLOW
Essex CM20 2BE
UK

Tel. +44 279 45000
Fax. +44 279 29149

Products/Services:
    Compilers
    Development Tools
    Consultancy

## ICL (UK) Ltd

Eskdale Road
Winnersh
WOKINGHAM
Berks RG11 5TT
UK

Tel. +44 734 693131
Fax. +44 734 693131-6004

Products/Services:
    Compilers
    Development Tools

## Imperial Software Technology

95 London Street
READING
Berks
UK

Tel. +44 734 587055
Fax. +44 734 589005

Products/Services:
    Development Tools

## Intel Corporation (UK) Ltd

Pipers Way
SWINDON
Wilts SN3 1RJ
UK

Tel. +44 793 696000

Products/Services:
    Compilers
    Development Tools

## Interactive Development Environments

40 Ocean Road
GUILDFORD
Surrey GU2 5YH
UK

Tel. +44 483 579000
Fax. +44 483 31272

Products/Services:
    Development Tools

## IPSYS Software

Marlborough Court
Pickford Street
MACCLESFIELD
Cheshire SK11 6JD
UK

Tel. +44 625 616722
Fax. +44 625 616780

Products/Services:
    Development Tools

## Knowledge Base Systems Ltd

1 Campus Road
Listerhills Technology Park
BRADFORD
West Yorks BD7 1HR
UK

Tel. +44 274 736895
Fax. +44 274 736553

Products/Services:
    Development Tools
    Training
    Consultancy

## Michael Jackson Systems Ltd

Technology House
Waterside Drive
Langley Business Park
LANGLEY
Berks SL3 6EZ
UK

Tel. +44 753 580111
Fax. +44 753 580141

Products/Services:
    Development Tools

## Milspec Systems Ltd

PO Box 162
COVENTRY
CV5 6SE
UK

Tel. +44 203 70770
Fax. +44 203 670770

Products/Services:
    Compilers
    Development Tools

## NAG Ltd

Wilkinson House
Jordan Hill Road
OXFORD
OX2 8DR
UK

Tel. +44 865 511245
Fax. +44 865 310139

Products/Services:
Reusable Components

## Napier Polytechnic

Department of Computer Studies
Sighthill
EDINBURGH
EH11 4BH
UK

Tel. +44 31 444 2266
Fax. +44 31 458 5089

Products/Services:
Training

## The National Computing Centre

Oxford Road
MANCHESTER
M1 7ED
UK

Tel. +44 61 228 6333

Products/Services:
Training Packages

## NA Software Ltd

Merseyside Innovation Centre
131 Mount Pleasant
LIVERPOOL
L3 5TF
UK

Tel. +44 51 7080123
Fax. +44 51 7095645

Products/Services:
Compilers
Numerical Libraries
Training Products
Consultancy

## Nokia Data Systems

Ada Tools
PO Box 209
SF-33101 Tampere
FINLAND

Tel. +358 31 37317

Products/Services:
Compilers
Development Tools

## PAFEC Ltd

Strelley Hall
Strelley
NOTTINGHAM
NG8 6PE
UK

Tel. +44 602 490000
Fax. +44 602 390695

Products/Services:
Development Tools
Consultancy

## P-E International

Systems Group
161 Fleet Road
FLEET
Hants GU13 8PD
UK

Tel. +44 252 625121
Fax. +44 252 617665

Products/Services:
Development Tools

## Program Validation Ltd

26 Queens Terrace
SOUTHAMPTON
SO1 1BQ
UK

Tel. +44 703 350001
Fax. +44 703 230805

Products/Services:
Development Tools
Consultancy

## Rational

18 rue Gounod
F-92210 Saint-Cloud
FRANCE

Tel. +33 47717232
Fax. +33 47717977

PO Box 225
HOVE
East Sussex BN3 1DX
UK

Tel. +44 273 204733
Fax. +44 273 25372

Products/Services:
Compilers, Training
Development Tools

## Ready Systems Ltd

33 Queen Street
MAIDENHEAD
Berks SL6 1NB
UK

Tel. +44 628 773100
Fax. +44 628 773044

Products/Services:
Compilers
Development Tools

## Real-Time Software

118-120 Warwick Street
LEAMINGTON SPA
Warwicks CV32 4QY
UK

Tel. +44 926 450858

Products/Services:
Development Tools
Training

## Rex Thompson and Partners

Newnhams
West Street
FARNHAM
Surrey GU9 7EQ
UK

Tel. +44 252 711414

Products/Services:
Development Tools

## SD-Scicon

SD Software Technology Centre
Pembroke House
Pembroke Broadway
CAMBERLEY
Surrey GU15 3XD
UK

Tel. +44 276 686200
Fax. +44 276 683511

Products/Services:
  Compilers
  Development Tools
  Consultancy
  Training

## SEMA Group

Orion Court
Kenarvon Drive
READING
Berks RG1 3DU
UK

Tel. +44 734 575900

Products/Services:
  Compilers

## Siemens AG

D VMP 133
Otto Hahn-Ring 6
D-8000 Munich 33
WEST GERMANY

Tel. +49 89 63647691

Products/Services:
  Compilers

## SQL Systems International plc

Latton Bush Centre
Southern Way
HARLOW
Essex CM18 7BL
UK

Tel. +44 279 641021
Fax. +44 279 451724

Products/Services:
  Development Tools

## Sun Microsystems Ltd

Sun House
31-41 Pembroke Broadway
CAMBERLEY
Surrey GU15 3XD
UK

Tel. +44 276 62111
Fax. +44 276 64220

Products/Services:
  Compilers
  Development Tools

## Systematica Ltd

3-7 St Stephens Road
BOURNEMOUTH
Dorset
UK

Tel. +44 202 297292
Fax. +44 202 291180

Products/Services:
  Development Tools

## Technical Training Ltd

17 Claremont Crescent
EDINBURGH
EH7 4HX
UK

Tel. +44 31 575111

Products/Services:
Training

## Tektronix UK Ltd

Fourth Avenue
Globe Park
MARLOW
Bucks SL7 1YD
UK

Tel. +44 6284 60000
Fax. +44 6284 74799

Products/Services:
Compilers
Development Tools

## TeleLOGIC Europe SA

33 Boulevard de la Cambre
1050 Brussels
BELGIUM

Tel. +32 2 6473640

Products/Services:
Compilers
Development Tools

## Verdix

123 Rue du Chateau
92100 Boulogne
FRANCE

Tel. +33 1 49 09 10 10
Fax. +33 1 46 04 17 19

Products/Services:
Compilers

## Yard Software Systems Ltd

Avonbridge House
Bath Road
CHIPPENHAM
Wilts SN15 2BB
UK

Tel. +44 249 656194
Fax. +44 249 655723

Products/Services:
Development Tools

## York Software Engineering Ltd

University of York
YORK
YO1 5DD
UK

Tel. +44 904 433745
Fax. +44 904 432767

Products/Services:
Compilers
Development Tools
Training

# 11

# Ada components

## 11.1    Reusable software components

Tony Orme
AEG (UK) Limited

Software reuse is an intuitively attractive idea and offers a rare prospect of radically improving the economics of software. The technology of reuse is a young one and there are difficulties associated which are now well known and described in the most recent literature. Briefly, they include :

— The Intellectual Property Rights issue

— The "Not Invented Here" Barrier to reuse

— The Creation of a Reusable Library will also require resources for its maintenance

— Identification of candidate components for reuse

— Effective Cataloguing

However those organisations who have instituted a discipline for reuse report that Ada is particularly suited to it. The separation of specification and body for Ada packages and subprograms mean that the reuser need only concern himself with the interface details that he needs to know. The strong typing of Ada largely avoids the accidental confusion of different data types. Generics are a kind of template which allow generalised packages and subprograms to be written. Last but not least, because Ada is normally used in the context of a software engineering discipline, greater readability and maintainability result, which aids the reuse process. As an example of what can be achieved, IBM estimates that Ada code reuse and new management methods have reduced the code-writing requirement by 25% on a 400,000 line-of-code circuit assembly project.

A number of organisations have set up reusable software libraries. Many are available to the public, their charges generally being commensurate with the support provided. The amount of Ada software already available is immense. Largely mathematical components are offered in the NAG (Numerical Algorithms Group) Library and in a product called Math Advantage. General components (stack, queue, etc.) on sale include the Booch components and GRACE. TACK includes Ada menus and Ada windows. There is a package called ASENTO with tools for Ada compiler writers. Ada support for the Graphical Kernel System (GKS) and other graphics systems are available. CAMP (Common Ada Missile Packages) is available to anyone with a legitimate interest. The U.S. Government-sponsored Ada Software Repository contains tens of megabytes of freely available programs, tools and educational materials.

One of the largest software research projects in the world is the U.S. STARS (Software Technology for Adaptable Reliable Systems) project. Part of its very ambitious goals are to create shared repositories with semi-automatic accession procedures and knowledge-based catalogue browsers. Each of the three main contractors, IBM, Unisys and Boeing, has collected hundreds of megabytes of reusable Ada source code.

# 11.2   The NAG Library

When the Ada language was announced it would have been a simple matter to take existing NAG code and simply translate the Fortran routines into Ada. To do so would throw away the advantages that the Ada language offers the user and would result in a library of diminished usefulness.

Instead NAG focused on the advantages offered by Ada:

(a) The ability to define new types, to overload operator and procedure names and to return a value of arbitrary type from a function. These features allow major improvements in the user interface compared with the Fortran Library.

(b) The package facility, which not only provides a well-defined and safe extension to the Fortran Library mechanism but allows the hiding of inessential information and guarding of essential information from misuse.

(c) The generic facility allows the provision of facilities much more general than those expressible in Fortran.

(d) The tasking mechanism which allows the expression of parallel and real-time programs with arbitrary synchronisation needs.

Whilst seeking to preserve these advantages NAG sought nevertheless to make the Ada Library easy to implement on a variety of machines under a variety of different compilers. The Library design therefore consists of a 'core' of basic facilities: type declarations, elementary functions, simple vector/matrix arithmetic, etc. and a set of application packages containing higher level routines.

Because Ada defines different declarations of a type to be distinct types, NAG needed to define some standard types globally so as to ensure consistency across the Library. To ensure uniformity of this Library with other library developments, these standard types closely follow the joint standardisation activities of the SIGAda Numerics and Ada Europe Numerics Working Groups. This also applies to the design of the elementary functions and basic random number generator.

These application packages have substantial source code bodies and a prime aim is therefore to reuse these packages as widely as possible. Much effort has thus been spent in designing them to make maximum use of the Ada generic facilities. NAG also provides specific instantiations for the more common data types. NAG's success with their Fortran Library would have enabled them to translate into Ada in a relatively short period of time. However, it was believed, and this has since been confirmed many times over, that this was not what our customers and Ada users expected.

Additional information is available from:

NAG Ltd
Wilkinson House
Jordan Hill Road
Oxford
OX2 8DR
UK
Tel. +44 865 511245
Fax. +44 865 310139

# 11.3   GRACE components

GRACE stands for Generic Reusable Ada Components for Engineering. GRACE is a library of production-ready reusable Ada software components, provided in source code form. These components implement fundamental data structures as abstract data types for use in the construction of any applications developed in the Ada programming language. Use of the GRACE library decreases development time and redundancy in the development effort while increasing the reliability, efficiency, and understandability of the application.

Grace is the result of many engineering man-years of effort. It is a library of twenty-three data structures for use in Ada software engineering, where each of the data structures is supplied in several different variations (or forms) to suit a wide variety of usage contexts. The variety of available forms permits the software engineer to choose the appropriate data structure for any design solution. For example, a list which must recycle the storage for deleted nodes to support extended execution would not be the same list selected for use in an application which executes briefly, but quickly. In one case the management overhead for reclaiming deleted nodes becomes an impediment, where it is a necessity in the other.

In the GRACE library, data structures are implemented as Ada packages which contain the data types to be structured and all of its operations. These packages are, in fact, generic Ada packages. The use of Ada generics allows a GRACE list to be a list of any data type. Then, using instantiation, software engineers can make the generic list into a list of items of a specified data type.

GRACE provides the following data structures:

- B-tree
- Binary search tree
- Binary tree
- Circular doubly-linked list
- Deque
- Directed graph
- Discrete set
- Doubly-linked list
- Hash table
- Heap
- List
- Map
- Matrix
- Multiset
- Priority queue
- Queue
- Ring structure
- Set
- Singly-linked list
- Stack
- String
- Undirected graph
- Weighted directed graph

## Features of the GRACE library

**Documentation:** There are 275 GRACE components implementing 23 families of abstractions, each in several different forms. For each component there are:

> *12 to 15 pages of requirement and object design* to support the engineer in understanding the purpose and usage of each component.

> *Rigorously commented Ada source code,* both specification and body. All component source code is portable, standard Ada in accordance with ANSI/MIL-STD-1815A-1983, with no Chapter 13 or Appendix F dependencies.

> *Portable Ada source code is provided for at least one test driver* for each component.

> *A bibliography specific to that component.*

**Component uniformity:** Each component exists in a uniform system of components, with properties such as standard interfaces, naming conventions, and error handling. The same engineering decisions have been applied consistently throughout GRACE.

**No royalties:** When GRACE components are used in the construction of a larger application of predominantly the licensee's creation, there is no royalty assessed on the sale or distribution of the application.

**Technical support:** Technical support includes: telephone support, revisions of existing components for a nominal fee, and reduced license fees for new components.

**The EVB warranty:** Each component is warranted to be error-free, or EVB will fix the error at no cost to the user, so long as the component is in the original form provided by EVB.

**Additional reuse services:** EVB will provide on an optional basis:

1.) an experienced consultant to advise with the installation of the GRACE library on a licensee's unique hardware and software configuration,

2.) a detailed technical briefing on library structure and components usage to a licensee's technical manager and engineers, and

3.) a course and software reuse with Ada.

**GRACE license options:** GRACE is offered in a variety of source code licenses including a CPU based license, a network license, and a limited site license. Support for the initial year of the license is included in the license fee.

GRACE has been field-proven since 1985. Governmental agencies and companies of all sizes – in application areas as diverse as defense, real-time embedded systems, scientific software and MIS software – are current GRACE users. This list includes: Boeing, CSF Thompson, GE, IBM, McDonnell Martin Marietta, NASA, NTT, Phillips, TRW, Siemens, the U.S. Air Force, and the U.S. Army.

Additional information available upon request by contacting:

Alison Wildblood
Director of Marketing
EVB Software Engineering Inc
5303 Spectrum Drive
Frederick, MD 32707
USA
Tel. +1 301 695-6965
Fax. +1 301 695-7734

# 12

# Benchmarks

Chris Nettleton
SD-Scicon UK Ltd

## 12.1   Introduction

Benchmark tests have long been used to measure the performance and capacity of computer equipment and more recently to measure the performance of compilers for high level programming languages. Benchmark results are widely used to compare the performance of competitive products.

Broadly speaking, there are three kinds of benchmarks tests which are known as "model", "synthetic" and "specific". Ada compiler evaluation tests such as the ACEC suite, and the AES suite are outside the scope of this section.

A model benchmark accurately implements some aspect of a proposed application program, and gives accurate and reliable results for that application. The benchmark is highly representative for its application, but of little value elsewhere.

A synthetic benchmark has roughly the same objective as a model benchmark but includes a statement mix that has been derived empirically from a representative sample of application programs. The results of synthetic benchmarks are widely quoted by Ada compiler vendors as a measure of product performance.

Specific benchmarks focus on individual language features and answer questions such as "how long does it take to perform a rendezvous?". The results of specific benchmarks can be used to compare products, but as with all benchmarks, the results should always be interpreted bearing in mind the limitations of the techniques used. It is easy to draw the wrong conclusion and of course the only truly representative benchmark test is the application software itself. However benchmark tests do provide valuable results and can be used to predict application software performance and to evaluate competitive products.

## 12.2   Model benchmarks

Since model benchmarks are representative of application programs they provide the most accurate and relevant results. But because they are only relevant for a given application program, their use is very restricted. However some have found their way into general suites of tests such as the PIWG tests, discussed later.

For an Ada user interested in evaluating the run-time performance of competing Ada compilers, the cost of writing a model benchmark and getting the results is generally thought to be a good investment. The majority of compiler vendors will be able to provide any assistance needed.

## 12.3   Synthetic benchmarks

The Whetstone benchmark published in 1975 by Curnow and Wichmann [1] is widely regarded as the first significant composite test that could be used to directly compare the performance of different computers. This test, originally written in Algol 60, expresses performance as a number of Whetstone instructions per second.

The Whetstone rating for a computer or high level language compiler is representative for scientific work, the principal application area of Algol 60. However, in 1984 a new synthetic benchmark test was published. This new test is written in the spirit of the Whetstone benchmark but representative for systems programming. Its name is Dhrystone [2].

Both Whetstone and Dhrystone are available in Ada and are commonly used to benchmark Ada compilers. The official version of Whetstone is held at the National Physical Laboratory in the UK.

Further work on synthetic benchmarks for hard real-time applications (that is real-time applications where a missed deadline is a failure) is being pursued at the Software Engineering Institute of Carnegie Mellon University where they have developed the Hartstone benchmark [3]. This measures the efficiency of task scheduling using Whetstone as a synthetic workload.

Hartstone is the first benchmark to consider the ability of a test program to meet specific deadlines. By increasing the workload until deadlines are missed, Hartstone measures the percentage of useful work the test can do.

## 12.4    Specific benchmarks

August 1986 saw the publication of a paper entitled "Towards Real-Time Performance Benchmarks for Ada" [4] which describes the methods being developed at the University of Michigan to measure the real-time performance of Ada programs. The benchmarks tests that resulted from this work are known as the "Michigan Tests" and are known to be founded on a sound theoretical base.

The Michigan team set out to create a suite of benchmark tests to measure the real-time performance of Ada. These tests are normally made available as part of the PIWG suite, but can be obtained from the University of Michigan.

The main areas covered by the Michigan tests are:

- timing and scheduling;
- memory capacity;
- subprogram overhead;
- dynamic storage allocation;
- exception handling;
- tasking;
- time arithmetic.

The Michigan team's theoretical work considered the difficult problems of isolating a specific programming language feature, and measuring the execution time. For this they devised the "dual loop" method where one loop is used to measure the overhead of another that encloses the test.

The Michigan team found that optimising compilers invalidated simple benchmarks, and investigated how to fool the optimiser into generating the required code.

# 12.5   PIWG

The principal source of benchmark tests for Ada compilers is PIWG. This is the Performance Issues Working Group of SIGAda which is a special interest group with the US Association for Computing Machinery.

PIWG was formed in November 1984 to provide the Ada community with performance information, and is responsible for collecting benchmark tests, distributing the tests to Ada vendors and Ada users, and for publishing the results.

The test suite was created in 1985 and following its distribution in 1986 it has been revised annually. The latest results are published in the Winter 1990 issue of Ada Letters, Volume 10, Number 3. This is the journal of SIGAda and this special issue also contains background information on the test suite and the work being done on the next revision.

The PIWG test suite includes most of the Ada tests available elsewhere, including many of the Michigan tests, a number of composite tests such as Whetstone and Dhrystone and a number of fragments of application programs. The suite also includes many compile-only tests for measuring the capacity of an Ada compiler.

The specific tests in the PIWG suite are similar to the Michigan tests but use an automatic method for terminating iterations, rather than the Michigan team's static method.

# 12.6   Rolling your own

Anyone wishing to write his own benchmark test should be aware of the main pitfalls.

Synthetic benchmarks (like Whetstone) are easier to write than specific benchmarks since it can be extremely difficult to isolate just one language feature, and even more difficult to interpret the results. Reference [4] contains a description of the dual loop method used in the Michigan tests and offers much valuable advice.

A good optimising compiler can make nonsense of specific benchmark results, and the tricks you need to employ to defeat the optimiser distort the Ada to the extent that the results may be meaningless. Compiler writers regularly dine out on tales of benchmark tests that have been optimised away.

Further problems are due to instruction alignment and pipelining. Some processors, the Motorola MC68020 for example, have an instruction cache. Small differences in the generated code can become significant differences in execution time, and invalidate the dual loop method.

# 12.7 Contacts

The chairman of PIWG is Daniel M. Roy who can be contacted at the following address.

> Software Engineering Institute
> Carnegie Mellon University
> Pittsburgh, PA 15213
> USA

For the Michigan benchmarks, queries should be sent to the following address marked for the attention of Russell M. Clapp.

> Advanced Computer Architecture Laboratory
> Department of Electrical Engineering and Computer Science
> The University of Michigan
> Ann Arbor
> MI 48109-2122
> USA

In the UK, copies of the PIWG distribution tape may be obtained from:

> Martin Davies
> BSI Quality Assurance
> PO Box 375
> Linford Wood
> Milton Keynes
> Bucks MK14 6LE
> UK

To get Hartstone, contact:

> REST Transition Services
> Software Engineering Institute
> Carnegie Mellon University
> Pittsburgh, PA 15213
> USA

The ACM can be contacted at:

Association for Computing Machinery, Inc
11 West 42nd Street
New York
NY 10036
USA

# References

1. Curnow, H.J. and Wichmann, B.A., "A Synthetic Benchmark", *The Computer Journal*, Vol. 19, No. 1, pp. 43 – 49, 1975.

2. Weicker, R.P., "Dhrystone: A Synthetic Systems Programming Benchmark", *Communications of the ACM*, 27 (10), pp. 1013 – 1030, October 1984.

3. Weiderman, N., "Hartstone: Synthetic Benchmark Requirements for Hard Real-Time Applications", *Ada Letters*, Vol. X, No. 3, pp. 126 – 136, Winter 1990.

4. Clapp, R.M., Duchesneau, L., Volz, R.A., Mudge, T.N. and Schultze, T., "Towards Real-Time Performance Benchmarks for Ada", *Communications of the ACM*, 29 (8), pp. 760 – 778, August 1986.

# 13

# Ada projects

This chapter provides an insight into a cross-section of Ada projects being undertaken in Europe.

## 13.1   Ada support in ESPRIT

David Callahan
Commission of the European Communities

**937 DESCARTES** Debugging and Specification of Ada Real-Time Embedded Systems.

> Contact: Mr O Maurel/C Bonnet
> GSI-Tecsi
> 6 Cours Michelet
> F-92064 Paris La Defense
> tel. +33 1 47 78 87 00

Results include the translation of Me-Too and Statelan specifications into Ada and a system for tracing and analysing execution histories of Ada programs.

**1500 DRAGON** Distribution and Reusability of Ada Real-Time Applications through Graceful and On-Line Operations.

> Contact: Mr Andrea di Maio
> TXT
> Via Socrate 41
> 20128 Milano
> tel. +39 2 260 00 160

The project developed an object-oriented approach to reuse. Included among the results is a software components library. The approach used involved extensions of existing Ada formalisms.

**32 PCTE** Portable Common Tool Environment.

Ada and C specifications of the PCTE interface are available. An Ada version of the PCTE OMS and tool interfaces is provided to ensure that PCTE can form the basis for an efficient APSE.

Contact: Mr R. Minot
Direction Recherche and Technologie
Bull SA
Route de Versailles 68
F-78430 Louveciennes
tel. +33 1 3902 5000

**390 PROSPECTRA** Program Development by Specification and Transformation.

**835 PROSPECTRA DEMO** The PROSPECTRA project used Ada/ANNA as a basis and developed its own wide spectrum version (PAfnndA-s). This has been experimented in PROSPECTRA DEMO which also produced a design support system.

Contact: Prof Krieg-Brueckner
Dept FB 3 Mathematik-Informatik
University of Bremen
Postfach 330330
D-2800 Bremen 33
tel. +49 421 218 2676

## Other contracts

**PCTE User Interface Ada Specification** This completes the Ada specification of PCTE by providing Ada interfaces for PCTE volume 2, the PCTE User Interface.

The specification is presently a draft, but comments received are quite minor.

Contact: Mr Thwaites
SD-Scicon
Pembroke House
Pembroke Broadway
Camberley
Surrey GU15 3XD
tel. +44 276 686200

# 13.2 The industrial installations supervision system at Madrid Airport

Jesus Aragoneses
Teice Control

During the last year the Spanish company Teice Control S.A. has developed a control and supervising system for the industrial installations of the Iberia Spanish Airline company in the industrial area of the Madrid Airport. The central surveillance software was entirely programmed in Ada. This system is currently installed and running, and its main objective is the control and supervising of heating, air-conditioning, power supply, fire-detection, and of other installations of 40 buildings in the industrial area of the Madrid Airport.

The system's main features are:

- a non-stop system running 24 hours per day, 365 days per year;
- strong time requirements for warning the operator of any alarm;
- friendly user interface (graphics, menus, semi-natural command language, etc.);
- communication among the different processor levels using a ring LAN;
- a big variety of data types are used, with complex relations among them;
- the system configuration can be modified by the user, when the installations change;
- user can write control automatisms using a Pascal-like language to optimize the installations use;
- user groups rights levels: not everybody can do everything.

Due to the computer naïvety of the users, the system offers a very easy user interface, based on graphic schemes, mouse, menus and a semi-natural command language with possibility of abbreviations. The user can draw and modify graphic schemes representing their installations, using a graphical editor also developed in Ada.

The system is structured in three functional levels:

- data acquisition panels;
- building control centres;
- surveillance centre.

The two lower levels are based on boards designed by Teice Control. The software running on them has been developed in PLM and concurrent Pascal. The highest level is supported by a Digital MicroVax 3300 with ULTRIX V3.1b, and was entirely developed in Ada using the Verdix 5.41 environment.

The design has been done hierarchically using abstract data type concepts. The final number of packages is 170. Of those, 120 are abstract data types and 50 are functional abstractions.

Due to implementation reasons, Ada tasking was not suitable: every task is a Unix process, so the IPC Unix mechanisms (shared memory, mailboxes, semaphores) were intensively used. In this sense, we did not find any problem interfacing with "C" language functions in order to perform system calls. The command interpreter was implemented using the "yacc" Unix tool.

The code was written "bottom-up", and every module was passed through its own module test. The total number of Ada statements is over 40,000. To simplify and facilitate the test coding and execution, we built an Ada programmed tool. The total number of test statements is over 15,000.

The manpower needed to accomplish this project (from the requirements specifications phase, until the beginning of the maintenance phase) was 6 man-years.

We can congratulate ourselves over this first experience of Ada. The language and the developed test tool gave us a high level of reliability during the development, making the team work and the integration phase very easy. On the other hand, the most negative aspect was the amount of mass storage and processor resources needed during the development phase.

# 13.3    Ada feedback in a large industrial project

Jean-Marc Poulet
Sema Group - Energy Division


## Introduction

Electricite de France's (EDF's) 1400 MW nuclear power plants are provided with a completely computerized control room.

SEMA Group, a European software company, is currently developing the needed system in a project called KIC-N4. This project started in September 1985 and the issued hardware and software will be delivered in different steps: the first one at the end of 1990 and the last one in July 1992.

This paper first gives some technical characteristics and key figures of the project, then gives the major reasons of the Ada choice and finally is focused on the feedback of 4 years of Ada use.


## Major technical characteristics and key figures of the KIC-N4 project

The KIC-N4 control system is based on a distributed hardware architecture, with several heterogeneous computers, all of them communicating with the others by means of local area industrial networks (this was needed to allow easy extensions to the system in the future) :

- level 1 deals with protection actions and regulations
- level 2 deals with processing the information of a high level of synthesis and ensures the interface with the control room operators
- level 3 deals with maintenance, servicing and technical management functions.

The three machines for which the choice of Ada has been made are part of level 2, these machines are called MC (for Main Computer), RC (for Recording Computer) and OWS (for Operator WorkStation).

The system capacity allows the control of approximately 10,000 devices (pumps, valves, analog sensors, motors, etc.), thanks to :

- 8,400 on/off commands
- 300 regulation commands
- 65,000 on/off data
- 2,500 analog data,

and also :

- 300 graphic control images
- 100 graphic regulation images
- 200 graphic monitoring images
- 10,000 data sheets
- 3,300 alarm sheets
- 3,000 pages of operating procedures.

The main response times of the KIC are as follows :

on/off command      : 500 ms in 90% of cases, 1 s as maximum time
regulation command : 300 ms in 90% of cases, 1 s as maximum time
display of any image : 1.5 s in 90% of cases, 2 s as maximum time
graphic CRT update : always less than 800 ms.

The overall software development effort of the KIC-N4 system is 1,800 person-months and up to 60 engineers worked on this project.

The target code for the first delivered version corresponds to :

- 80,000 Ada source lines for the RC machine
- 180,000 Ada source lines for the MC machine
- 200,000 Ada source lines for the OWS machine

    (these figures neither include blank lines, nor pure comment lines),

and about 300,000 Ada source lines have been produced for the different testing phases : test drivers, specific tools.


Ada choice

This paragraph is written in the past tense because it expresses what was expected from Ada when the choice was made.

Life duration of the application (30 to 40 years) involved a high degree of software portability and maintainability. Ada, because it was an international standard (ISO standard) before the first compiler appeared, gave an answer to portability problem, and because it took into account the fact that a program is written once and read 100 times, Ada gave also an answer to maintainability.

Among a lot of new features provided by Ada, the enforced typing of data types and the exception handling seemed to be good foundations for building a safe system.

The separate compilation feature provided very powerful help for a modular design from which would follow a good human resources organization.

Finally, another non purely technical reason has to be mentioned : Ada was very attractive and will generate a strong motivation on people having to produce a very long (several years) development effort.

## Ada feedback

- after about 40 hours of work on a good computer aided training system, plus one month dedicated to practice based on exercises, engineers were able to begin writing good Ada programs (complex features such as tasking or low level I/O can be, in a big project, reserved to a small and especially trained subteam)

- Ada compilers are powerful :

  - correcting compilation errors is very easy because of the level of detail of the error messages

  - some errors that one used to uncover at execution time with less powerful languages are detected in Ada at compilation time

- no PDL (Programming Design Language) is needed : Ada avoids redundancy between PDL and programming language (and distortion which can raised from going from one to the other)

- writing Ada was said to be painful (Ada is verbose) but simple tools such as editor macros, or more important tools such as syntactic editors, make writing Ada quite fast

- the breakdown of effort between the different development phases is changed, going from :

|  |  |
|---|---|
| design | about 40% |
| coding and unit testing | about 30% |
| integration | about 40% |

to :

|  |  |
|---|---|
| design | about 55% |
| coding and unit testing | about 15% |
| integration | about 30% |

- automatic generation has been used for test drivers and 'stubs' of missing (not yet ready to be integrated) units, this automatic generation is based on the specifications of the related packages; the effort saved by this automatic generation is devoted to test cases improvement (content and numbers) and hence test coverage ratio is improved

- unit testing process (in most cases) is just going from one exception to another and so, errors can be quickly identified and in cases where the source of error is not obvious and requires a diagnostic phase, the investigations are made on a 'clean' context (no degradation of the error context due to error propagation)

- a precise accounting of errors tackled during the integration phase (sub-system integration and system integration) reveals that the number of residual errors at the end of the unit testing phase, is quite small : between 0.8 and 1.3 errors for 1,000 lines of code; this does not mean that integration tests are no longer needed but means that Ada contributes to software reliability improvement

- reusable parts of software have been easily and quickly ported from N4's target machines to different ones, for instance a 3 person-month effort was needed for porting of 60,000 lines of Ada code : Ada improves portability

- Ada real-time features such as tasking, rendezvous or interrupt management have been intensively used and the conclusion is that they can fit requirements of an application such as KIC-N4,

but :

- the compiler validation process just provides the guarantee that the compiler complies with the Ada LRM (Language Reference Manual), no performance constraints are defined by the norm so a validated compiler may be poor in compilation speed or may be associated with a bugged run-time

- Ada is greedy for MIPS and disk space Megabytes, good ratios are about 0.5 MIPS and 50 Megabytes by person for each developer of a big development team (more than 30 persons)

- using Ada does not need only a compiler, it needs a set of tools (called an APSE for Ada Programming Support Environment), each of those tools being as important as the compiler itself (library manager, symbolic debugger, 'ada_make', etc.)

## Conclusion

Ada has now come to maturity and can be involved in big industrial projects. Ada real-time features (tasking, interrupt management) fit the requirements of an application such as the one hereupon described.

Some precautions have to be taken when starting with Ada but choosing Ada will always mean going ahead in software engineering.

# 13.4   Ada projects at Siemens Plessey Defence Systems

Dr Mel Selwood
Siemens Plessey Defence Systems
Grange Road
Somerford
Christchurch
Dorset
BH23 4JE
UK
Tel. +44 202 404341
Fax. +44 202 404221

## Introduction

Siemens Plessey Defence Systems at Christchurch, Dorset has been involved in some ten major Ada projects (four have already been successfully completed), involving a variety of host (typically VAX/VMS, Sun/Unix workstation and IBM PC) and target (e.g., Intel embedded microprocessors) computers. A resume of a number of these projects is provided below. These have been supported by some 150 Ada software engineers, making the site one of the foremost centres of Ada project experience in the UK. This capability has been founded on extensive and ongoing software methods and tools and Ada technology issues, as well as close technical liaison with key Higher Education Establishments and a number of well-known tool vendors. The company is also involved in a number of project definition studies and bids associated with programmes to be implemented in Ada.

### AWHQ

AWHQ is a system which will provide mobile Command and Control for Supreme Headquarters Allied Command Europe and Allied Forces in Central Europe. The overall contract is valued at around £40m and involves collaboration between a number of companies from Europe and the United States. File and Communications Servers control access to about 100 workstations in vehicles.

Some commercial off the shelf software is used but all new software is written in Ada. A key activity is the integration of applications written in Ada with commercial relational database management systems.

## QID

The Quadrilateral Interoperability Demonstrator (QID) is an implementation of the ISO seven layer model which will provide for the automatic exchange of information between the Army field command systems of the United States, Germany, France and the United Kingdom.

The programme involves analysis of communications and information protocols and utilises a Real-Time Structured Analysis and Object-Oriented Design approach tailored for an Ada implementation. This ten man year programme involves liaison with similar programmes in the United States, France and Germany.

## VIXEN

Vixen is a £36.5m tactical eavesdropping system that will greatly enhance the British Army's ability to collect and analyse radio transmissions, in providing the effectiveness in battlefield intelligence gathering and in the deployment and use of electronic countermeasures. The project is the first of its kind to be using the NATO and MoD approved Ada programming language.

Ada is combined with a Real-Time Structured Analysis and Object-Oriented Design approach. In addition, the use of Sun / Unix host development workstations targeting to multiple embedded Intel microprocessors makes the porting of the Ada software to the target on this scale an interesting aspect of the programme.

Software tools to support the development include TeamWORK, ORACLE database, TeamWORK/Ada and INTERLEAF (a desktop publishing tool).

The method and language being used ensure that loose coupling and maximum cohesion of software is obtained. This allows each programmer to be responsible for designing, coding and testing portions of the total system, whilst being part of an overall team approach.

## GENERICS, CISAT and ASWEAP

GENERICS is a suite of Ada software that forms the core elements of a Command and Control Information System. It consists of a number of "products", each with a well-defined interface. These products are a relational database, an ISAM driver, a man–machine interface (MMI) and foundation software. The database is fully relational with mechanisms for enhancing the integrity and robustness of the data storage. It consists of a transaction manager, a relational algebra processor, and a remote node handler as well as packages for handling security and data event monitors. It is provided with a number of recovery procedures suitable for military environments. Uniquely, the GENERICS database is able to replicate data over a wide area network in a poor communications environment.

The ISAM driver provides the database with a set of indexing and accessing procedures for mapping the logical data structures in the database on to the physical file structures on the disk. The ISAM is also responsible for managing the cache. A well-defined interface to the ISAM driver allows it to be used directly in other applications.

The MMI is based on X-Windows. It provides a Windows, Icons, Menus and Pointer (WIMP) interface familiar to PC users between the user and the GENERICS database and applications. The MMI has many graphical features and can use maps to provide a background for the display of information.

The foundation software provides GENERICS with a layered functionality that eases porting of the system to a variety of hardware bases. The foundation has buffer management and message passing mechanisms and a central error handling function.

GENERICS was the first major Ada project at Siemens Plessey Defence Systems and has involved over 100 man years of effort. More than 90% of the code is written in Ada (a small amount of "C" code is used for interfacing purposes) and this has helped reduce the effort required for integration and for porting to other platforms. Currently GENERICS runs on SUN 3, VAX/VMS and bare Intel 80286 computers. It is planned to port it to HP equipment shortly.

CISAT and ASWEAP are GENERICS application projects. CISAT is a simulation and rapid prototyping tool which embraces real-time simulation capabilities, while ASWEAP is an application which supports analysis and debriefing of anti-submarine warfare exercises.

# 14

# Ada users

## 14.1 Profiles of Ada users

The profiles of a number of Ada users are given which indicate the application areas, the development and host/target environments and, in some instances, give an overview of the work carried out.

### AXL4

Address: ARE Portsdown
Portsmouth PO6 4AA
Hants.

Project title: The Implementation of a MASCOT 3 Design in Ada

Application area: Naval $C^3$ Systems

Number of lines of Ada (non-comment semicolons): 33,000

Target machine(s): 68030/VAX

Development host(s) (if different): VAX

Supplier of compiler: DEC/Ready Systems (Telegen)

Other key tools used: MDSE (Alvey) & MASCOT 3 Organiser

## BATS S.A.

Address: Avenue des Noisetiers
Parc Indusktriel de Recherches du Sart Tilman
B - 4900 ANGLEUR
Belgium

Project title: Radar Training Simulator

Application area: Military and Civilian operator training

Number of lines of Ada (non-comment semicolons): 80,000

Target machine(s): 386

Development host(s) (if different): VAX/VMS

Supplier of compiler: Telelogic Europe S.A.

Other key tools used: Case TeamWORK/Ada

Man-years for total development: 20

Contact name: Georges Jean-Claude, Program Manager

Telephone: +32 41 67 08 88

## Bofors Electronics AB

Address: S-175 88 Jarfalla
Sweden

Project title: Ship System 2000 or 9LV MK 3

Application area: Complete naval systems ($C^3$ + Weapon Control)

Number of lines of Ada (non-comment semicolons): approx. 1,000,000

Target machine(s): M68020

Development host(s) (if different): Rational, VAX

Supplier of compiler: Rational

Other key tools used: VAX based CMS, EXCO

Contact name: Bjorn Kaillberg    Berlil Carlsson
Senior Scientist  Information Dept.

Telephone:       +46 758 84813  +46 758 22147

## Brighton Polytechnic

Application area: Teaching

Target machine(s): VAX, IBM PC

Supplier of compiler: DEC for VAX

Contact name: Mike Smith

Telephone: +44 273 600900 Ext. 2268

Teaching of second year undergraduate degree program.


## British Aerospace (Military Aircraft) Ltd

Address: Saltgrounds Road
         Brough
         North Humberside

Project title: ETA

Application area: Military Airborne Applications

Number of lines of Ada (non-comment semicolons): 60K

Target machine(s): 68020

Development host(s) (if different): VAX

Supplier of compiler: SD-Scicon

Other key tools used: CORE/HOOD/LDRA/MDS

Contact name: D. S. Wynn

Telephone: +44 482 667121 Ext. 5596

## Cranfield Institute of Technology

**Address:** Department of Electronic System Design
Bedford MK43 0AL

**Project title:** Simulation of a Royal Navy Lynx Helicopter Tactical Data System

**Application area:** Real-time simulation

**Number of lines of Ada (non-comment semicolons):** 1500

**Target machine(s):** IBM PC

**Development host(s) (if different):** IBM PC/AT

**Supplier of compiler:** RR Software Inc. Janus Ada

**Man-years for total development:** 6 man months

**Contact name:** Dr. Stuart J. Handley

**Telephone:** +44 234 750111 Ext. 2444

### Simulation of a Royal Navy Lynx helicopter tactical data system

The project covered the development of a software simulation of the Lynx Helicopter Centralised Tactical System Tactical Situation Display. The requirement for this simulation arose from the need to train aircrew how to operate this new type of equipment. The Simulator was developed on an IBM PC/AT computer or compatible machine, and will make use of optional hardware such as a maths co-processor, joystick, and second terminal, if fitted.

Software engineering techniques were strictly adhered to throughout the project. Requirements analysis was carried out using the actual system's functional specification as a guideline. Functional Decomposition and Ada rendezvous diagrams were then used for the software's high level design. Low level design used Program Design Language techniques. A testing strategy was developed and employed.

The project achieved all its aims and objectives, and a successful simulation was produced. Ada software libraries were developed to meet the graphics and serial communications requirements of the project, and auxiliary software was produced to allow simulation parameters to be altered, in real time, from a second terminal. The project proved the feasibility of using low cost personal computers, and of using Ada, for simulations of this type.

# Ferranti International Plc, Naval Systems

**Address:** Submarine Control Group
North Crawley Road
Newport Pagnell MK16 9HT

**Project title:** Ferranti AP2000 Autopilot Ada Testbed

**Application area:** Submarine Autopilot

**Number of lines of Ada (non-comment semicolons):** approx. 3000

**Target machine(s):** 68020

**Development host(s) (if different):** VAX

**Supplier of compiler:** SD-Scicon

**Man-years for total development:** approx. 2/3

**Contact name:** D. J. Chetwynd

**Telephone:** +44 908 613746

**Ferranti AP2000 autopilot Ada testbed***

This was a feasibility exercise to demonstrate that a novel autopilot algorithm could be implemented in Ada and run in real time on a 68020-based target. The algorithm employs modern control theory and is heavy on matrix arithmetic and floating point calculation.

The testbed supplies both a simulation environment (i.e. submarine dynamics mathematical model) and a program environment (i.e. a harness). The testbed is run under the Ada Programming Systems debugger, which supplies input data and captures results in its log file.

The exercise showed that the implementation was feasible and provided valuable experience of using Ada. The testbed software will be reused as the vehicle for testing of future developments of the algorithm and for a real-time submarine dynamics simulator.

# Hunting Engineering Ltd

**Address:** Reddings Wood
            Ampthill
            Bedford MK45 2HD

**Project title:** Smart Weapon Anti-Armour (SWAARM)

**Application area:** Defence

**Number of lines of Ada (non-comment semicolons):** 20K

**Target machine(s):** Motorola MC68020/Mips R3000

**Development host(s) (if different):** DEC VAX

**Supplier of compiler:** Verdix(target) DEC(host)

**Other key tools used:** Cadre TeamWORK, LDRA Testbed, Yard Lifespan, VAXset

**Contact name:** Ian Simpson

**Telephone:** +44 525 841000

## SWAARM

The Smart Weapon Anti-Armour (SWAARM) is an air-launched, stand-off weapon which dispenses a number of intelligent submunitions against armoured targets on the ground.

For guidance and control the SWAARM project made use of an in-house developed On-board Processor system. The On-board Processor is a general purpose, Ada programmable, controller based around high speed, 32 bit, military specification, processors communicating over a VME bus to application specific interface cards. SWAARM used a two processor configuration of the On-board Processor to achieve the very high control bandwidth required to maintain vehicle stability during flight and submunition deployment, with the software source code written in the Ada language.

The application software for SWAARM was designed, coded and tested within a highly integrated computer aided software engineering (CASE) environment hosted on a cluster of DEC VAX workstations. The design for the software was based on the results of research into the application of Ada to high speed, time-critical, applications carried out at Hunting Engineering over a number of years. Testing was conducted within a closed loop, fully representative, simulation of the dispenser aerodynamics, again written in Ada.

The success of Ada on this and other projects has resulted in Hunting Engineering's commitment to the use of Ada for future software projects.

# Link-Mills Ltd

Address: Churchill Industrial Estate
Lancing
W. Sussex.

Project title: Ada Transition

Application area: Training Simulation

Target machine(s): Intel 386

Development host(s) (if different): SUN 3

Supplier of compiler: Telesoft

Other key tools used: CASE

Contact name: Carol Fishbourne (Ms.)

Telephone: +44 903 755881 Ext. 2282

## The Link-Miles Ada Transition programme

The Link-Miles Ada Transition programme has successfully established a centre of excellence in the areas of Object Oriented Design (OOD) and Ada development skills. Papers describing the project results have been given at ITEC and Ada UK over the past two years.

A flight simulator major function, digital control loading, has been designed and implemented, using OOD and Ada, as proof of concept. The results conclusively demonstrated that this approach has no performance disadvantages for real-time embedded software.

Current R & D work is focused on a more in-depth evaluation of different flavours of OOD. Using Real-Time Structured Analysis (RTSA) combined with various OOD paradigms, a complete simulator subsystem is being built in Ada. The results will be used to establish the most effective OOD approach for real-time simulation.

Work is continuing to develop run environments, and associated real-time executive and debug facilities, suitable for distributed multi-processor systems.

Future work will include defining and establishing an appropriate Ada programming support environment (APSE) and developing the potential of Object Oriented Analysis (OOA) as an alternative to RTSA.

The skill of the programme team is used to support the development of Ada expertise throughout the company.

## The Numerical Algorithms Group Limited

**Address:** Wilkinson House
Jordan Hill Road
Oxford OX2 8DR

**Project title:** NAG Ada Library

**Application area:** Solution of Numerical Problems

**Number of lines of Ada (non-comment semicolons):** about 500,000

**Target machine(s):** VAX, MICROVAX, Sun Workstation

**Development host(s) (if different):** MICROVAX

**Supplier of compiler:** DEC, Alsys, Verdix, Telesoft, DDC

**Man-years for total development:** 20

**Contact name:** Dr. Zohair A. Maany and Dr. Graham S. Hodgson

**Telephone:** +44 865 511245

**The NAG Ada Library**

The NAG Ada Library is a comprehensive collection of "algorithms" for the solution of numerical problems. To encourage expandability and reusability the NAG Ada Library makes extensive use of generic templates. Most of the library units are generic with respect to some number of generic parameters in order to provide greater generality of use as envisaged in the Ada language. In particular, library units are often generic with respect to a type so that computations can be carried out with different arithmetics. However, to avoid the need for users to instantiate library templates with common floating-point types (or complex types or integer types), the library provides a number of standard instances of these templates. The NAG Ada Library is being implemented on different computer systems. It is divided into "chapters", each devoted to a branch of numerical analysis or statistics. Mark 2 of the NAG Ada Library contains twelve chapters. These chapters are:

**A01** Basic Arithmetic

**A02** Input/Output

**A03** Array Sections (two-dimensional arrays slicing and trimming)

**A04** Extended Arithmetic

**D01** Quadrature

**D02** Ordinary Differential Equations

**D03** Partial Differential Equations

**E02** Curve and Surface Fitting

**F04** Simultaneous Linear Equations

**G05** Random Numbers

**P01** Error Trapping

**S01** Elementary Functions

## N.A. Software Ltd

**Address:** The Merseyside Innovation Centre
131 Mount Pleasant
Liverpool L3 5TF

**Project title:** Numerical Libraries

**Application area:** Numerical Analysis

**Target machine(s):** Various

**Supplier of compiler:** Various

**Man-years for total development:** 6 (to date)

**Contact name:** Stuart Gascoyne

**Telephone:** +44 51 708 0123

### The Numeric Libraries project

We decided in 1987 to develop a range of Ada numeric libraries for the following two reasons:

1. The increasing recognition of the benefits of Ada coupled with the mandatory use of Ada by most Western defence ministries would assure a strong future for the language.

2. In recognition that one of the stated aims of Ada is to facilitate a software components industry.

We are currently developing five libraries, each of which will have an increased number of functions with each release.

A scalable computer systems library which is a general purpose numerical library designed to run on hardware ranging from an IBM PC to a CRAY.

The statistics library is similarly scalable.

We have developed a fixed-point library essentially aimed at real-time and avionics users.

The signal processing library reflects the increasing use of Ada for SP applications.

The fifth library is a variable precision floating-point library which was developed out of a research project at Liverpool University.

Our experience of Ada is that the maintenance and porting of programs has been easier than with FORTRAN. We have not gained as much productivity benefit from using Ada because of the immaturity of the compilers. This, however, is beginning to change.

We believe that the use of a modern block structured language such as Ada helps users produce clear maintainable code. In particular the support for abstraction provided by such features as packages and generics aid design. Finally from a numerics point of view the attribute functions are extremely useful.

The production of these libraries obviously represents a strong commitment by N.A. Software to the Ada language and demonstrates our confidence in its future.

# PAFEC Ltd

**Address:** 39 Nottingham Road
Stapleford
Nottingham NG9 8AD

**Project title:** HORSES

**Application area:** Software tools for developing engineering/scientific applications and some end-user engineering applications

**Number of lines of Ada (non-comment semicolons):** 200,000

**Target machine(s):** Apollo, VAX, SUNsparc

**Development host(s) (if different):**

**Supplier of compiler:** Telesoft, Verdix, Alsys, DEC

**Other key tools used:** ORACLE RDBMS

**Man-years for total development:** 75

**Contact name:** Mark Toole

**Telephone:** +44 602 357060

## Ada at PAFEC

PAFEC, Europe's largest independent engineering software house, develops markets and supports a wide range of integrated software products principally for technical computing applications. With its origins in research that started in the mid 1960s, PAFEC has grown from its foundation in 1976 into an international company with distributors in over 30 countries worldwide. It now employs around 300 staff, mainly in its two offices in Nottingham, England.

Since 1986 PAFEC has been using Ada as its principal programming language. HORSES is PAFEC's software developers' toolkit, consisting of software tools and reusable utility modules to reduce life cycle costs for engineering and scientific applications. Principal tools within the toolkit include user interface management systems, and integrated graphics and database utilities.

As well as being commercially available to other software developers, PAFEC also has used HORSES to develop engineering applications. By late 1990 3D modelling, finite element analysis pre-processor and GIS viewer applications were nearing first release.

Using the combination of HORSES tools and Ada, development times have been reduced by a factor of five, and preliminary results show a decrease in maintenance costs of around 75 percent.

## Racal Communications Systems Ltd

**Address:** Western Road
Bracknell
Berks. RG12 1RG

**Application area:** Military command and control

**Number of lines of Ada (non-comment semicolons):** 62,000

**Target machine(s):** 386 PC

**Supplier of compiler:** Alsys

**Man-years for total development:** 19

**Contact name:** John Hole

**Telephone:** +44 344 4832446

### Racal Communications Systems

The system controls specialist radio equipment manufactured by the company and provides information to operators fulfilling various command and control functions. The system is installed in military vehicles and operates as a distributed network with data communications over narrow band combat net radio and wide band local area networks.

The software architecture is interesting in that it consists of a single Ada program which elaborates differently in each processor node to provide the set of operational facilities required for that node. Flexibility is a key property of the design — different configurations of controlled equipment, applications functions and network elements all have to be supported from a set of reusable software components.

The use of Ada was not a mandatory requirement for this project. It was chosen for commercial reasons because, being based on sound software engineering principles, it was felt likely to result in improved development productivity and better code quality.

Although this was the first Ada project undertaken by the company and had to bear the introductory costs of acquiring new tools and skills, the investment has been well justified. Significant gains in productivity and reliability have already been achieved and further improvements are expected as our Ada expertise and our library of reusable Ada components continue to grow.

# University of Southampton

Address: Dept. of Electronics and Computer Science
Southampton SO9 5NH

Project title: Distributed systems

Application area: Ada language and runtime systems

Number of lines of Ada (non-comment semicolons): 2000 (for experimental programs)

Target machine(s): transputers

Supplier of compiler: Alsys

Other key tools used: Occam, TDS, itoolset

Man-years for total development: 5

Contact name: Dr. J. M. Bishop

The Stadium project

The Stadium project investigated the implementation of Ada on distributed computers. A categorisation of implementations was devised and a phased approach to distribution proposed. As part of the study several parallel programs were implemented in Ada and run on multiple transputers on the Supernode developed at Southampton. Work is progressing to link Ada into the PUMA software for through routing on transputers in anticipation of the new H1.

# Systematic Software Engineering A/S

**Project title:** IRIS

**Application area:** Military Communication

**Number of lines of Ada (non-comment semicolons):** 220,000

**Target machine(s):** 80x86

**Development host(s) (if different):** PC's

**Supplier of compiler:** Alsys

**Other key tools used:** Cadre's CASE tool TeamWORK

**Man-years for total development:** 16

**Contact name:** Michael Holm

**Telephone:** +45 86 15 18 66

## IRIS

IRIS is an unique military message formatting tool for entry, editing, formatting and distribution systems, with possibilities for user definition of message structures and composition. IRIS provides preparation of error-free ADatP-3 messages and supports the ACP 127 message structure.

IRIS can be acquired as executable ready-to-run programs or as Ada application libraries for integration within own systems.

**Project title:** GRACE

**Application area:** Radar Control

**Number of lines of Ada (non-comment semicolons):** 80,000

**Target machine(s):** 80x86

**Development host(s) (if different):** 80286 PC

**Supplier of compiler:** Alsys

**Other key tools used:** Cadre's CASE tool TeamWORK

**Man-years for total development:** 2

**Contact name:** Michael Holm

**Telephone:** +45 86 15 18 66

## GRACE

A full-graphic finger-touch based, combined radar monitor/controller and clutter-map display, running on PC-DOS mode. By means of multitasking, GRACE can communicate with 12 radars simultaneously on either synchronous (HDLC, X.25) or asynchronous data lines. All radar management orders are executed by finger-touch on graphic push-pull buttons, pop-up calculators and multiple-choice selections. Cluttermaps data can be combined with land-map and coast-line maps.

**Project title:** Alsys Ada MetaGraphic interface

**Application area:** All

**Target machine(s):** 80x86

**Development host(s) (if different):** PC 80286

**Supplier of compiler:** Alsys

**Man-years for total development:** 0.5

**Contact name:** Michael Holm

**Telephone:** +45 86 15 18 66

## MetaWINDOW

Systematic's MetaWINDOW/Alsys Ada interface provides the full functionality of MetaWINDOW from MetaGraphics Software Corporation.

MetaWindow/Alsys Ada provides PC programmes and application developers with a powerful set of graphic drawing functions, plus an expanded set of advanced utilities for developing multi-window desktop applications.

# The University College of Wales

Address: Department of Computer Science
         Penglais
         Aberystwyth
         SY23 3BZ

Application area: Teaching and research

Target machine(s): Sun 3

Supplier of compiler: Alsys, Verdix

Contact name: Frank Bott

Telephone: +44 970 622424


## Ada at Aberystwyth

Several members of the academic staff at UCW were involved in early Ada developments so it is not surprising that, as soon as the first version of the York Ada compiler became available, a final year course was mounted to introduce students to the language. At that time (1982), the main programming language used for teaching purposes was Pascal.

The undergraduate course at UCW was, and is, firmly oriented towards software engineering and there was growing dissatisfaction with Pascal. Early in 1986, we decided that Pascal had to be replaced and, after careful consideration, we decided to change to Ada.

Our experience with Ada as the main teaching language has been good. Most importantly, student reaction has, on the whole, proved very positive and we are convinced that the quality of our courses has improved significantly as a result of the switch to Ada.

The one serious difficulty we experience is that interfaces between Ada and other system software (such as SunView, X-Windows, or the basic operating system calls) either do not exist or are mysterious, undocumented and ridden with bugs. The result is, too often, that students who have spent two years of their course learning to write good programs in Ada have to resort to C for large parts of their final year projects.

In our research, we have been involved with IPSEs and Tool Support Interfaces. We have evaluated both CAIS and PCTE and this work led to a prototype implementation of CAIS (in Ada) and a prototype implementation of the Ada Interfaces to PCTE.

# YARD Ltd

**Address:** Charing Cross Tower
Glasgow G2 4PP

**Project title:** Implementation of a MASCOT 3 Design in Ada

**Application area:** Command & Control Systems

**Number of lines of Ada (non-comment semicolons):** 32,000

**Target machine(s):** MUME 147

**Development host(s) (if different):** VAX station II

**Supplier of compiler:** Host: DEC, Target: Ready Systems (Telesoft Compiler)

**Other key tools used:** MDSE (MASCOT Design Support Environment), Ready Systems RTTAda, GKS

**Man-years for total development:** 3

**Contact name:** Alastair O'Brien

**Telephone:** +44 41 204 2737 Ext. 2365

## Implementation of a MASCOT 3 Design in Ada

The aims of the project are to demonstrate the feasibility of designing and constructing real-time Ada systems using MASCOT 3, and to establish a benchmark against which various target compiler/hardware combinations can be measured.

The system is a simulation of the Close-In-Weapons (CIW) facility of a hypothetical command and control system. Targets detected by the CIW are attacked unless the operator intervenes to veto the attack.

The software comprises two main programs, a sensor systems simulation program which runs on the Host and communicates through Ethernet with a display driver program which may run either on the Host or the Target. These allow evaluation and performance measurements on the system distributed over 2 programs. In addition, a minimal Data Fusion program was produced which runs on the Host and sends additional messages to the display driver program, to allow the evaluation of a more complex system divided among 3 programs.

Ada proved generally satisfactory as an implementation language with extensive use being made of generics in the mapping from MASCOT 3 components.

There were no problems in writing portable Ada code. In particular, the use of numeric subtypes overcame the differences in the underlying representation of numeric values between the Host and the Target.

## University of York

**Address:** Department of Computer Science

**Project title:** Real-time use of Ada

**Application area:** Research into the suitability of Ada for real-time use

**Number of lines of Ada (non-comment semicolons):**
None — coding in C!

**Target machine(s):** M68000

**Development host(s) (if different):** SUN, HLM Orion

**Supplier of compiler:** own

**Man-years for total development:** 6 man years

**Contact name:** I. C. Wand

**Telephone:** +44 904 432725

# 14.2    The 1990 survey of Ada users

Compiled by John Hole
Racal Communications Ltd

The information used to compile this report was kindly supplied by members
of Ada UK. The survey was carried out in September 1990. It is intended to
arrange annual surveys so that trends in the application of Ada can be
reported in future issues of the Yearbook.

## Areas of activity

The prime areas of activity of the organisations which participated in the
survey were:

|  |  |
|---|---|
| Product Development | 43% |
| Education and Training | 35% |
| Turnkey System Development | 13% |
| Consultancy | 9% |

Those organisations producing Ada software were involved in the following
application areas:

|  |  |
|---|---|
| Products with Embedded Microprocessors | 38% |
| Software Tools | 31% |
| Military Command and Control Systems | 15% |
| Avionics Systems | 8% |
| Software Components | 8% |

There were no organisations participating in the survey concerned with civil
command and control systems, telecommunications systems and industrial
process control systems.

## Ada software engineers

The survey asked those organisations which have been developing Ada
programs to indicate the number of software engineers and their experience
with Ada:

|  |  |
|---|---|
| 46% | of the organisations had less than 20 |
| 46% | had between 21 and 50 |
| 8% | had between 51 and 100 engineers |

Thirty-eight percent of organisations reported substantial depth of Ada experience with at least 75% of their engineers having more than one year of practical experience. Thirty-one percent of the organisations had a low level of Ada experience, with less than 5% of their engineers having used Ada for more than one year. Across all of the organisations it was estimated that around 14% of the software engineers had been using Ada for more than one year.

## Ada projects

The survey revealed that 79% of the organisations were actively using Ada on commercial projects whilst the remainder were in the process of deciding whether to use Ada.

The survey discovered that the contributing organisations had completed 12 projects and were currently working on 25 projects. The use of Ada was a mandatory customer requirement in only 7 of those projects.

Approximately 1.6 million Ada statements had been delivered. Interestingly the breakdown by application area was:

| | |
|---|---|
| Software Components | 46% |
| Software Tools | 42% |
| Military Command and Control Systems | 9% |
| Products with Embedded Microprocessors | 2% |
| Avionics | under 1% |

Around one third of the organisations had so far delivered less than 10,000 Ada statements. The average size of completed projects was around 120,000 Ada statements.

The survey showed that around 60% of the Ada users had critical real-time applications. Of these about half were already using Ada for these applications and the others were expecting to use Ada.

No organisation has yet used Ada in a safety critical application; one avionics company indicated that it expected to use Ada.

## Use of Ada constructs

The survey attempted to find out whether users, as a matter of technical policy, restricted the use of the language. We found out that 75% of users forbade the use of certain Ada constructs for two main reasons:

1. to avoid using constructs which resulted in non-deterministic behaviour such as dynamic storage allocation;

2. to avoid Chapter 13 constructs which affect portability.

About half of the users did make substantial use of generics but some were restricted because of compiler deficiencies in this area. Only about half of the organisations producing Ada programs indicated that the Ada tasking model was sufficient for their applications. The others, mostly those concerned with critical real-time applications, had found it necessary to use a run-time system with additional facilities. Some developers of software tools did not use Ada tasking at all.

# Benefits of Ada

Organisations were asked whether Ada was proving to be a commercial success;

45%   said that their investment had definitely been justified.
45%   said that it was too soon to judge.
10%   said that their investment had resulted in a marginal benefit.

No organisation reported that investment in Ada had not been justified.

Most organisations confirmed that Ada had demonstrated positive benefits in the software lifecycle when compared with other languages. They found that the software was more reliable, more easily maintained and integration time was reduced.

Ada was used alongside a wide variety of other programming languages and was the dominant language in 27% of the user organisations.

# Ada development tools

Nearly 70% of user organisations had purchased several different Ada compilation systems from more than one supplier. Only 18% had purchased a single compilation system. On average each organisation had purchased 3 different compilation systems with 18% buying 6 or more.

The survey asked users if they were satisfied with the Ada compilers, run-time kernels and source debuggers they had purchased. In general the response was encouraging:

|                            | Compilers | Kernels | Debuggers |
|----------------------------|-----------|---------|-----------|
| Very satisfied             | 20%       | 13%     | 14%       |
| Moderately satisfied       | 60%       | 60%     | 57%       |
| Dissatisfied but usable    | 20%       | 27%     | 29%       |
| Dissatisfied and unusable  | None      | None    | None      |

The main reasons for dissatisfaction with compilers were the number of bugs present and limits imposed by the compiler on the size of the program and levels of generic nesting.

Problems with kernels and debuggers were mostly inadequate performance and unreliability. Some debuggers were reported as unusable with complex programs.

The survey indicated that amongst Ada developers:

- 70%  applied an established design methodology
- 50%  had purchased tools to support the design methodology
- 30%  used a host/target debugging environment
- 25%  used an integrated Ada programming support environment
- 20%  used test analysis tools

Around half of the surveyed users were expecting to purchase additional Ada development tools during 1991. Overall indications were that:

- 25%  of users would purchase additional compilers
- 12%  would purchase test and performance analysis tools
- 9%  would purchase syntax directed editors
- 9%  would purchase design tools

## Problems with Ada

The survey revealed that the main reason which would prevent Ada from being used more widely in the future was the cost of compilers. This was the view of 35% of the surveyed users. The second most likely reason (given by 17% of users) was the perceived run-time performance for certain critical real-time applications when compared with other languages. Other reasons given which could restrict the spread of Ada included:

1. Lack of Ada bindings to standardised graphics (eg OSF-MOTIF) and database interfaces.

2. Compiler reliability.

3. Lack of support in the language for object-oriented concepts such as inheritance.

4. The need to build on reusable software existing in another language (e.g. image processing systems in FORTRAN).

Thirty percent of the organisations said there were no obstacles which would prevent them using Ada in the future.

High quality cross compilers were not currently available for target processors used in many process control applications; in particular for the Motorola M68000.

Several educational establishments stated that good quality inexpensive compilers were required for educational use on small PCs.

## Ada hosts and targets

By far the most popular platform for hosting Ada compilers was the PC, with 70% of the surveyed user base. The second most popular was the VAX range (57%) and the third was the SUN 3 range (35%).

The ratings of the most widely used target environments were:

| Intel 386 | 74% |
| Motorola 68k Range | 57% |
| VAX Range | 43% |

## Ada training

Perhaps not surprisingly most organisations have strong views about Ada training. The consensus of opinion was that the software engineering concepts supported by Ada must be taught first. It is essential that students understand and then learn how to apply these concepts in the design of programs before teaching them how to write programs using the Ada language. Several organisations stated that emphasis should be placed on a top-down object-oriented approach. Students should not be taught a Pascal-like subset first. (One organisation however had the opposite view.)

Many educational establishments had found that students with no previous programming experience who had been taught the concepts generally had little difficulty in mastering the Ada language and applying it successfully. The ability of undergraduate students to learn how to design and program in Ada should not be underestimated. On the other hand, experienced programmers from industry often had great difficulty with Ada because they lacked the conceptual background.

Ada, more so than other languages, provides mechanisms for implementing good design. It is how well the design is formulated to take advantage of these features that determines whether a good Ada implementation is produced. A competent Ada software engineer can very often design an efficient and maintainable program which is a fraction of the size and takes a fraction of the effort when compared with the work of an inexperienced programmer. It is very easy to produce a bad Ada program.

The Ada software engineer needs to be equipped with abstract reasoning skills and to be able to draw on compatible methods to transform requirements into a detailed Ada design. Clearly learning to use Ada productively is an ongoing process and users expressed the need for regular refresher workshops to help improve their skills. It was also emphasised that for training to be effective students must have access to good quality fast compilers.

In conclusion it is necessary to get the message across to business managers that it takes much more than a two week programming course for software engineers to acquire the skills to succeed with Ada.

# 15

# Education and training

## 15.1 Training companies and courses

Compiled by Tony Orme
AEG (UK) Ltd

A list of training companies and courses in Ada is given below. Of course, it cannot possibly include every course that might be relevant to Ada practitioners, and the editor reluctantly had to leave out quite a few interesting courses which were not language-specific. The courses below are either directly about Ada, or assume a knowledge of Ada (rather than any other language), and/or use Ada for their practical work.

The courses listed below are publicly announced and available. Very short courses of less than one day in length have been excluded, as have been courses which rely on instructors coming specially from outside the U.K.

The courses are divided into two groups: in the first subsection are the live courses with instructors, and in the second subsection are the media-based courses (where instructors may or may not be on hand to answer queries, set up practicals, etc).

## 15.1.1  Live courses

## Ada Training Ltd

Address: Astra Centre
        Edinburgh Way
        Harlow, Essex. CM20 2BE

Tel. +44 279 450000
Fax. +44 279 429149

Contact Name: Sarah Board

Course 1

Course title: Ada Programming
Normal course location: At Company Address
Normal duration: 5 days
Frequency held: Monthly
This course has practical/lab sessions using the following Ada
compiler system(s): Meridian
The 2 categories of staff likely to be most interested in this
course: (1) Programmer/Software Engineers (2) Programming Team Leaders

Brief Description: For those who require a working knowledge of Ada. It
combines lectures and practicals, and covers the language features, plus the
use of Ada programming facilities.

Course 2

Course title: Advanced Ada Workshop
Normal course location: At Company Address
Normal duration: 5 days
Frequency held: Every 2 months
This course has practical/lab sessions using the following Ada
compiler system(s): Meridian
The 2 categories of staff likely to be most interested in this
course: (1) Systems/Software Engineers (2) Group/Team Leaders

Brief Description: An intensive second-level course which focuses on the
design and application of Ada in large embedded systems, and includes a
guided mini-project.

## Course 3

Course title: Ada Issues for Managers
Normal course location: At Company Address
Normal duration: 2 days
Frequency held: Every 2 months
This course has no practical/lab sessions.
The 2 categories of staff likely to be most interested in this
course: (1) Technical Managers (2) Business Managers

Brief Description: Where knowledge of the practical issues involved in
using Ada is required, this course provides an objective introduction, with
advice on exploiting the benefits of Ada.

## Course 4

Course title: Introduction to HOOD
Normal course location: At Company Address
Normal duration: 2 days
Frequency held: Every 2 months
This course has no practical/lab sessions on the computer.
The 2 categories of staff likely to be most interested in this
course: (1) System Designers (2) Software Engineers

Brief Description: Covers all the design aspects of HOOD and presents
the general concepts, limitations and benefits of Object-Oriented Design,
together with exercises.

## Course 5

Course title: Ada Design Seminar
Normal course location: At Company Address
Normal duration: 1 day
This course has no practical/lab sessions.
The 2 categories of staff likely to be most interested in this
course: (1) Systems/Software Engineers (2) Consultants

Brief Description: Provides impartial and informed answers to the typical
questions raised about the design of Ada software and the selection of
appropriate design techniques.

# Alsys Ltd

Address: Partridge House
        Newtown Road
        Henley-on-Thames, Oxon. RG9 1EN

Tel. +44 491 579090
Fax. +44 491 571866

Contact Name: Dr A. Tlusty-Sheen

## Course 1

Course title: Understanding Ada Seminar and Workshop
Normal course location: Henley
Normal duration: 5 days
Frequency held: Bi-monthly
This course has practical/lab sessions using the following Ada
compiler system(s): Alsys
The 2 categories of staff likely to be most interested in this
course: (1) Project Leaders (2) Software Engineers

Brief Description: Gives a thorough grounding in the theoretical and
practical aspects of the Ada language.

## Course 2

Course title: Object-Oriented Design and Ada (in conjunction with Napier
Polytechnic)
Normal course location: Henley/Edinburgh
Normal duration: 10 days
Frequency held: Quarterly
This course has practical/lab sessions using the following Ada
compiler system(s): Alsys
The 2 categories of staff likely to be most interested in this
course: (1) Project Leaders (2) Software Engineers

Brief Description: Combines the Understanding Ada course with a detailed
examination of the OOD paradigm, covering its development from academic
roots to its implementation in Ada.

# Datel Technology Ltd

Address: 323 Clifton Drive
Lytham St Annes
Lancs. FY8 1HN

Tel. +44 253 713311
Fax. +44 253 714369

Contact Name: Steve Williamson

Course 1

Course title: Ada Programming
Normal course location: Poulton-le-Fylde (Blackpool)
Normal duration: 5 days
Frequency held: 2.5 months
This course has practical/lab sessions using the following Ada
compiler system(s): Meridian Adavantage
The 2 categories of staff likely to be most interested in this
course: (1) Programmers (2) Designers

Brief Description: Provides a detailed working knowledge of Ada and will
develop the skills necessary for good programming practice through lectures
and hands-on.

# Digital Equipment Co Ltd

Address: Shire Hall
Shinfield
Reading, Berks. RG2 9XU

Tel. +44 734 869766
Fax. +44 734 854094

Contact Name: Customer Training Support Desk

Course 1

Course title: Programming in Ada
Normal course location: At Company Address

Normal duration: 5 days
Frequency held: Monthly
This course has practical/lab sessions using the following Ada
compiler system(s): VAX/VMS
The 2 categories of staff likely to be most interested in this
course: (1) Programmers (2) System Programmers

Brief Description: Teaches the syntax, format and structure of the
language.

# Encore Computer (UK) Ltd

Address: Marlborough House
         Mole Business Park
         Randalls Road
         Leatherhead, Surrey. KT22 7BA

Tel. +44 372 363363
Fax. +44 372 362928

Contact Name: Terry Knowles

Course 1

Course title: Introduction to Ada
Normal course location: At Company Address
Normal duration: 2 days
Frequency held: Quarterly
This course has no practical/lab sessions.
The 2 categories of staff likely to be most interested in this
course: (1) Software & Systems Engineers (2)

Brief Description: Introduces the Ada language covering the objectives
and strategies employed as well as the key language features.

Course 2

Course title: Ada Programming Language Package 1
Normal course location: At Company Address
Normal duration: 5 days
Frequency held: On demand

This course has practical/lab sessions using the following Ada compiler system(s): (Generic)
The 2 categories of staff likely to be most interested in this course: (1) Programmers (2)

Brief Description: Covers the necessary skills to write and execute basic Ada programs.


# GEC-Marconi Software Systems

Address: Elstree Way
         Borehamwood
         Herts. WD6 1RX

Tel. +44 81 906 6788
Fax. +44 81 906 6362

Contact Name: Sue Prince


Course 1

Course title: Overview of Software Engineering with Ada
Normal course location: At Customer Site
Normal duration: 1 day
Frequency held: On demand
This course has no practical/lab sessions.
The 2 categories of staff likely to be most interested in this course: (1) Managers (2) Team Leaders

Brief Description: An insight into the main features of Ada and Ada environments. Implications of Ada from both technical and management points of view.


Course 2

Course title: Software Engineering with Ada
Normal course location: At Customer Site
Normal duration: 5 days
Frequency held: Quarterly or On demand
This course has practical/lab sessions using the following Ada compiler system(s): VADS

The 2 categories of staff likely to be most interested in this course: (1) Software Engineers (2) Programmers

Brief Description: Intensive practical course aiming to provide working knowledge of Ada syntax and its relevance to the design process within software engineering.

# KBSL

Address: 1 Campus Road
        Listerhills Science Park
        Bradford, West Yorks. BD7 1HR

Tel. +44 274 736895
Fax. +44 274 736553

Contact Name: Dr John Robinson

Course 1

Course title: HOOD Workshop
Normal course location: Various
Normal duration: 3 days
Frequency held: Bi-monthly
This course has practical/lab sessions using the following Ada compiler system(s): Various
The 2 categories of staff likely to be most interested in this course: (1) Team Leaders (2) Programmer/Engineers

Brief Description: Presents an integrated approach to HOOD using HOIST (Hierarchical Object Identification STrategy), a KBSL developed technique for identifying objects from structured requirements analysis.

Course 2

Course title: Ada for Technical Managers
Normal course location: Various
Normal duration: 2 days
Frequency held: Bi-monthly
This course has no practical/lab sessions.

The 2 categories of staff likely to be most interested in this
course: (1) Technical Managers (2) Business Managers

Brief Description: Provides an objective and balanced appraisal of Ada
allowing them to plan for the successful introduction of the language.


Course 3

Course title: Advanced Ada
Normal course location: Various
Normal duration: 5 days
Frequency held: On demand
This course has practical/lab sessions using the following Ada
compiler system(s): Various
The 2 categories of staff likely to be most interested in this
course: (1) Team Leaders (2) Programmer/Engineers

Brief Description: An opportunity for delegates to work on a mini-project
within a team led by experienced Ada consultants. Design methods used
include HOOD, Booch and Buhr.


Course 4

Course title: OOD Workshop
Normal course location: Various
Normal duration: 3 days
Frequency held: Bi-monthly
This course has practical/lab sessions using the following Ada
compiler system(s): Various
The 2 categories of staff likely to be most interested in this
course: (1) Team Leaders (2) Programmer/Engineers

Brief Description: Presents an integrated approach to Buhr-based OOD
using HOIST (Hierarchical Object Identification STrategy), a KBSL developed
technique for identifying objects from structured requirements analysis.


Course 5

Course title: Ada Programming
Normal course location: Various
Normal duration: 5 days

Frequency held: Bi-monthly
This course has practical/lab sessions using the following Ada
compiler system(s): Various
The 2 categories of staff likely to be most interested in this
course: (1) Team Leaders (2) Programmer/Engineers

Brief Description: Presents the complete Ada language emphasizing how
language features should be used to maximize their effectiveness. The course
makes extensive use of practical exercises.


# Real Time Software Ltd

Address: 118-120 Warwick St
          Leamington Spa
          Warwickshire. CV32 4QY

Tel. +44 926 450858
Fax. +44 926 422165

Contact Name: Paul Rumph


Course 1

Course title: Ada Language
Normal course location: At Client's Premises
Normal duration: 4 days
Frequency held: On demand
This course has practical/lab sessions using the following Ada
compiler system(s): Client's own
The 2 categories of staff likely to be most interested in this
course: (1) Programmers (2)

Brief Description: Intensive course for experienced users of a
block-oriented language.


Course 2

Course title: Ada Design
Normal course location: At Company Address or Client's Premises
Normal duration: 5 days
Frequency held: On demand

This course has practical/lab sessions using the following Ada compiler system(s): IBM PC
The 2 categories of staff likely to be most interested in this course: (1) Designers (2) Analysts

Brief Description: Intended for experienced development staff with some knowledge of Ada.

# SD-SCICON (UK) TRAINING

Address: Carlton House
Ancells Road
Fleet, Hants. GU13 8UN

Tel. +44 252 812244
Fax. +44 252 811803

Contact Name: Mrs S. Tilley

Course 1

Course title: Ada Programming
Normal course location: At Company Address
Normal duration: 5 days
Frequency held: One to two months
This course has practical/lab sessions using the following Ada compiler system(s): Dec VAX Ada
The 2 categories of staff likely to be most interested in this course: (1) Programmers (2) Designers

Brief Description: Provides delegates with a fundamental grounding in Ada programming.

Course 2

Course title: Ada Design
Normal course location: At Company Address
Normal duration: 3 days
Frequency held: Monthly
This course has practical/lab sessions using the following Ada compiler system(s): Dec VAX Ada

The 2 categories of staff likely to be most interested in this course: (1) Software Engineers (2) Designers

Brief Description: Covers the integration of Ada with good design practice.

## York Software Engineering Ltd

Address: University of York
Heslington
York. YO1 5DD

Tel. +44 904 433745
Fax. +44 904 432767

Contact Name: Dr K. G. Mander

Course 1

Course title: Introduction to Ada: a course for Experienced Programmers
Normal course location: York
Normal duration: 5 days
Frequency held: Thrice Yearly
This course has practical/lab sessions using the following Ada compiler system(s): York ACE under Unix
The 2 categories of staff likely to be most interested in this course: (1) Programmers (2) Analysts

Brief Description: Introduces the whole language with practical sessions using the fully validated York Ada Compiler Environment.

## 15.1.2 Media-based courses (no live instructor)

## Alsys Ltd

Address: Partridge House
Newtown Road
Henley-on-Thames, Oxon. RG9 1EN

Tel. +44 491 579090
Fax. +44 491 571866

Contact Name: Dr A. Tlusty-Sheen


Course 1

Course title: Lessons on Ada
Media based on: Computer
Typical duration: 50 hours
Computer hardware assumed: VAX/VMS or PC or PS/2
There are particular Ada compiler system(s) associated with the
course: Alsys
The 2 categories of staff likely to be most interested in this
course: (1) Project Leaders (2) Software Engineers

Brief Description: A two volume Computer Aided Instruction course
mixing tutorials and exercises and providing a detailed explanation of the full
Ada language.


Course 2

Course title: Ichbiah, Barnes & Firth on Ada
Media based on: Video
Typical duration: 18 hours
Computer hardware assumed: Generic
There is no particular Ada compiler system associated with the
course.
The 2 categories of staff likely to be most interested in this
course: (1) Technical Managers (2) Engineers

Brief Description: The lectures, organised by subject into 27 tapes,
include the original "Ada launch". Augmented by examples, illustrated by
advanced computer graphics. Student transcripts are provided.

# Applied Learning

Address: 1 Hogarth Business Park
          Burlington Lane
          Chiswick, London. W4 2TJ

Tel. +44 81 994 4404
Fax. +44 81 994 5611

Contact Name: P. F. Hutchings

Course 1

Course title: Ada: Ichbiah, Barnes & Firth
Media based on: Video
Typical duration: 5 days
Computer hardware assumed: Generic
There is no particular Ada compiler system associated with the
course.
The 2 categories of staff likely to be most interested in this
course: (1) Programmers (2)

Brief Description: Provides an in-depth introduction to the Ada
programming language. Topics cover Programming Construction, Tasking,
Exception Handling and Technical Questions.

# Digital Equipment Co Ltd

Address: Shire Hall
          Shinfield
          Reading, Berks. RG2 9XU

Tel. +44 734 869766
Fax. +44 734 854094

Contact Name: Customer Training Support Desk

Course 1

Course title: Lessons in Ada
Media based on: Computer and Text

Typical duration: 10 days
Computer hardware assumed: Dec VAX
There are particular Ada compiler system(s) associated with the
course: VAX/VMS Ada
The 2 categories of staff likely to be most interested in this
course: (1) Programmers (2)

Brief Description: Any programmer interested in programming in Ada.

# N.A. Software Ltd

Address: Merseyside Innovation Centre
131 Mount Pleasant
Liverpool L3 5TF

Tel. +44 51 708 0123
Fax. +44 51 709 5645

Contact Name: Stuart Gascoyne

Course 1

Course title: Ada Tutor
Media based on: Computer
Typical duration: 5 days
Computer hardware assumed: PC
There are particular Ada compiler system(s) associated with the
course: Meridian AdaVantage
The 2 categories of staff likely to be most interested in this
course: (1) Programmers (2)

Brief Description: Online tutorial with examples and exercises.

Course 2

Course title: Lessons on Ada
Media based on: Computer
Typical duration: 7 days
Computer hardware assumed: PC or VAX
There is no particular Ada compiler system associated with the
course.

The 2 categories of staff likely to be most interested in this course: (1) Programmers (2)

**Brief Description:** 28 lessons, each composed of tutorials including examples and exercises.

**Course 3**

**Course title:** You know Fortran — Ada is simple
**Media based on:** Computer
**Typical duration:** 5 days
**Computer hardware assumed:** PC or VAX
**There is no particular Ada compiler system associated with the course.**
The 2 categories of staff likely to be most interested in this course: (1) Programmers (2)

**Brief Description:** A tutorial which assumes some knowledge of Fortran. It includes examples and exercises.

# 15.2   Public sector Ada education

Compiled by Judy Bishop
Southampton University

A survey was conducted of all universities and polytechnics to gauge the usage, and potential usage, of Ada in higher education. The survey was carried out in October 1990. The results of the survey are summarised below.

| | |
|---|---|
| Questionnaires sent out | 80 |
| Questionnaires returned | 27 |
| Return rate | 34% |

## Institutions using Ada

1. Number of responding institutions using Ada: 15

2. Place of Ada in the curriculum:
   First year                    7
   Second year                   5
   Third and higher years   3

3. Importance of Ada in the curriculum:
   Main language                         6
   One of several other languages   9

4. Year the move to Ada took place:
   1985   3   1988   2
   1986   2   1989   3
   1987   2   1990   3

5. Satisfaction with Ada:
   Very happy                      3
   Reasonably happy            9
   Unhappy                          0
   Good for concurrency      3

6. Hardware and software used:
   DEC VAX VMS                                   6
   Meridian or Janus on IBM PC         5
   York on Orions and Suns                3
   Alsys on Suns                                  2
   Unix workstations                          2
   Verdix on Apollo                            1
   Sequent Balance                            1
   HP850                                           1

7. Student numbers involved:

200 +   2
100 +   3
50 +   5
< 50    3

8. Institutions using Ada who answered the questionnaire (non-computer science departments identified):

Birmingham Polytechnic
Brighton Polytechnic
Bristol Polytechnic
Hatfield Polytechnic
Keele University
King's College London
Leeds University
Liverpool Polytechnic
Liverpool University (Statistics and computational mathematics)
Newcastle Polytechnic
Queen's University of Belfast
Southampton University
South Bank Polytechnic
Polytechnic of Wales, Pontypridd
York University

9. Comments:

The high cost of Ada compilers is still a problem, and may cause some to drop the language. Institutions with networked VAX's seem to be able to cope with resources better than those with stand-alone workstations or PCs.

## Institutions not using Ada

1. Number of responding institutions not currently using Ada: 12

2. First language used by students:
   Pascal      6
   Modula-2   5
   BASIC      1

3. Main language used by students:
   Pascal      5
   Modula-2   5
   C           4
   Fortran     1
   C++         1

4. Still considering Ada or no interest:
   Still considering   5
   No interest         6

5. Hardware in use by those considering Ada:
   Suns        1
   HP          1
   Sequent     1

6. Hardware in use by those not considering Ada:
   Suns or UNIX w/s   6
   PCs                4
   VAX                1

7. Reasons for not using Ada:
   High cost of compilers and high resource usage   6
   Unsuitable for undergraduate teaching            5

8. Institutions not using Ada who answered the questionnaire
   (non-computer science departments identified):
   Essex University
   Heriot-Watt University
   Hull University
   Kingston Polytechnic
   Nottingham University (Mathematics)
   Reading University
   Royal Holloway, Bedford and New College, London
   Sheffield University
   Strathclyde University
   Sussex University (Engineering and Applied Sciences)
   University of Wales College of Cardiff
   Warwick University

9. Comments:
   The high cost of a switch to Ada in real terms (price of compilers and
   usage of memory and processor time) is clearly an issue. It is mostly the
   universities that consider Ada unsuitable, whereas polytechnics are
   happier to embrace it for software engineering and even first year
   teaching.

# 16

# Approved Uniformity Issues

Edited by:
P D Kenward and B A Wichmann
National Physical Laboratory, TW11 OLW, UK

## 16.1 Introduction

The Uniformity Rapporteur Group (URG) is a technical working group which reports to the part of the International Organization for Standardization which handles the standardization of Ada. The purpose of the URG is to fulfil an item of work which was assigned to WG9.

The Ada programming language is very rigorously standardized, and the standard explicitly excludes subsets and supersets in order to encourage portability (both of programs and programmers). In spite of this successful standardization, the Ada language does have significant barriers to portability. The reason for this is that the standard specifically allows implementations to vary in ways that can influence the program. Some of these differences are essential for the provision of an effective Ada system on very different underlying hardware. Other differences have no obvious purpose and therefore act as a needless barrier to portability.

The problems that have arisen have been divided into individual issues, each one being addressed in isolation and the issues give recommendations to increase the portability of existing Ada text. After detailed discussion and agreement by the URG, each issue is sent to WG9 for approval.

A Uniformity Issue (UI) gives a *recommendation* and not a *requirement*. This implies that an implementation is quite free to ignore the recommendation and stay within the Standard. Of course, if a Uniformity Issue is not followed, then portability costs to users could increase, which might well encourage users to request implementations which support the recommendations.

The database of the URG material is maintained at the National Physical Laboratory. See the URG report to WG9 issued on April 1990 for further details of the workings of the URG.

## 16.2   Summary of approved issues

The issues which have been approved by WG9 are UI-0000, UI-0008, UI-0016, UI-0023, UI-0030, UI-0035 and UI-0052. The summaries of these seven issues follow :

### Issue : UI-0000

Title : Conformity to Issues
Editor : B Wichmann

This "issue" gives the meaning of conformity to a recommendation of any of the uniformity issues. A vendor is recommended to conform to all the approved issues, but there may be good reasons why this is inappropriate. In such cases, the vendor should produce a justification for not complying with the recommendation. Such a justification could be hardware, operating system or compilation problems.

### Issue : UI-0008

Title : Integer Types
Editor : B Wichmann

The RM gives very large freedoms for the implementor in the provision of integer types, including the size of INTEGER and this issue gives guidelines on integer types. It recommends that SYSTEM.MAX_INT $>= 2^{31} - 1$ and that the implementation has a mode of operation in which INTEGER'LAST $>= 2^{31} - 1$. It advises that the only allowable forms of other predefined integer types are SHORT_INTEGER, SHORT_SHORT_INTEGER (etc) and LONG_INTEGER, LONG_LONG_INTEGER (etc).

# Issue : UI-0016

Title : Definition of Type DURATION
Editor : R Dewar

This issue gives guidelines to govern the selection of implementation defined parameters for the type DURATION. It recommends that the type DURATION be implemented using at least 32-bit signed representation. It advises that DURATION'SMALL is as small as possible consistent with the requirement that the range be at least one day and that the value 1.0 (one second) is a model number.

# Issue : UI-0023

Title : Files must be Closed Automatically on Termination
Editor : R Dewar

The RM specifically leaves it up to implementations whether or not files are automatically closed on program termination. This issue recommends that implementations must guarantee that all files are closed when a program completes normally or abnormally.

# Issue : UI-0030

Title : Incorrect Order Dependences
Editor : J Pedersen

Incorrect order dependences occur when the execution order of parts of certain constructs are allowed to be determined by the implementation and different orders lead to different effects. A construct with this property is said to be "incorrect" (or have an "incorrect order dependence"). This issue recommends that implementations should not attempt to raise PROGRAM_ERROR for incorrect order dependences. The effect of such dependence is merely to make the program potentially non-deterministic (from the Ada semantics point of view).

# Issue : UI-0035

Title : Source Line Length
Editor : R Dewar

The RM does not specify the maximum identifier length which is determined by the maximum line length. This issue recommends that all compilers support a line length of at least 250 characters. There may be portability problems between compilers supporting different maximum line lengths.

## Issue : UI-0052

Title : Never raise NUMERIC_ERROR
Editor : B Wichmann

AI-00387 already recommends that CONSTRAINT_ERROR should be raised instead of NUMERIC_ERROR. This issue makes the same recommendation on grounds of uniformity by issuing a warning at compile-time on an explicit raising of NUMERIC_ERROR that this exception is no longer raised by the predefined operations. A warning at compile-time is also recommended if NUMERIC_ERROR is handled in an exception handler separate from CONSTRAINT_ERROR since these predefined exceptions cannot be safely distinguished.

# 16.3   Testing the issues

Work has been undertaken at NPL in collecting and writing test programs for the issues agreed by the URG to test the recommendations given for each issue. For each issue, the test program will pass if the implementation satisfies the requirements of the recommendations or fails by giving warnings of any shortcomings. These programs are available for distribution to evaluate the approved issues on different implementations at various sites. Results of the test runs are collected from different implementations and collated in a report.

List of available test programs

| Issue | Title |
|---------|-------------------------------------------|
| UI-0008 | Integer Types |
| UI-0016 | Definition of Type DURATION |
| UI-0018 | Treatment of Undefined Variables |
| UI-0023 | Files Closed Automatically on Termination |
| UI-0030 | Incorrect Order Dependences |
| UI-0035 | Source Line Length |
| UI-0052 | Never raise NUMERIC_ERROR |

Some URG members have been willing to run these tests and report the
results back to NPL but more testers are required to run these short test
programs on the many different Ada implementations to get a better
coverage. Please send an e-mail message to pdk@seg.npl.co.uk if you would
like copies of the sources of these test programs to run on your computer and
to report the results to NPL.

# 16.4   Complete index to issues

| Issue/ Version | Date | Editor | Title | Current Status |
|---|---|---|---|---|
| 0000/2 | 90-08-08 | B.Wichmann | Conformity to Issues | Agreed WG9 |
| 0001/2 | 89-07-11 | P.Hilfinger | Tasking and I/O | Await revision |
| 0002/1 | 89-11-14 | No editor | Bindings | Await editor |
| 0003/1 | 89-11-14 | No editor | Heterogeneous Tasking | Await editor |
| 0004/1 | 89-11-16 | R.Dewar | I/O on Unconstrained Types | To be discussed |
| 0005/3 | 90-06-07 | K.Bowles | Bare Target I/O | To be discussed |
| 0006/2 | 90-05-16 | B.Wichmann | Storage Management Policies | To be discussed |
| 0007/3 | 90-05-04 | B.Wichmann | Unchecked_Conversion for Equal Sizes | Agreed in principle |
| 0008/6 | 90-03-02 | B.Wichmann | Integer Types | Approved WG9 |
| 0009/2 | 89-07-16 | B.Wichmann | Predictable Floating Point | To be discussed |
| 0010/1 | 89-04-05 | No editor | Fixed Types and Operations | Not considered |
| 0011/1 | 89-04-20 | R.Dewar | Records with Dynamic Arrays | Await revision |
| 0012/6 | 90-04-11 | B.Bardin | Unsigned Arithmetic | Agreed in principle |
| 0013/1 | 89-11-14 | No editor | Integration | Abandoned |
| 0014/1 | 89-11-14 | No editor | System Interface Sets | Abandoned |
| 0015/1 | 89-11-14 | D.Emery | Package SYSTEM | To be developed |
| 0016/3 | 89-11-16 | R.Dewar | Definition of type DURATION | Approved WG9 |
| 0017/1 | 90-08-06 | A.Gargaro | Generic Instantiation | Agreed in principle |
| 0018/4 | 89-12-28 | B.Wichmann | Treatment of Undefined Variables | Agreed in principle |
| 0019/2 | 89-06-07 | K.Bowles | Order of Elaboration | Agreed in principle |
| 0020/1 | 89-04-17 | R.Dewar | pragma SHARED | Not considered |
| 0021/1 | 89-04-24 | R.Dewar | pragma SUPPRESS | Not considered |
| 0022/1 | 89-04-24 | C.Mitchell | Implementation defined pragmas | Not considered |
| 0023/3 | 89-11-16 | R.Dewar | Files closed automatically on termination | Returned WG9 |
| 0024/1 | 89-04-24 | R.Eachus | Call by Reference or Value/Return | Abandoned |
| 0025/1 | 89-11-14 | No editor | Allowed Character Sets in Comments | Abandoned |
| 0026/2 | 89-05-31 | K.Bowles | File Names | Not considered |
| 0027/1 | 89-04-24 | D.Eilers | Form Strings | Not considered |
| 0028/1 | 89-11-14 | C.Mitchell | File Sharing | To be discussed |
| 0029/1 | 89-04-17 | D.Emery | Text File Interoperability | Not considered |
| 0030/4 | 90-01-03 | J.Pedersen | Incorrect Order Dependences | Approved WG9 |
| 0031/1 | 89-04-24 | R.Dewar | Preemptive Scheduling is required | Agreed in principle |
| 0032/1 | 89-04-24 | R.Dewar | Time slicing is required | Agreed in principle |
| 0033/1 | 89-04-03 | No editor | Select Strategy | Not considered |
| 0034/1 | 89-11-14 | R.Eachus | Abort Statement | To be discussed |
| 0035/3 | 89-11-16 | R.Dewar | Source Line Length | Agreed WG9 |
| 0036/1 | 89-11-16 | R.Dewar | Pragma INTERFACE Extensions | To be discussed |
| 0037/2 | 89-05-31 | K.Bowles | Interface to Ada | Not considered |
| 0038/1 | 89-11-16 | J-P.Rosen | Interactive I/O | To be discussed |
| 0039/2 | 90-07-12 | R.Dewar | Non-Blocking I/O | Approved URG |
| 0040/1 | 89-11-14 | No editor | Source Code Interchange | Abandoned |
| 0041/1 | 89-11-16 | J.Pedersen | Erroneous Execution | To be discussed |
| 0042/1 | 89-11-14 | B.Eachus | Distributed Processing | Abandoned |
| 0043/1 | 89-08-23 | D.Emery | Meaning of Address Attribute/Clause | To be discussed |
| 0044/2 | 90-06-07 | K.Bowles | Delay 0.0 | Agreed in principle |

| 0045/1 | 89-11-14 | R.Dewar | 64-bit Fixed Point | Agreed in principle |
|--------|----------|---------|--------------------|---------------------|
| 0046/1 | 89-11-14 | R.Dewar | Decimal 'SMALL | Agreed in principle |
| 0047/1 | 89-05-22 | R.Dewar | IEEE Floating Point | Not considered |
| 0048/2 | 90-04-16 | J.Squire | Floating Point Names | Agreed in principle |
| 0049/1 | 89-11-15 | R.Dewar | System'Address/Access Types Conversion | To be discussed |
| 0050/5 | 90-04-14 | A.Gargaro | Time Resolution | Agreed in principle |
| 0051/1 | 89-11-15 | R.Dewar | Specifying Default Task Priorities | To be discussed |
| 0052/4 | 89-11-21 | B.Wichmann | Never raise NUMERIC_ERROR | Approved WG9 |
| 0053/1 | 89-11-15 | C.Mitchell | Pragma INLINE_GENERIC | To be discussed |
| 0054/1 | 89-07-07 | B.Wichmann | Capacity Limits in Compilers | Agreed in principle |
| 0055/1 | 90-02-08 | N.Cohen | Deallocation of Task Storage | To be discussed |
| 0056/1 | 89-11-15 | R.Dewar | Uniformity of representations | To be discussed |
| 0057/1 | 90-01-29 | R.Dewar | Ranges in Record Representation Clauses | To be discussed |
| 0058/1 | 90-01-29 | No editor | Packed Bit Arrays Storage Representation | Await editor |
| 0059/1 | 90-05-14 | N.Cohen | Code Justified by Erroneous Execution | To be discussed |
| 0060/1 | 90-07-12 | N.Cohen | Membership Tests on Invalid Values | To be discussed |
| 0061/2 | 90-08-15 | A.Gargaro | Time-Related Data | Agreed in principle |
| 0062/1 | 90-04-16 | J.Squire | Unchecked_Conversion of Unequal Sizes | Not considered |
| 0063/1 | 90-04-16 | J.Squire | Unchecked_Conversion of Unconstraints | Not considered |
| 0064/1 | 90-06-04 | D.Emery | Address Arithmetic Operations | Not considered |
| 0065/2 | 89-12-06 | D.Emery | Standard name for null address | Agreed in principle |
| 0066/0 | 90-02-14 | R.Eachus | Relationship of delay, duration and time | To be developed |

# 16.5 Conformity to Issues

**UI:** 0000

**Version:** 2

**Date:** 90-08-08

**Editor:** Brian Wichmann

**AI references:** AI-00325

**UI references:** UI-0035, UI-0052, UI-0054

**Section:** RM 1.1.1(6)

**History:** Agreed in principle, February 90; Agreed in principle by WG9, returned for editorial review, June 90

**Status:** Agreed WG9

### Issue

This "issue" recommends the meaning of conformity to a recommendation of any of the uniformity issues.

### Recommendation

A vendor is recommended to conform to all the agreed issues, but there may be good reason why this is inappropriate. In such cases, the vendor should produce a justification for not complying with the recommendation.

### Discussion

A uniformity issue makes a recommendation which is not a requirement of the Ada 83 standard. Hence vendors are free to follow the recommendations or not as they wish, without any criticism that they are not implementing Ada.

However, the goal of the Unformity Rapporteur Group is to increase portability by reducing the actual differences between implementations. Therefore the group wishes to encourage vendors to comply with the recommendations.

In many cases, a uniformity issue arises because of a well-chosen flexibility in the language. In this case, it is acknowledged that a uniformity recommendation may not be appropriate for all systems. A justification should be given for non-compliance along the same lines as AI-00325. Three classes of non-uniformity (which are not exhaustive) are:

**Performance.** In this case, the penalty for conformity is too high to be practical. As an example, a uniformity recommendation could be that floating point overflow should cause an exception to be raised. However, on some machines, three or four additional machine instructions may be needed for every floating point instruction to ensure this. This would be a good reason for non-compliance.

**Hardware environment.** The agreed UI-0035 recommends a minimum line length of 250 characters. If the hardware and the underlying operating system cannot support this, then that would be a good reason for non-compliance. (The URG knows of no such system — hence the recommendation.) These limits could be due to the host system or the target.

**Small compiler.** An issue being discussed is that of the size and complexity of programs that should be acceptable to any implementation (UI-0054). It is acknowledged that either the limits need to reflect the size of the host environment, or a specific exception needs to be made for educational compilers.

For most of the issues, the URG can see no reason why all implementations should not follow them. An example of this is UI-0052 (Never raise NUMERIC_ERROR). These issues are clearly candidates for a language change from Ada 83 to Ada 9X.

WG9 has discussed the possibility that the uniformity recommendations should become an optional secondary standard for Ada. The ISO New Work Item does not allow this and hence the current formulation is in terms of recommendations contained in a Technical Report.

# 16.6   Integer Types

**UI:** 0008

**Version:** 6

**Date:** 90-03-02

**Editor:** Brian Wichmann

**Section:** RM 3.5.4

**History:** Discussed, October 1988 and February 1989; Approved by URG, June 1989; Approved by WG9, June 1990.

**AI references:** AI-00459.

**Status:** Approved WG9

### Issue

The RM gives very large freedoms for the implementor in the provision of integer types, including the size of INTEGER. This issue provides recommendations to increase the portability of programs.

### Recommendation

The recommendations are:

1. SYSTEM.MAX_INT >= 2**31 - 1.

2. That the implementation has a mode of operation in which INTEGER'LAST >= 2**31 - 1.

3. That the names of the other predefined integer types (if any) are SHORT_INTEGER, SHORT_SHORT_INTEGER (etc) and LONG_INTEGER, LONG_LONG_INTEGER (etc). Although such types could have the same range (see AI-00459), the number of such types should be minimized. No other named predefined integer types are allowed.

### Discussion

Since type INTEGER has special properties (base types of loop parameter, default type for the bounds of a discrete range, right operand of **, use in

STRING, CALENDAR, I/O etc) which are built into the language, an
implementation which has a restricted size for INTEGER has problems in
porting code to it. This can significantly undermine one of the goals of Ada.

The use of integer type definitions can increase the portability of programs by
reducing the dependence upon the predefined integer types. The direct use of
user-defined types involves unnecessary constraint checking which can be
avoided by the following technique:

```
type Thirty_Two is range -2**31+1 .. 2**31-1;
-- The above will always be acceptable, given that we are
--   assuming that SYSTEM.MAX_INT >= 2**31-1.
type My_Long is range
            Thirty_Two'BASE'FIRST .. Thirty_Two'BASE'LAST;
```

From this one concludes that the names of the predefined types are not so
important, but that the value of SYSTEM.MAX_INT is, as in the size of
INTEGER.

The additional type names introduced by an implementation can have an
undesirable effect as can be seen from the following example:

```
package MY_TYPES is
   type TINY_INTEGER is range -128..127;
end MY_TYPES;

with MY_TYPES;
package P is
   X: MY_TYPES.TINY_INTEGER;
   use MY_TYPES;
   Y: TINY_INTEGER := X;
end P;
```

The problem here is that if an implementation has its own type
TINY_INTEGER in STANDARD, then Y will be of this type rather than the users
own type. Hence the code here would not compile, but in other cases, the
code could compile but with different semantics which could be hard to trace.
The moral is that the predefined identifiers in STANDARD should be subject to
uniformity recommendations.

The current recommendation is based upon the view that 16-bit
implementations restrict the programmer excessively and that this restriction
is not needed given modern hardware. Some machines provide much more
efficient support for 16-bit integers than for 32 bits. In recognition of this, it is
clear that on such machines, an implementor needs to provide a mode of

operation in which INTEGER is 16 bits. However, to ensure portability to such machines (rather than to such libraries), it is recommended that a mode of operation is provided in which INTEGER is 32 bits (or more). This mode of operation may not be as efficient on these machines.

Note that the RM requirements for fixed point types are more severe than that for integer types in spite of the fact that implementations typically use the same machine instructions for fixed and integer types. The reason for this is that type DURATION requires at least 24 bits.

## Current Practice

Several implementations of Ada for microprocessors provide INTEGER with 16 bits. At least one vendor of such a system regards this decision as a mistake in view of the difficulty in porting code from true 32-bit systems. Having common source code with larger systems then forces implementations on 32-bit machines to have INTEGER with 16 bits for compatibility. This is clearly inappropriate except for host systems designed for 16-bit targets. Validations have been concluded with INTEGER having 16, 32, 36, 46 and 64 bit ranges.

The ACVC makes checks on SHORT_INTEGER and LONG_INTEGER if such types are supported. In version 1.10 of the ACVC, three tests are made on any other predefined integer type, if such a type exists (the tests require that the type name be added).

# 16.7   Definition of type DURATION

UI: 0016

Version: 3

Date: 89-11-16

Editor: Robert Dewar

UI references: UI-0044, UI-0050

Section: RM 9.6

History: Approved 7-0-0, subject to editorial review, March 1988; finally approved by URG, June 1989; Approved by WG9, June 1990.

Status: Approved WG9

## Issue

What guidelines should govern the selection of implementation defined parameters for the type DURATION in package STANDARD?

## Recommendation

The type DURATION must be implemented using at least a 32-bit signed representation, with a DURATION'SMALL as small as possible consistent with the requirement that the range be at least one day and that the value 1.0 (one second) is a model number. In any case, the quantity DURATION'SMALL must not exceed $2^{-14}$ seconds (61.035 microseconds).

## Discussion

The RM says (section 9.6 (4))

> "Any implementation of the type DURATION must allow representation of durations (both positive and negative) up to at least 86400 seconds (one day); the smallest representable duration DURATION'SMALL must not be greater than twenty milliseconds (whenever possible, a value not greater than fifty microseconds should be chosen)."

This definition implies at least 24 bits are needed for type DURATION, and it seems reasonable to guess that any implementation which can provide 24 bits can equally easily use 32 bits. With 32 bits signed, the recommended 50 microseconds can only be achieved using a non-binary value for 'SMALL which would require an appropriate representation clause to be added to package STANDARD.

It is presumably valid for an implementation to provide such a representation clause in STANDARD, even though a very strict reading of the reference manual would seem to prohibit this addition (the permitted additions to the specification of STANDARD being carefully enumerated in the RM). However, requiring an implementation to use a non-binary 'SMALL for DURATION seems too aggressive at this point, given that there are still questions of whether or not such representation clauses must be provided at all.

Given this, the question is how to read the intent of the above section. It seems clear that a small DURATION, as close as possible to 50 microseconds is desirable, subject to the one day minimum range requirement. In particular, it is undesirable for implementations (as some have already done) to use a coarser 'SMALL in an attempt to widen the range beyond one day, since this causes portability problems. It is perfectly possible to write programs in Ada which handle event timing over arbitrarily long periods without requiring that DURATION be able to represent the time intervals involved, and such programming approaches are expected as part of the normal approach to handling timed events in an Ada program.

A related issue concerns model numbers of type DURATION. It seems highly desirable that delay values expressed in integral numbers of seconds be exact. This means that the quantity 1.0 should be a model number of type DURATION. There is no such requirement in the RM, but in practice this requirement is not onerous and will contribute to portability.

Two related issues are the effect of delay 0.0 (UI-0044); and the resolution of the clock (UI-0050).

## Current Practice

Virtually all compilers use a 32-bit fixed type to represent DURATION. No compilers provide a representation clause to achieve the recommended 50 microsecond value for 'SMALL. The delta chosen varies. Some implementations are consistent with the recommendation as stated above, but others have deliberately expanded the range of DURATION by using a much coarser precision. All compilers implement types where 1.0 seconds is a model number.

# 16.8   Files must be Closed Automatically on Termination

UI: 0023

Version: 3

Date: 89-11-16

Editor: Robert Dewar

AI references: AI-00399

Section: RM 14.2.1

History: Approved (7-0-0), subject to editorial review, March 1988; Approved finally by URG, June 1989; Returned by WG9 for editorial review, June 1990.

Status: Returned WG9

Issue

The RM specifically leaves it up to implementations whether or not files are automatically closed on program termination.

Recommendation

Implementations must guarantee that all files are closed when the main program terminates. The semantics of this automatic close operation is identical to the semantics of a normal Ada CLOSE call.

Discussion

The probable motive for the freedom granted by the RM was that operating systems differ on whether or not files are automatically closed on exit. In fact the issue in practice is a higher level one, since closing files in the Ada sense presumably involves other actions than the actual system level close, for example flushing buffers. It is quite simple to implement automatic closing of files even if the operating system does not have this semantics, and most (all?) existing Ada implementations do in fact do this automatic close. There is no point in leaving an undefined condition where it is not sufficiently helpful to compilers to do so. See also AI-00399 which discusses the general issue of program termination.

**Current Practice**

Most implementations close files automatically, at least in the case of normal termination.

# 16.9   Incorrect Order Dependences

UI: 0030

Version: 4

Date: 90-01-03

Editor: Jan Storbank Pedersen

AI references: AI-00030, AI-00284, AI-00365

UI references: UI-0019

Section: RM 1.6

History: Approved by URG, October 1989; Approved by WG9, June 1990

Status: Approved WG9


Issue

Incorrect order dependences occur when the execution order of parts of certain constructs are allowed to be determined by the implementation and different orders lead to different effects. A construct with this property is said to be "incorrect" (or have an "incorrect order dependence").

A currently unanswered AI (AI-00284) questions the definition of incorrect order dependence with reference to the vagueness of the term "effect."


Recommendation

Implementations should not attempt to raise PROGRAM_ERROR for incorrect order dependences. The effect of such dependences is merely to make the program potentially non-deterministic (from the Ada semantics point of view).


Discussion

The freedom to determine certain execution orders is quite deliberately granted to the implementation. It is an attempt to give compilers freedom to reorder operations, with the assumption that for most programs (i.e. those not containing functions with inappropriate side-effects) the reordering will not change the effect. Nevertheless, the variance in ordering is a non-uniformity and non-portable programs depending on the differences can easily be written.

The RM defines (by using the phrase (evaluated/executed/elaborated) "in some order that is not defined by the language" (1.6(9))) the following constructs as potentially having an incorrect order dependence:

1. default expressions (3.2.1(15))

2. simple expressions of a range constraint (3.5(5))

3. index constraints and component subtype indications of an array type definition (3.6(10)) and index constraints of a subtype indication (3.6.1(11))

4. discriminant associations of a discriminant constraint (3.7.2(13))

5. the prefix and index expressions of an indexed component (4.1.1(4))

6. the prefix and discrete range of a slice (4.1.2(4))

7. choices and component expressions of an aggregate (4.3.1(3), 4.3.2(10))

8. operands of an infix expression not involving short-circuit control forms (4.5(5))

9. the variable name and expression of an assignment statement (5.2(3))

10. parameter associations (6.4(6))

11. copy back of in out or out parameters (6.4(6))

12. implicit package bodies (9.3(5)) [This rule does not use the exact phrase but is probably to be interpreted in this manner.]

13. conditions, delay expressions, and entry indices in a selective wait (9.7.1(5), AI-00030)

14. task names in an abort statement (9.10(4))

15. library units (that are to be elaborated) (10.5(5), UI-0019)

16. expressions that are (part of) explicit generic actual parameters (12.3(17), AI-00365)

The RM allows an implementation to raise PROGRAM_ERROR in cases where incorrect order dependences are detected (1.6(10)). Because the possible behaviours of a program containing an incorrect order dependence are limited to those corresponding to different orderings of well-defined operations, incorrect order dependence is "less severe" than erroneous execution. Indeed, an incorrect order dependence can be seen simply as introducing a well-defined non-deterministic behaviour in the program execution.

In general, detecting an incorrect order dependence at run-time is not feasible, because the definition refers to "different" orders and only *one* order is actually chosen (the other orders will not be "tried," in particular, side-effects

must not take place more than once). Incorrect order dependences may be
detected at compile time in certain cases. However, the uncertainty as to
what is meant by "effect of a program" still exists. Consider for example the
following program:

```
with TEXT_IO;
procedure MAIN is
   I : INTEGER := 0;

   function INCI(J : INTEGER) return INTEGER is
   begin
     I := I + J;
     return I;
   end INCI;

begin

   -- This program will print either 7 or 8

   TEXT_IO.PUT_LINE(INTEGER'IMAGE(INCI(2) + INCI(3)));

end MAIN;
```

Does this program have an incorrect order dependence? The comment
indicates that the non-determinism is intended (or at least expected). If the
PUT_LINE statement were changed to:

```
I := INCI(2) + INCI(3);
```

Would the answer be changed (does the effect include not externally visible
changes to the values of variables)?

Due to the unresolved issue of what "effect" means, and because not all
incorrect order dependences will be detected by an implementation, the most
uniform behaviour is to never raise PROGRAM_ERROR for incorrect order
dependences.

## Current Practice

Existing compilers certainly choose various orders of elaboration and evaluation where freedom exists, and therefore programs with side-effects yield different results when ported from one system to another. No known compiler attempts any level of checking, either at compile time or execution time, for incorrect order dependences.

# 16.10   Source Line Length

UI: 0035

Version: 3

Date: 89-11-16

Editor: Robert Dewar

UI references: UI-0054

Section: RM 2.3

History: Approved by URG, June 1989; Agreed in principle by WG9, returned for editorial review, June 1990.

Status: Agreed WG9

### Issue

The maximum identifier length is determined by the maximum line length, which is not specified by the RM. Possible portability problems exist between compilers supporting different maximum line lengths.

### Recommendation

All compilers must support a maximum line length of at least 250 characters, that is, a source program containing no lines longer than 250 characters must be accepted by all compilers.

### Discussion

Clearly we would not accept a compiler whose maximum line length is 16, even though such a compiler is in compliance with the RM (16 is chosen to be long enough to spell any of the reserved words). What is the minimum acceptable maximum line length? The suggested choice of 250 seems reasonably safe. On the one hand it is unlikely that any compiler will have difficulty with this maximum. On the other hand, it seems that restricting identifier lengths to 250 characters in portable programs is probably reasonable. Note that the limitation also applies to strings and other literals. A long line length could be required by some tools, such as one which inserts automatic qualification (without changing the layout). The limit has been made as long as seems reasonable without introducing additional overheads into a compilation system.

See also UI-0054 for other compiler limits.

## Current Practice

One compiler has recently had its limit increased so that it will satisfy this limit. Another compiler has a slightly lower limit, while typical UNIX systems have no limit.

# 16.11    Never raise NUMERIC_ERROR

**UI:** 0052

**Version:** 4

**Date:** 89-11-21

**Editor:** Brian Wichmann

**AI references:** AI-00387

**Section:** RM 11.01

**History:** Discussed briefly in November 1988 and February 1989; Approved finally (11-0-0) by URG, June 1989; Approved by WG9, June 1990.

**Status:** Approved WG9

### Issue

AI-00387 already recommends that CONSTRAINT_ERROR should be raised instead of NUMERIC_ERROR. This issue makes the same recommendation on grounds of uniformity.

### Recommendation

To follow the recommendation of AI-00387, as stated above. To issue a warning at compile-time on an explicit raising of NUMERIC_ERROR that this exception is no longer raised by the predefined operations. To issue a warning at compile-time if NUMERIC_ERROR is handled in an exception handler separate from CONSTRAINT_ERROR since it has been agreed that the predefined exceptions cannot be safely distinguished.

### Discussion

For detailed discussion on the problem of attempting to distinguish between the situations in which either exception should be raised, see AI-00387. The conclusion in terms of uniformity is clearly stronger in the sense that the recommendation removes a potential non-uniformity between conforming implementations. AI-00387 was approved by WG9 on 86-05-09.

It should be noted that users can always merge the two exceptions in an exception handler so that the program will not be able to distinguish between the two exceptions. Hence the consequences of not accepting this recommendation for a careful user is not severe.

## Current Practice

Validations to ACVC 1.9 determine whether CONSTRAINT_ERROR or NUMERIC_ERROR is raised in five situations:

1. when an array is declared with INTEGER'LAST+2 components,

2. when an array type is declared with SYSTEM.MAX_INT+2 components,

3. when a packed Boolean array is declared of INTEGER'LAST components,

4. when a packed two-dimensional Boolean array is declared of more than INTEGER'LAST components,

5. when a null array is declared with one dimension having a length greater than INTEGER'LAST.

It appears that at least some compilers still raise NUMERIC_ERROR. It does not seem worthwhile to survey the situation further, since WG9 has already agreed on a recommendation here.

Model Numbers

# 17

# Towards an Ada standard for the elementary functions*

Kenneth W. Dritz
Mathematics and Computer Science Division
Argonne National Laboratory
Argonne, Illinois 60439, USA

## Abstract

Since the conclusion of its three-year development period in 1989, the proposed Standard for a Generic Package of Elementary Functions for Ada has been working its way through a hierarchy of committees towards achieving the status of a secondary ISO standard in the Ada area. This article introduces the contents of the proposed standard and discusses some of the decisions that influenced it.

As is well known, Ada — unlike other languages — does not include built-in or predefined elementary functions such as SQRT, SIN, and EXP. Instead, it contains numerous features that directly support the construction of high-quality, portable mathematical software [5]. Not the least of these is a *model* of floating-point arithmetic that, by specifying the result interval for floating-point operations, provides a semantic target for compiler implementers and a formalism for programmers to use in reasoning about their programs (in either an implementation-independent or an implementation-specific way). Because the elementary functions pervade scientific and engineering computations, compiler vendors have typically supplied them in the form of math libraries. However, since the composition of these libraries has not been the subject of any standard, they differ in the

---

*This work was supported by the U.S. Strategic Defense Initiative Organization, Office of the Secretary of Defense, under WPD B423.

functions they offer, in the functions' names (e.g., LOG vs. LN) and parameter profiles, and even in the use or avoidance of genericity; consequently, most Ada scientific and engineering codes are not portable.

In 1986, following preliminary recommendations for standards in this area [10, 4] as well as pioneering implementation efforts, an activity to draft and formally recommend a standard specification for a package of elementary functions for Ada was launched under the auspices of SIGAda, the ACM special interest group for Ada. A committee — the SIGAda Numerics Working Group ("NumWG"), chaired by G. Myers — was formed in that year and has met every few months since then. Much of its early work was based on [9], and through its European members it has communicated and collaborated with the Ada-Europe Numerics Working Group ("A-ENWG"). In 1989, a subcommittee of ISO-IEC JTC1/SC22/WG9 (Ada), known as the Numerics Rapporteur Group ("NRG"), was constituted and charged formally with the drafting of proposed numeric standards for Ada. The NRG received a joint proposal for an elementary functions standard from the NumWG and A-ENWG and passed a slightly revised version of it to WG9, which in turn approved it after further minor revisions and passed it to SC22. At the current time, it has been initially processed by SC22, and the standardization effort is at a momentary pause while the NumWG and NRG contemplate small changes that would permit implementations to exploit certain features of IEEE arithmetic [6, 7]. In addition, the NumWG — again with the help of the A-ENWG — is working on proposals for other standards.

The document describing the proposed elementary functions standard [8] contains a one-page specification for a generic package called GENERIC_ELEMENTARY_FUNCTIONS and a small auxiliary package called ELEMENTARY_FUNCTIONS_EXCEPTIONS (see Figure 17.1). In addition, the document contains information for each function, including its mathematical definition, examples of its use, the domain over which the function is defined, the range of values that can be returned, and the accuracy requirements to which implementations must conform. Prefatory material explains the meaning of the domain and range specifications and the accuracy requirements.

The elementary functions are encapsulated in a generic package having one generic formal parameter, which is the generic formal floating-point type used in the parameter and result profiles of all the functions. The generic package can be instantiated with a generic actual parameter that is any floating-point subtype, including one having a range constraint. Range constraints might interfere, of course, with the ability of an elementary function to receive its argument(s) or deliver its computed result; avoiding that problem is necessarily the user's responsibility. However, the user is guaranteed by an explicit requirement of the proposed standard that range constraints will have no other

```
package ELEMENTARY_FUNCTIONS_EXCEPTIONS is
   ARGUMENT_ERROR : exception;
end ELEMENTARY_FUNCTIONS_EXCEPTIONS;

with ELEMENTARY_FUNCTIONS_EXCEPTIONS;
generic
   type FLOAT_TYPE is digits <>;
package GENERIC_ELEMENTARY_FUNCTIONS is

   function SQRT     (X          : FLOAT_TYPE)         return FLOAT_TYPE;
   function LOG      (X          : FLOAT_TYPE)         return FLOAT_TYPE;
   function LOG      (X, BASE    : FLOAT_TYPE)         return FLOAT_TYPE;
   function EXP      (X          : FLOAT_TYPE)         return FLOAT_TYPE;
   function "**"     (X, Y       : FLOAT_TYPE)         return FLOAT_TYPE;

   function SIN      (X          : FLOAT_TYPE)         return FLOAT_TYPE;
   function SIN      (X, CYCLE   : FLOAT_TYPE)         return FLOAT_TYPE;
   function COS      (X          : FLOAT_TYPE)         return FLOAT_TYPE;
   function COS      (X, CYCLE   : FLOAT_TYPE)         return FLOAT_TYPE;
   function TAN      (X          : FLOAT_TYPE)         return FLOAT_TYPE;
   function TAN      (X, CYCLE   : FLOAT_TYPE)         return FLOAT_TYPE;
   function COT      (X          : FLOAT_TYPE)         return FLOAT_TYPE;
   function COT      (X, CYCLE   : FLOAT_TYPE)         return FLOAT_TYPE;

   function ARCSIN   (X          : FLOAT_TYPE)         return FLOAT_TYPE;
   function ARCSIN   (X, CYCLE   : FLOAT_TYPE)         return FLOAT_TYPE;
   function ARCCOS   (X          : FLOAT_TYPE)         return FLOAT_TYPE;
   function ARCCOS   (X, CYCLE   : FLOAT_TYPE)         return FLOAT_TYPE;
   function ARCTAN   (Y          : FLOAT_TYPE;
                      X          : FLOAT_TYPE := 1.0) return FLOAT_TYPE;
   function ARCTAN   (Y          : FLOAT_TYPE;
                      X          : FLOAT_TYPE := 1.0;
                      CYCLE      : FLOAT_TYPE)         return FLOAT_TYPE;
   function ARCCOT   (X          : FLOAT_TYPE;
                      Y          : FLOAT_TYPE := 1.0) return FLOAT_TYPE;
   function ARCCOT   (X          : FLOAT_TYPE;
                      Y          : FLOAT_TYPE := 1.0;
                      CYCLE      : FLOAT_TYPE)         return FLOAT_TYPE;

   function SINH     (X          : FLOAT_TYPE)         return FLOAT_TYPE;
   function COSH     (X          : FLOAT_TYPE)         return FLOAT_TYPE;
   function TANH     (X          : FLOAT_TYPE)         return FLOAT_TYPE;
   function COTH     (X          : FLOAT_TYPE)         return FLOAT_TYPE;

   function ARCSINH (X          : FLOAT_TYPE)         return FLOAT_TYPE;
   function ARCCOSH (X          : FLOAT_TYPE)         return FLOAT_TYPE;
   function ARCTANH (X          : FLOAT_TYPE)         return FLOAT_TYPE;
   function ARCCOTH (X          : FLOAT_TYPE)         return FLOAT_TYPE;

   ARGUMENT_ERROR : exception renames ELEMENTARY_FUNCTIONS_EXCEPTIONS.ARGUMENT_ERROR;

end GENERIC_ELEMENTARY_FUNCTIONS;
```

Figure 17.1.   Specification of GENERIC_ELEMENTARY_FUNCTIONS and ELEMENTARY_FUNCTIONS_EXCEPTIONS

untoward effect, such as raising an exception when a result satisfying the range constraints and the accuracy requirements is deliverable. For all practical purposes, this means that implementations of the elementary functions in Ada must not declare variables of the generic formal type to hold intermediate results. One alternative to that is illustrated in [11], while another involves a second-level call to an inner function in a generic package instantiated with the appropriate predefined floating-point type. Peculiarities of use clauses can be exploited to make the latter technique portable with respect to the unpredictable number of predefined floating-point types available [1].

Two versions of each of the trigonometric functions, and of their inverses, are provided: the one without a CYCLE parameter measures the angle in units of radians, whereas the one with a CYCLE parameter provides for arbitrary units of measure (CYCLE => 360.0 corresponds to degrees; CYCLE => 6400.0, to mils; etc.).

Early in the development of the elementary functions standard, it was thought that the natural cycle of $2\pi$ radians and the arbitrary user-specified cycle could both be accommodated in a single version of each of the trigonometric functions — in particular, one having an optional CYCLE parameter with a default value of $2\pi$. Inverses included, this technique would have shortened the generic package specification by eight functions, which is certainly appealing. However, since the value given by the default expression would necessarily be only an approximation to $2\pi$, its use as if it were the exact cycle would lead to a function that would not meet the accuracy requirements for large arguments, or even for certain small arguments. The fact that argument reduction relative to a cycle of $2\pi$ demands special techniques effectively makes the natural-cycle trig functions different from their arbitrary-cycle counterparts. The difference is reflected in the use of subprogram overloading to accommodate two versions of the trig functions, one with and one without a CYCLE parameter. (The preceding discussion touches on one of many issues that came up during the development of the standard; further details can be found in its "rationale" document [3].)

For similar reasons, the natural — or Napierian — logarithm and logarithms to an arbitrary base are accommodated by a pair of overloaded subprograms for LOG, with and without a BASE parameter, rather than by a single subprogram with an optional BASE parameter having a default value.

An example of a domain definition is the familiar one for the square root function, SQRT, which says that the argument, X, must be greater than or equal to zero. As the prefatory material in the standard explains, this means that SQRT must raise ARGUMENT_ERROR when X < 0.0. As another example, the exponential function, EXP, has a mathematically unbounded domain (it is mathematically defined for all arguments), even though overflow prevents a result from being delivered when X is sufficiently large. This means that EXP never raises ARGUMENT_ERROR, even for those large arguments. The raising of ARGUMENT_ERROR is the chosen way of informing the application that it has supplied an argument for which the function being invoked has no mathematical definition. If the mathematically defined result is so large that it overflows, then (according to the prefatory material) overflow is signaled in the natural way, which in Ada is by the raising of a particular predefined exception (CONSTRAINT_ERROR or, in systems not yet implementing AI-00387, NUMERIC_ERROR).

At the present time, the proposed elementary functions standard calls for ARGUMENT_ERROR to be raised at isolated poles of a function — i.e., arguments for which the mathematical result is infinite are excluded from the domain. A change that would include poles in the domain is, however, being considered. Thus, the response *at* a pole (namely, the signaling of overflow) would be the same as the response *near* a pole, rather than abruptly different. This change would facilitate the extension of IEEE *infinities* [6, 7] to GENERIC_ELEMENTARY_FUNCTIONS when they are introduced by a proposed IEEE binding for Ada [2]; without the change, this feature of IEEE arithmetic could not be exploited by implementations of GENERIC_ELEMENTARY_FUNCTIONS.

An example of a range definition is the familiar one for the sine function, SIN, which says that the result must lie between -1.0 and 1.0. Range definitions serve several purposes.

One purpose of the range definitions is to guarantee that delivered results will satisfy certain familiar properties. A result from SIN that is slightly greater than 1.0 could wreak havoc with an especially sensitive computation; its inverse, ARCSIN, cannot be computed, for example. On the other hand, although no finite argument is mathematically mapped by the exponential function into zero, zero *is* included in the range of EXP; this is because EXP can underflow for negative arguments of sufficiently large magnitude, and zero is a valid result when underflow occurs in Ada. Range definitions are not carried beyond the point of practicality, however. Although the mathematical range of the arcsine function is $-\pi/2$ to $\pi/2$, and in fact that is what the proposed standard appears to require for ARCSIN, the prefatory material explains that a range limit that is not a safe number may be exceeded — up to the next safe number — because, in general, that is the best that can be achieved in a portable implementation.

A second purpose of the range definitions is to reduce a multivalued mathematical function to a single-valued one, by specification of its principal range, for implementation purposes. A third purpose is mentioned later.

Compared with treatments of the elementary functions in other programming languages, the proposed standard would seem to be unique in its inclusion of accuracy requirements. The purposes of the accuracy requirements are to give the user some assurance of reasonable quality, to allow the user to perform an error analysis of complete computations that use the elementary functions, and to serve as the basis for the eventual validation of implementations. Two forms of accuracy requirements are embodied in the standard — maximum relative error ("MRE") bounds and prescribed results.

Every function has a maximum relative error bound, which constrains the computed result to be relatively close to the true result over the entire domain, with certain exceptions. (One exception is that the MRE bounds of the trigonometric functions with natural cycle apply only over a limited portion of the domain; another is that they do not apply to any function where the true result is zero, since the relative error is undefined there; and a third is that a uniform maximum absolute error bound is substituted in the vicinity of zeros, where underflow to zero causes all relative accuracy to be lost.) The MRE bounds were chosen by numerical analysts with broad implementation experience; while these bounds will rule out quick-and-dirty implementations, they do nevertheless permit a reasonable range of implementation techniques, and a careful implementer should have no difficulty meeting and even exceeding the requirements.

With one exception, the maximum relative error bounds (see Figure 17.2) take the form of a constant coefficient, which depends on the function, times FLOAT_TYPE'BASE'EPSILON. The approximate effect of this is to constrain the result to lie within a certain number of units in the last place, relative to the predefined floating-point type implicitly selected by the Ada implementation as the representation of the generic formal type. Basing the MRE bounds on the precision of the base type of FLOAT_TYPE, rather than that of FLOAT_TYPE itself, compels implementations to exploit the accuracy achievable with the hardware representations they are given. It is motivated by the rule for Ada's predefined floating-point arithmetic operators, which also demands base-type accuracy. (Incidentally, discussions of accuracy issues during the development of the standard caused a reexamination and eventual repeal of AI-00407.)

The prescribed results go beyond the MRE requirements by stipulating that certain functions must deliver particular results exactly for arguments of special significance. A few of the prescribed results are the following: SQRT(0.0) = 0.0; LOG(1.0) = 0.0; X ** 1.0 = X; COS(0.0) = 1.0; and TAN(X, CYCLE) = 0.0 when $X = k \cdot \text{CYCLE}/2.0$, for integer $k$. Besides

| Function or operation | Coefficient of FLOAT_TYPE'BASE'EPSILON |
|:---:|:---:|
| SQRT | 2.0 |
| LOG | 4.0 |
| EXP | 4.0 |
| "**" | $4.0 + \lvert Y \cdot \log_e X \rvert / 32.0$ |
| SIN | 2.0 |
| COS | 2.0 |
| TAN | 4.0 |
| COT | 4.0 |
| ARCSIN | 4.0 |
| ARCCOS | 4.0 |
| ARCTAN | 4.0 |
| ARCCOT | 4.0 |
| SINH | 8.0 |
| COSH | 8.0 |
| TANH | 8.0 |
| COTH | 8.0 |
| ARCSINH | 8.0 |
| ARCCOSH | 8.0 |
| ARCTANH | 8.0 |
| ARCCOTH | 8.0 |

Figure 17.2. Maximum relative error bounds

being easy to implement, prescribed results help to ensure the integrity of computations, especially sensitive ones, in limiting or degenerate cases. They also serve as the primary means for constraining the computed result at the zeros of a function, where the MRE requirements do not apply. Some prescribed results, such as ARCCOS(-1.0) = $\pi$, would appear to be impossible to implement, until one reads in the prefatory material that this notation really means that any value in the smallest safe interval containing, or defined by, the right-hand side can be delivered. The convention is analogous to the one that applies to range limits that are not safe numbers.

A third purpose of the range definitions, alluded to earlier, is to function as additional accuracy requirements — i.e., as a kind of prescribed result in the form of an inequality, rather than an equality. For example, for X close to $\pi$, COS(X) is close to -1.0, and the MRE requirements might actually permit a result slightly less than -1.0; the range definition for COS rules out results less than -1.0, however.

Implementations of the proposed standard have been completed at several locations and are under way at others, and some Ada compiler vendors already support it. It will likely be recommended for inclusion in Ada 9X as a separate annex. Eventually there will be a high-quality validation suite for implementations; some unsophisticated test suites have already been written, and a very rigorous portable test suite is under development.

# References

[1] J.-M. Chebat. Personal communication, March 21, 1990.

[2] R. B. K. Dewar. Proposed Ada Interface for the IEEE Standard for Binary Floating-Point Arithmetic, August 1989. Version 4.

[3] K. W. Dritz. Rationale for the Proposed Standard for a Generic Package of Elementary Functions for Ada. ANL Report ANL-89/2 Rev. 1, Argonne National Laboratory, Argonne, IL, October 1989. Later (August 1990) revision available from author.

[4] R. Firth. Preliminary Draft Specification of a Basic Mathematical Library for the High Order Programming Language Ada. Royal Military College of Science, Shrivenham, Swindon, Wiltshire, England, March 1982.

[5] B. Ford, J. Kok, and M. W. Rogers, editors. *Scientific Ada*. Cambridge University Press, Cambridge, 1986.

[6] IEEE. IEEE Standard for Binary Floating-Point Arithmetic. ANSI/IEEE Std. 754-1985, IEEE, New York, 1985.

[7] IEEE. IEEE Standard for Radix-Independent Floating-Point Arithmetic. ANSI/IEEE Std. 854-1987, IEEE, New York, 1987.

[8] ISO-IEC/JTC1/SC22/WG9 (Ada) Numerics Rapporteur Group. Proposed Standard for a Generic Package of Elementary Functions for Ada, October 1989. Draft 1.1.

[9] J. Kok. Proposal for Standard Mathematical Packages in Ada. CWI Report NM-R8718, Centrum voor Wiskunde en Informatica, Amsterdam, November 1987.

[10] J. Kok and G. T. Symm. A Proposal for Standard Basic Functions in Ada. *Ada Letters*, IV(3):44–52, November/December 1984.

[11] P. T. P. Tang. Portable Implementation of a Generic Exponential Function in Ada. ANL Report ANL-88-3, Argonne National Laboratory, February 1988.

# 18

# Ada 9X Requirements Document, December 1990*

The Ada 9X Project Report "Ada 9X Requirements Document, December 1990" is reproduced here verbatim, except that essentially empty pages have been omitted. The copyright of the report resides with the Ada 9X Project Office and it is reprinted with their permission.

---

# Table of Contents

## Table of Contents

**Table of Contents**

**Table of Contents**

# Foreword

The revision of ANSI/MIL-STD-1815A, the Ada programming language, is being conducted by the Ada 9X Project Office located at the Air Force Armament Laboratory at Eglin AFB, Florida. The Ada 9X Project is sponsored by the Ada Joint Program Office in the Office of the Under Secretary of Defense for Acquisition. The Project was initiated in October 1988 with an invitation to the public to submit revision requests. Over 750 revision requests were submitted world-wide between October 1988 and October 1989. In addition, several international workshops and meetings were organized by the Ada 9X Project Office for the purpose of further refining and prioritizing user needs in order that they might better be addressed in the revision effort.

While many individuals have greatly contributed to the requirements process, one person deserves special recognition. John Goodenough, at the Software Engineering Institute (SEI), has made enormous contributions to the Ada 9X Project since its inception. John not only orchestrated the Ada 9X Complex Issues Studies but also led the team that successfully completed the Ada 9X Requirements. That Team consisted of John, Arthur Evans, Jr., also at the SEI, Benjamin Brosgol from Alsys, Inc., and Robert Dewar from New York University. They are to be congratulated for a difficult job superbly accomplished.

I would also like to thank participants of the initial phase of the requirements process for their dedication in collecting and analyzing the revision requests from the Ada community. This team, based at the Institute for Defense Analyses (IDA), consisted of Cy Ardoin (IDA), Paul Baker (CTA), Douglas Dunlop (Intermetrics), Audrey Hook (IDA), Joseph Linn (IDA), Catherine McDonald (IDA), Reginald Meeson, Jr. (IDA), Steven Michell (Prior Data Sciences: Canada), and Karl Nyberg (Grebyn Corp).

I would also like to thank the Ada 9X Project technical experts, the Distinguished Reviewers, who,

under the very capable chairmanship of Erhard Ploedereder of Tartan Laboratories, performed many intense reviews of the material leading to the publication of this document. The Distinguished Reviewers are: G. Booch (Rational), B. Brosgol (Alsys), N. Cohen (IBM), R. Dewar (NYU), G. Dismukes (TeleSoft), D. Fisher (Incremental Systems), A. Gargaro (Computer Sciences), M. Gerhardt (ESL), J. Goodenough (SEI), E. Guerrieri (Boston University), T. Harrison (SPC), S. Heilbrunner (IABG: Germany), M. Henne (Sverdrup), P. Hilfinger (UC/Berkeley), Jean Ichbiah (Alsys: DR emeritus), M. Kamrad II (UNISYS), R. Landwehr (CCI: Germany), C. Lester (Portsmouth Polytechnic: UK), R. Leavitt (Prior Data Sciences: Canada), L. Månsson (Telelogic AB: Sweden), R. Mathis (Contel), M. Mills (US Air Force), C. Mitchell (DEC), E. Ploedereder (Tartan), D. Pogge (US Navy), K. Power (Boeing), O. Roubine (Consultant: France), T. Taft (Intermetrics), W. Taylor (Ferranti: UK), E. Vasilescu (GNV), and T. Wheeler (US Army).

Defining the requirements for the revision of Ada 83 has been a challenging task. The overall goal has been to balance the necessary changes for Ada's continued growth in the 1990s with the need for stability in terms of preserving the integrity of existing Ada software and tools. The requirements as stated in this document are intended to enhance Ada's usability and strengthen its position in the marketplace.

I wish to express my sincerest thanks to all of the Ada 9X Project Team members and to those of you in the Ada community who have so generously given of your time to attend workshops and special meetings, submit revision requests, and review and comment on interim reports.

Publication of this document is a major milestone but we still have a long way to go. I look forward to your continued participation and support in the remaining phases of the Project.

Christine M. Anderson
Ada 9X Project Manager

# 1 Introduction

The purpose of this document is to specify needs that are considered to be the appropriate focus of the Ada 9X revision effort and to identify revision requirements that are to be addressed by the Mapping/Revision Team.

## 1.1 Background

This document is the result of a collective effort to identify the most appropriate kinds of revisions that should be made to the Ada Programming Language (ANSI/MIL-STD-1815A-1983 and ISO 8652-1987). The effort began in January 1988 when the Ada Board was asked to prepare a recommendation to the Ada Joint Program Office (AJPO) on the most appropriate standardization process to use in developing a revised Ada standard, known as Ada 9X. The recommendation [4] was delivered in September 1988 to Virginia Castor, Director, Ada Joint Program Office, who subsequently established the Ada 9X Project for conducting the revision of the Ada Standards. Christine M. Anderson was appointed Project Manager in October 1988.

The Ada 9X effort consists of several phases. The output of the Requirements Definition Phase is this document, which specifies the revision needs to be addressed. The next phase is performed by the Mapping/Revision Team, which is responsible for defining changes to the standard that meet these requirements. The purpose of the Requirements Definition Phase is to identify and prioritize the revision requirements to be addressed by the Mapping/Revision Team.

The requirements definition effort and the mapping/revision efforts are both constrained by the overall objective of the Ada 9X effort [1]:

> Revise ANSI/MIL-STD-1815A-1983 to reflect current essential requirements with minimum negative impact and maximum positive impact to the Ada community.

A revision was undertaken because, according to the Ada Board, "some omissions, limitations, and minor errors have been discovered ... since the ANSI standard was approved. Although a major revision does not appear to be necessary to correct these problems, some revision is warranted." [4] The Ada Board further recommended that the scope of the revision be defined in a document that captures the high-level requirements to be satisfied by the revision. The Board then went on to say, "The objective of the proposed revision should be to select only those changes that improve the usability of the language while minimizing the disruptive effects of changing the standard."

## 1.2 Scope of the Revision

Several key issues affecting the scope of the Ada 9X revision are evident in the revision requests received from the general public [3] and in the results of various workshops and special meetings dealing with the revision (e.g., [2]):

- Dissimilar Needs for Change: Users from different application domains want different changes, and changes that are important to some domains are either unnecessary or detrimental to others. For example, support for decimal arithmetic is important if Ada is to satisfy the needs of information systems developers, but real-time and embedded systems programmers typically have no need for such numeric represen-

## 1: Introduction

tations and would prefer that compiler vendors devote time and effort to supporting other specialized capabilities (often ones that are not critical to information systems).

• Expanding Ada's Domain of Use: There are some Ada users who feel strongly that if Ada 9X is not enhanced in certain areas (e.g., by providing support for distributed systems, object-oriented programming, or information systems), it will fail to attract enough new users to ensure the continued improvement and availability of compilers. In this event, neither the Department of Defense (DoD) nor Ada's non-DoD users would obtain the benefits of a strong competitive market.

• Extent of Change: Many in the Ada community are worried that if Ada 9X incorporates too many changes, Ada 9X compilers will be less efficient, less reliable, and more costly than existing compilers (at least initially). Indeed, the mere prospect of major changes may lead people to delay or reduce their commitment to use Ada because of fears about the length of time it will take for the revised language to stabilize.

• Unstandardized Tailoring of Implementations: Quite a few application-specific needs are being met today by providing implementation-defined (and hence, nonstandard) pragmas, attributes, packages, support tools, etc. Of course, if compiler vendors cater to the needs of special classes of customers by providing specialized compiler support that is not under control of the standard, Ada programs become more vendor-dependent and the benefits of language standardization are increasingly lost. Changes that lead to more implementation uniformity would be helpful here, but increased uniformity is somewhat in conflict with the diversity of user needs and concerns about the potential scope of the revision.

We[1] believe that these concerns can best be met by providing *annexes* in the 9X standard that address specialized application needs. In particular, such annexes should be limited to the following kinds of specifications:

a) Specialized packages. Standard packages of subprograms are often an appropriate means of providing special capabilities needed in given application areas. For example, a package for supporting dynamic priorities might be provided for use by real-time applications, and a package supporting COBOL's "picture" format might be specified for use by information systems applications. Standardizing the interface for such capabilities in annexes should improve Ada's ability to meet specialized needs.

b) Pragmas and Attributes. In Ada 83, only a basic set of required pragmas and attributes is defined. In cases where a special pragma or attribute is the appropriate solution to a specialized need, then a relevant annex will prescribe its exact form and meaning.

c) Representation clauses. The extent to which Ada 83's representation clauses must be supported by all implementations is currently a subject of review by the Ada Rapporteur Group (the group responsible for recommending interpretations of the standard). When this review is completed, there will still be some representation clause behavior that is implementation-dependent. In Ada 9X, it is expected that annexes will impose further restrictions on representation clause support required for the application area addressed by the annex.

---

[1]The Requirements Team.

**1: Introduction**

    d) Performance specifications. Since inefficient support for certain uses of language constructs is tantamount to non-support as far as some applications are concerned, each annex is expected to address critical performance issues that cannot or need not be satisfied by all implementations.

In short, Ada 9X annexes will permit the standard to address specialized needs without requiring support by all compilers. This will improve the degree of uniformity that can be achieved as compared with the current standard because the annexes will impose restrictions on capabilities where the current standard imposes none. For example, an Information Systems annex might specify how representation clauses are to be used to support packed decimal representations and it might specify that at least 18 digits of precision are required. Such a requirement probably should not be imposed on all implementations. Consequently this requirement is not addressed at all in Ada 83 and the result is lack of uniform support for this capability even for implementations that are attempting to address the needs of Information Systems applications.

The annex concept should give greater freedom to the Mapping/Revision Team to address the needs of specialized application areas without having to be overly concerned that a specified capability is inappropriate for some community of users (since not every implementation will have to support the required capability).

A possible advantage of this approach is that it allows for incremental transition to an Ada 9X implementation that supports all the annexes — implementers can decide to concentrate initially on supporting just those annexes of greatest interest to their customer base. Of course, some implementers (e.g., those targeting the education market) may decide not to support any of the annexes, thereby allowing them to implement Ada 9X with less effort. The other advantage, of course, is that the annexes allow the specialized and critical needs of different user communities to be addressed explicitly in the standard.

The role of the annexes in compiler validation needs to be kept in mind during the revision. The Mapping/Revision Team should assume that validation policy can be developed to help ensure that the purpose of the specialized annexes is achieved. One possibility is that validation certificates would mention only those annexes that are fully supported by an implementation. Moreover, it is probably reasonable to allow an implementation to provide only partial support for additional annexes without claiming validation status for such support.[2] The details need to be worked out during the revision and depend to some extent on the nature of the specialized annexes.

Of course, the notion of annexes needs to be refined further during the revision. The Mapping/Revision Team must determine how many annexes are necessary (there should not be many) and their interrelationship (e.g., whether a specified pragma appears in more than one annex). In refining this concept, the Mapping/Revision Team should keep in mind that the main purpose of the annex notion is to allow Ada 9X to address a broader spectrum of user needs than might otherwise be possible, thereby expanding Ada's domain of use while respecting the incompatible nature of some required capabilities and the need to limit the overall extent of change.

---

[2]Some existing compilers might already support some of the capabilities required by a given annex.

1: Introduction

## 1.3 Structure and Terminology

This document is organized to reflect groups of needs for improving the usability of Ada. Each chapter is devoted to a different group of needs. After specifying a revision need in user-oriented terms, we specify topics to be addressed by the Mapping/Revision Team. The topics are prioritized as either *Requirements* or *Study Topics* with the intent that the Mapping/Revision Team work primarily on satisfying the *Requirements*. Revisions that are not covered by either a Requirement or a Study Topic are considered outside the scope of the 9X revision effort.

It is expected that some revision needs will be satisfied by providing additional language features (syntax, semantics, attributes, or pragmas) while others may simply impose performance constraints on implementations. Having the revised standard address performance issues reflects the fact that the *way* in which a feature is supported is sometimes critical to its usability in particular applications. It is expected that performance issues of particular interest to different user communities will be addressed in separate annexes of the standard.

Generally we do not specify whether the solution to a particular requirement[3] should be given in one of the special annexes or in the main body of the standard. This decision is left to the Mapping/Revision Team because it depends on the nature of the solutions to the requirements. On the other hand, some requirements seem sufficiently specialized to merit being addressed in a special annex; we sometimes mention this in our discussion of a requirement to remind the reader that we realize the requirement could lead to solutions that are of little general interest or are inapplicable for programming some applications.

A user need or requirement may be appropriate for more than one application domain. If so, we generally state the need or requirement for only that domain considered to be the dominant source for the requirement (based on the results of the various workshops and written materials submitted during the Requirements Phase).

Not all user needs are reflected in the stated Requirements because it is not clear that all such needs can be satisfied with the requisite minimal impact on implementations. Also, for some needs it is unclear whether the benefits of making a change are worth the potential costs. Such needs are sometimes reflected in Study Topics when it was felt that it would be appropriate for the Mapping/Revision Team to give attention to the topic, but not at the cost of neglecting the more important topics stated as Requirements. Revisions addressing Study Topics must have a low negative impact.

Requests for language changes came from a variety of sources, including Revision Requests (RRs) submitted by the public [3], various Workshops and special meetings sponsored by the Ada 9X Project (e.g., [2], and Ada Commentaries [5]. A separate document, "Rationale for the Ada 9X Requirements," will list all submitted RRs and will discuss how each is related to the Requirements and Study Topics presented here. A few RRs, workshop proceedings, Ada commentaries, and other sources are cited directly in this document when they provide additional explanation and background that could not be presented directly while keeping the document short. We

---

[3]The lack of an initial capital "R" means we are neutrally referring to one of the topics to be addressed by the Mapping/Revision Team without distinguishing whether it is classified as a Requirement or as a Study Topic.

**1: Introduction**

also acknowledge RRs and other sources when they have been directly helpful in suggesting the wording of specific requirements or user needs. A revision request is cited as RR-dddd, which is the number of the RR that can be found in [3]. An approved Ada Commentary is cited as AI-ddddd, which is the number of the commentary as found in [5].

## 1.4 General Guidelines for the Mapping/Revision Team

The following guidelines provide overall guidance to the Mapping/Revision Team. The Mapping/Revision Team must make appropriate tradeoffs when the guidelines cannot be satisfied simultaneously.

**G-1: Minimum Disruption:** Changes shall minimize disruption to the Ada community while satisfying as many of the recognized needs as possible. In particular, this guideline covers the following criteria:

- **Implementation Ease:** The recommended changes shall be relatively easy to implement with existing compiler technology.

- **Execution Efficiency:** Changes to Ada shall not negatively affect object code efficiency.

- **User Need:** The extent of a change shall not be out of proportion with the degree of user need for the change.

- **Upward Compatibility:** In general, any legal Ada 83 program must also be a legal Ada 9X program and must have the same effect allowed or required by Ada 83. However, to improve the portability of Ada programs, and to satisfy other requirements, it may be necessary to eliminate some effects allowed by Ada 83 or to make some Ada 83 programs illegal. In these cases, the following guidelines shall apply:

    - No implementation-dependent behavior allowed in Ada 83 shall be excluded in Ada 9X if that behavior is actually supported by a significant number of implementations and is important to a significant number of users.

    - No Ada 83 program shall be illegal in Ada 9X unless it is relatively easy to correct the illegal program or it is expected that very few existing legal programs will be affected (since the programs are either pathological or erroneous).

    - No legal Ada 83 program shall have a different semantic effect in Ada 9X unless it is expected that extremely few existing programs will be affected (e.g., it might be acceptable to modify the optimization rules in ways that affect when the evaluation of an expression requires CONSTRAINT_ERROR or NUMERIC_ERROR to be raised).

    Any non-upward-compatible changes shall be justified by the Mapping/Revision Team and where possible, accompanied by an analysis of techniques for detecting possible incompatibilities in existing programs.

**G-2: Reliability/Safety/Maintainability:** Support for the reliability, safety, and long-term maintainability of large, complex systems shall take precedence over convenience of Ada coding. For example, this means greatly favoring statically checkable rules over rules checked at run-time, and favoring run-time checks over uncheckable rules (erroneous behavior).

## 2 General Requirements

There are a number of revision requirements that almost go without saying, since the revision of any language standard must at least address the small defects that have been discovered during the use of the standard. In addition, the overall structure and style of the revised standard present fundamental issues that must be addressed by the requirements. These basic requirements are addressed here.

## 2.1 Presentation Requirements

<u>User Need U2.1-A</u>: **Improve Wording to Reflect the Intended Meaning:** A number of commentaries on the existing standard have been approved by the Ada Joint Program Office (AJPO) or by the ISO Working Group responsible for the standardization of Ada (ISO-IEC/JTC1/SC22/ WG9). The commentaries serve to correct unintended implications of the wording of the current standard and to point out places where some users have had difficulty in understanding the standard's intent. To minimize different interpretations among Ada users and implementers, the wording of the standard should be revised, where necessary, to reflect these clarifications.

**Requirement R2.1-A(1) — Incorporate Approved Commentaries:** Ada 9X shall incorporate the approved Ada Commentaries [5] to the extent that they do not conflict with changes dictated by other requirements and to the extent that incorporation makes the wording of the standard clearer.

**Discussion:** WG9's Ada Rapporteur Group (ARG) has been developing a report (the *Ada Commentary Integration Document* (ACID)) that reflects the impact of the approved commentaries by suggesting revised wording for appropriate sections of the standard. ACID would be a good starting point for satisfying this requirement. Of course, some of the approved commentaries may be inconsistent with changes suggested by the Mapping/Revision Team to meet other requirements, and in this case, the commentary should not be incorporated into the revised standard. In addition, since the process for developing the commentaries was limited to maintenance changes, some of the clarifications proposed by the commentaries may not be appropriate given the latitude for change allowed by the Ada 9X revision process. In short, the approved commentaries should be reflected in the revised standard only when the intent of the commentary is consistent with the overall nature of the Ada 9X revisions.

**Requirement R2.1-A(2) — Review Other Presentation Suggestions:** Ada Commentaries in the "Presentation" class as well as the Revision Requests shall be examined for suggested wording improvements. Appropriate suggestions shall be incorporated into the revised standard.

**Discussion:** Commentaries in the "Presentation" class have not generally been formally approved by the Ada Rapporteur Group and WG9, but some of them make useful suggestions for improving the presentation of the standard. Similarly, some revision requests point out areas where the clarity of the wording can perhaps be improved.

<u>User Need U2.1-B</u>: **Maintain Continuity with the Existing Standard:** Since most users of Ada 83 are familiar with the structure and format of the existing standard, it is important that the revised standard retain that structure and format.

### 2: General Requirements

**Requirement R2.1-B(1) — Maintain Format of Existing Standard:** The Ada 9X standard shall be similar in style and structure to the existing standard. Chapter and section headings and their order shall be retained to the largest extent possible. The presentation style shall also be retained.

**Discussion:** The structure and style of the Ada 83 standard must be retained by Ada 9X in order to preserve continuity with Ada 83. Maintaining the same document structure and style will also help to minimize the impact of changes on programmers.

**User Need U2.1-C: Derivative Use of the Standard:** Compiler vendors and other organizations have found it helpful to provide annotated versions of the standard that reflect vendor implementation decisions or approved commentaries. Providing a machine-readable version of the standard would facilitate such use.

**Requirement R2.1-C(1) — Machine-Readable Version of the Standard:** A machine-readable version of the Ada 9X standard shall be made available using a widely supported formatting language.

**Discussion:** Providing a version of the standard that contains formatting commands will make it easier to incorporate its content into data bases. In addition, some implementers and other organizations have produced annotated versions of the current standard that are helpful to users. This is easier to do if the standard is made available with machine-readable formatting codes.

## 2.2 Efficiency, Simplicity, and Consistency

**User Need U2.2-A: Minimize Compilation and Execution Costs:** The language must permit efficient compilation and execution of useful combinations of language features. Appendix Section A.1 on page 57 includes some of the cases that shall be considered.

**Requirement R2.2-A(1) — Reduce Deterrents to Efficiency:** Combinations of language features shall not incur compilation and execution costs (in time and space) that are significantly increased primarily because of extremely unlikely interactions with other language features.

**Discussion:** For example, AI-00867 notes that the ability to access a task outside its master makes it difficult for an implementation to decide when it can release the task's space, especially when the task is returned as part of a composite object. Similar cases need to be identified and resolved as part of the Ada 9X revision.

**User Need U2.2-B: Ease of Learning:** Language rules should be easy to teach and easy to remember.

**Requirement R2.2-B(1) — Understandability:** Rules that have proven to be confusing or error-prone to users shall be reviewed and eliminated when possible. Appendix Section A.2 on page 57 includes some of the rules that shall be considered for revision.

**User Need U2.2-C: Generality:** Sensible uses and combinations of language constructs should be allowed.

**Requirement R2.2-C(1) — Minimize Special-Case Restrictions:** To the extent consistent with Requirement R2.2-B(1), Ada 9X shall minimize exceptions to general rules specifying how language constructs interact. Special uses and combinations of language constructs shall be eliminated. Appendix Sections A.3 on page 58 and A.4 on page 60 list some of the existing rules that shall be considered for revision.

**Discussion:** Experience with Ada 83 has revealed a number of opportunities for simplifying, generalizing, or otherwise revising the language rules so as to avoid unusually large compilation or execution costs and to make the language easier to learn. The above Needs and Requirements direct the Mapping/Revision Team to reexamine the rationale for the original language rules in such areas. If the reasons are no longer applicable, appropriate corrections should be made, consistent with the general guidelines **G-1** and **G-2**.

It should be noted that the above requirements directly conflict with each other. Minimizing costs of unused capabilities is typically satisfied by having special case restrictions, thus violating User Need 2.2-B (Ease of Learning) and User Need 2.2-C (Generality). User Need 2.2-B can be satisfied by making the language very general and orthogonal, risking inefficiencies that would violate User Need 2.2-A, or by simplifying and restricting the language, which could violate User Need 2.2-C. The Mapping/Revision Team must find an appropriate balance among these conflicting requirements.

## 2.3 Error Detection

**User Need U2.3-A: Minimize Consequences of Programmer Error:** Violations of language rules should be detected by pre-execution checks whenever practical. When such checks are not practical, violations should be detected by run-time checks, so exception handlers can recover from the error, or so programs can be abandoned in a safe and predictable manner. Whenever practical, violations should not place a program in an undefined state with unpredictable consequences.

**Study Topic S2.3-A(1) — Improve Early Detection of Errors:** If an implementation is able to detect that certain run-time program errors are present (e.g., that execution will necessarily be erroneous or that initialization of a declared object will necessarily raise an exception), the implementation shall provide an option for rejecting the compilation (that is, not adding it to the program library). A similar option shall also be provided when a restriction associated with a pragma has been violated.

**Discussion:** Implementations can sometimes detect at compile-time that the execution of a program will be erroneous or will raise a predefined exception such as CONSTRAINT_ERROR or STORAGE_ERROR. Such situations, especially those that can be easily detected at compile-time, are almost always programmer errors. In general, programmers want as much help in detecting possible problems as they can get. Moreover, they want to be able to count on the nature of such help as they port applications among compilers. Ada 9X can help achieve these goals by specifying more clearly that implementations are allowed to reject compilations containing probable run-time errors of the kind specified in the requirement. This recognition of errors also applies to the use of certain pragmas, e.g., pragmas that inform an implementation of the programmer's intent to avoid the use of certain language features (e.g., see Requirement R9.3-A(1) on page 47).

## 2: General Requirements

Of course, implementations today are allowed to issue "warning" messages in these situations, and they can provide an optional mode of operation in which certain kinds of warnings cause compilations to be rejected, but this potentially useful behavior is not uniformly provided. For some applications (such as safety critical and trusted system applications), a special annex might specify that implementations must definitely detect certain kinds of these situations, requiring that a compilation be rejected if such situations are detected.

On the other hand, there are some compilations that should not be rejected even though they appear to contain these kinds of errors. For example, a program might appear to reference an uninitialized variable but the programmer may know that the variable is given a valid value when the system is loaded. In such cases, there must be some standard way for programmers to ensure that the compilation is not rejected.

This requirement is classified as a "Study Topic" because it is not completely clear how far the Ada 9X standard should or can go in specifying situations that *must* be detected. Such a list might be application-dependent, e.g., trusted and safety-critical systems might want to impose more severe constraints on error detection than would be considered cost-effective for other application areas. Moreover, not all such errors can be easily detected at compile-time. Requiring that all compilers detect certain errors of this kind could impose an unacceptable implementation burden on some compilers, e.g., inexpensive compilers that are intended for the education market.

**Requirement R2.3-A(2) — Limit Consequences of Erroneous Executions:** Run-time violations of language rules shall have narrowly defined consequences. Whenever practical, a violation shall result in the raising of an exception. When the raising of an exception is not practical, the possible consequences of the violation shall be few, confined to limited aspects of the computation state, and defined in the standard. This definition shall be in terms of those aspects of the computation state addressed elsewhere in the standard. To the extent possible, catastrophic consequences shall be excluded.

**Discussion:** In Ada 83 most rules are enforced either by compile-time or run-time checks. For a small number of rules, neither compile-time nor run-time checks are practical. In general, violation of such rules can have unpredictable consequences. Execution is said to become "erroneous" when such a rule is violated.

The consequences of erroneous execution can be devastating. For example, an arbitrary storage location can be overwritten when assigning to an array component if the array index is known to have an appropriate range but has an undefined value. In such a case, Ada 83 does not require that a range check be performed because an implementation is allowed to assume that the index has an acceptable value. Ada 9X could require that a range check be performed in such cases (except when RANGE_CHECK has been suppressed), but the net effect of such a rule might be to discourage implementations from removing truly unnecessary range checks, so the solution in this case is not obvious.

The possibility of devastating consequences is more easily eliminated in other cases. For example, execution is rendered erroneous by a subprogram call whose effect depends on the parameter-passing mechanism, but for any reasonable implementation only a small number of precisely defined effects are possible — the call proceeds normally with each parameter passed either by copy or by reference. Such a rule change would tighten the language while probably having little or no effect on implementations.

In short, the problem addressed by the requirement is a difficult one. The situations giving rise to erroneous program executions were given close attention in the original design. Nonetheless, it is important that these situations be re-examined in the Ada 9X revision.

## 2.4 Controlling Implementation-Dependent Choices

**User Need U2.4-A:** **Uniformity of Compiler Behavior:** Because Ada is intended to be a language that enhances the portability of software, Ada programs should behave in the same way for different implementations. In some cases, Ada 83 has deliberately permitted implementation freedom to reflect expected variations in user needs as well as in target and operating system environments. For example, the range of the subtype PRIORITY is not specified since the intention is that this range reflect both user needs and operating systems capabilities. There is a need to minimize these implementation-dependent choices, since in practice they cause difficulty in porting programs.

**Requirement R2.4-A(1) — Minimize Implementation Dependences:** Implementation dependences permitted in Ada 9X shall be justified by considerations of target architecture variations and different needs of applications. Ada 9X shall specify performance parameters and constraints affecting the use of critical constructs, although, since such constraints are typically application dependent, they should usually be specified in annexes.

**Discussion:** In some cases, Ada 83 permits implementation-dependent behavior in anticipation of operating system and target variability, but experience has shown that more uniformity can be achieved. WG9's Uniformity Rapporteur Group (URG) has been systematically investigating such variations and is in the process of producing uniformity recommendations. For example, Ada 83 specifies that the status of unclosed files at program termination is undefined, but the URG recommends that external files be closed on program termination. In some cases, it is not possible to completely eliminate variations among implementations, but their effect can be minimized. For example, the behavior of the I/O packages has proven to be more implementation dependent than seems necessary (e.g., with respect to the ability to open the same external file with different data types or the behavior of TEXT_IO when applied to terminals).

Another source of implementation dependence is in the efficiency with which certain constructs and combinations of constructs are supported by an implementation. If an application's use of time or space is critically dependent on how an implementation supports a particular construct, then application programmers should be able to determine or control the performance associated with their use of the construct. Such constraints have typically not been a part of a language standard, but given their importance in fostering the usability of Ada implementations and the portability of Ada programs, it is appropriate for Ada 9X to attempt improvements in this area.

# 3 Requirements for International Users

Ada is an international language. However Ada 83 does not adequately address the need for handling non-English character sets. In addition, the Ada 83 syntax is inconvenient for use by non-English speaking programmers. These issues were identified during the ISO standardization process for Ada 83 and a commitment was made by ISO-IEC/JTC1/SC22/WG9, the ISO group responsible for the Ada standard, that the character set issue would be addressed when the ISO standard was next revised. Since a goal of the Ada 9X effort is to maintain Ada as an international standard, this ISO commitment must be addressed.

## 3.1 International Character Sets

**User Need U3.1-A:** **International Character Set:** The character set of Ada 9X must be convenient for international use. In particular:

1. It must be convenient to write applications that deal with character sets of languages other than English.

2. Ada must be convenient to use for programmers whose native language is not English.

3. Despite differences in national character sets, there must be no country-specific variations affecting Ada's syntax and lexical rules; these rules must continue to be completely defined by the standard.

**Discussion:** The Ada 83 character set represents a rather small subset of the graphic symbols used in natural languages throughout the world. This fact complicates writing programs and handling character and string data in non-English-speaking communities. Enhancement of Ada's character set will help extend the world-wide use of Ada.

It follows from item 1 of the User Need that the alphabet of character and string literals must include additional characters and that there must be functionality equivalent to the present TEXT_IO package for such alphabets.

A minimum response to item 2, already reflected in commentary AI-00339, is that non-English characters must be permitted in comments; it is desirable that they also be permitted in identifiers. However, various meetings with members of the international community have indicated that the translation of reserved words is not considered to be a requirement, and indeed such a translation would be difficult to achieve in a manner that did not conflict with item 3.

Item 3 reflects the need to guard against variations in Ada rules that could make it difficult to process Ada code (such as standard packages) using compilers produced in different countries. In particular, despite the needed extension of Ada's character set, any Ada lexical element accepted by one Ada compiler must be accepted by all.

**Requirement R3.1-A(1) — Base Character Set:** The Ada 9X type STANDARD.CHARACTER shall be based on ISO 8859 [22], an 8-bit standard for character representation, in the same way that the Ada 83 character set is based on the ISO 646 [21], a 7-bit standard.

**Discussion:** This requirement introduces the potential for incompatibility with existing programs (for example, in constructs such as case statements and array aggregates that might require

**3: Requirements for International Users**

choices for every value of type CHARACTER), but it has been widely recognized that an 8-bit standard is more appropriate as the base character set. ISO 8859 actually defines a number of different 8-bit character sets, and the Ada 9X design must take this into account.

It is intended that the semantics of the predefined ordering operators for STRINGs continue to be based on the ordering of the elements of the (extended) type CHARACTER, even though this ordering will not be "lexicographic" with respect to graphic symbols (e.g., ' ê ' will not be sorted next to ' e ', since the underlying character codes are not adjacent).

**Requirement R3.1-A(2) — Extended Graphic Literals:** Ada 9X shall permit the use of character and string literals containing non-English characters, including those from international character sets with more than 256 graphic symbols.

**Requirement R3.1-A(3) — Extended Character Set Support:** Ada 9X shall provide input/output facilities and other operations for extended character sets (specifically, for international character sets with more than 256 graphic symbols). The operations shall be comparable to those provided for the current base character set.

**Discussion:** The two requirements above address the issue of very large character sets, in particular, those of Asian countries such as Japan, China, and Korea. Ada 9X must provide a way to support these and other international languages. Where possible, Ada 9X should be consistent with ISO standards that are developing in this area.

These requirements should not be interpreted as mandating a method of displaying extended graphic symbols in source text. Instead, the point is that Ada 9X must support character types that require more than eight bits for their representation (typically 16 or 32), and must support the corresponding string types, file operations, etc. The Ada 9X report on character set issues [9] discusses these points in more detail.

**Requirement R3.1-A(4) — Extended Comment Syntax:** The use of international character sets (including those with more than 256 characters) shall continue to be permitted in comments in Ada 9X source code.

**Discussion:** The inclusion of extended characters in comments raises no conceptual problems since this is allowed in Ada 83 (see AI-00339).

**Study Topic S3.1-A(5) — Extended Identifier Syntax:** Ada 9X shall permit the use of extended character sets in identifiers while continuing to keep Ada's syntax and lexical rules independent of source code representation.

**Discussion:** The identifier issue is somewhat complex. Among issues to be considered is the applicability of the upper-lower case equivalence rule. The various parts of the ISO 8859 standard present difficulties here. For example, a character code that represents a letter in one part of ISO 8859 may represent a non-alphabetic graphic symbol in another part.[4] A general solution providing completely satisfactory use of identifiers for all languages may be unacceptably complex. One suggestion is that at least Latin-1 be permitted, which fully meets the needs of all

---

[4]For example, the character code representing the Greek letter $\chi$ in Part 7 of ISO 8859 represents the + symbol in Part 1 (Latin-1).

### 3: Requirements for International Users

Western European countries. It is reasonable to move at least this far — the question of how much further to go needs study.

It is highly desirable that the Ada 9X solutions in this area be compatible with the recommendations of WG9's Character Rapporteur Group (CRG), since the CRG's recommendations are likely to be used as guidelines for accommodating international character sets in existing Ada 83 implementations.

In considering possible extensions of identifier syntax, it should be kept in mind that Ada 83 does not specify the physical form of source programs, and this approach could be continued in Ada 9X — the standard does not need to specify how to convert alternative source code representations into the representation accepted by a given compiler. Separate standards for representing source code may be desirable since methods for representing text are not well standardized, but such standards are outside the scope of the Ada 9X revision effort.

# 4 Support for Programming Paradigms

This Chapter deals with a variety of issues related to expressive power — the ability to use Ada in a way that is consistent with modern software engineering practice and that meets the needs inherent in programming a broad variety of applications. Some of the needs expressed in this Chapter derive from experience in using Ada and some are derived from experience in using other languages.

## 4.1 Subprograms

**User Need U4.1-A: Dynamic Subprogram Selection:** One common programming idiom involves deciding at run time which subprogram is to be applied to a particular parameter list. This style of programming arises naturally in a number of situations, e.g.

- when processing input messages and the action to be taken depends partly on the content of certain fields in a message;

- when traversing a data structure and different actions are to be taken depending on the values found at each point in the structure;

- when associating actions with user-interface buttons. The action to be taken can depend on the current input mode. When the mode changes, the set of actions to be taken is easily and quickly changed simply by pointing to a different table of subprograms. Moreover, the user sometimes determines what subprogram is to be associated with a given button, mouse key, etc. This means the action to be taken in response to some selection criterion is not known at compile time.

- when needing to change the effect of a group of subroutines without passing the same subprogram to each subroutine as a parameter. This can occur when specifying a "trap" procedure that is to be called when an exceptional situation occurs and the routine detecting the situation doesn't want to raise an exception (e.g., because the routine is written in another language or because the trap procedure is expected to take a recovery action that allows processing to continue at the point where the exception situation was detected). Such a need has arisen in defining Ada bindings to the IEEE floating point standard and to SQL (e.g., see [11]).

In addition, some programs can be updated more easily and reliably if the subprograms to be selected are stored separately from the selection code; updating a table of subprograms that are called in certain situations can be less error-prone than modifying the selection code itself and promotes better program modularity. This "table-driven" programming style is a common paradigm that should be supported directly by Ada.

**Study Topic S4.1-A(1) — Subprograms as Objects:** Ada 9X should provide:

1. an easily implemented and efficient mechanism for dynamically selecting a subprogram that is to be called with a particular argument list;

2. a means of separating the set of subprograms that can be selected dynamically from the code that makes the selection.

**Discussion:** An obvious solution to this requirement is to provide subprogram types and variables.

### 4: Support for Programming Paradigms

This requirement is presented as a Study Topic because there are a number of well-known and difficult language design issues posed by such a solution (e.g., ensuring that non-local entities referenced by subprograms exist when the subprogram is called). In addition, there are problems unique to Ada such as possible interactions with overloading rules, the propagation of exceptions, and the notation for distinguishing between a reference to a parameterless function variable and a call on the value of the variable. Given the complexity of the design issues, it is appropriate to categorize this requirement as a Study Topic.

Of course, one way to select subprograms at run-time in Ada 83 is to use a case statement; each case alternative calls a different subprogram with the same argument list for each call. The case statement approach does not, however, satisfy item 2 of the Study Topic since the unit containing the case statement must be modified directly when changing the subprograms to be called. Direct modification is not necessary if the subprograms are contained in a data structure that is separate from the selection code.

This Study Topic interacts strongly with Study Topic S4.3-B(1) on page 21.

**User Need U4.1-B: Interfacing with Non-Ada Subprograms:** Ada programs must interface with non-Ada procedures and functions, including some that pass subprograms as parameters. Ada 9X should ensure greater uniformity in how implementations support such interfaces.

**Requirement R4.1-B(1) — Passing Subprograms as Parameters:** Ada 9X shall provide a uniform means of passing subprograms as parameters to non-Ada procedures and functions.

**Discussion:** Because the ability to pass subprograms as parameters to procedures and functions is provided by other widely used languages (particularly, FORTRAN and C), there exist important libraries of subprograms that make use of this capability (e.g., standard FORTRAN mathematics libraries, interfaces to windowing systems, database manager interfaces, etc.). Ada programs need the ability to call such "foreign" routines in a standard and reliable way.

The use of generic formal subprograms is not a solution to the problem of interfacing with non-Ada subprograms that require subprogram parameters since pragma INTERFACE cannot be applied to a generic unit. Consequently, less reliable workarounds must be used in implementations today that support this requirement (e.g., the subprogram parameter is declared as an access type and unchecked conversion is used to pass the address of the desired subprogram).

The ability to pass subprograms directly as parameters to any Ada procedure or function (not just to those that interface with foreign code) is a viable solution to this requirement that could be justified by the requirement for generality (see Requirement R2.2-C(1) on page 8). Moreover, such a capability would provide an easily implemented solution to one situation in which generic code sharing is required (see Requirement R4.4-C(1) on page 23). Finally, the need to manipulate subprograms as objects (see Study Topic S4.1-A(1) above) also leads naturally to a general ability to pass subprograms as parameters. However, the ability to pass subprograms as parameters does not pose as many complex language design issues as does the general ability to manipulate subprograms as objects.

**Requirement R4.1-B(2) — Pragma INTERFACE:** Ada 9X shall provide standard methods for specifying the link name of an externally defined subprogram and for specifying the parameter passing mechanism that is to be used. Other capabilities associated with pragma INTERFACE that are commonly provided by implementations today shall also be considered for standard-ization (e.g., see [15]).

**Discussion:** There are a variety of implementation-dependent pragmas that in effect, extend the functionality of pragma INTERFACE. The most common extension is to define the link name of the external subprogram (since the name might not conform to Ada's syntax for subprogram names). Another, somewhat less common extension allows a programmer to specify the parameter passing mechanism. Extended support for pragma INTERFACE is one of the most common areas in which implementation-dependent pragmas have been created [15]. Ada 9X needs to standardize the means of providing this information.

## 4.2 Storage Management

<u>User Need U4.2-A</u>: **Control of Storage Use:** In many applications the programmer requires precise control over the allocation and deallocation of data storage. In the extreme (and realistic) case of a long-running application, allocation without reclamation is unacceptable, whether the storage is allocated explicitly by the programmer or implicitly by the run-time system.[5] In addi-tion, the ability to provide specialized storage management algorithms is often essential when tuning an application's performance.

**Requirement R4.2-A(1) — Allocation and Reclamation of Storage:** Ada 9X shall allow an application to ensure that storage is allocated and reclaimed efficiently and predictably.

**Discussion:** In some applications, it is necessary to predict when storage is reclaimed and to ensure that the time taken to reclaim storage is not greater than some bound. In other applica-tions, it is only important to be sure that storage will be reclaimed without needing to know exactly when or how long it will take. At the minimum, implementations should ensure against storage leaks, that is, the inability to reuse storage that no longer contains values of interest to a program.

**Study Topic S4.2-A(2) — Preservation of Abstraction:** To the extent possible, Ada 9X shall meet Requirement R4.2-A(1) in a manner that allows storage allocation and reclamation to be controlled reliably for user-defined data types.

**Discussion:** A programmer implementing an abstract data type in terms of dynamic data struc-tures needs to be able to determine when memory used for values of that type may be reclaimed. At a minimum, the programmer should be able to gain control whenever storage is allocated and whenever a scope is deactivated. (Note that user-defined assignment and finalization appear to be needed here.)

Meeting this requirement will assist the programmer in controlling storage deallocation. In Ada 83, it can be difficult to insulate a user of a type from the decision to use dynamic data structures for its implementation unless garbage collection is provided; there is no way for the implementer of a type to determine when an abstract object is no longer needed. For time-critical applications,

---

[5]For example, some implementations allocate storage implicitly on the heap when an object's size can vary widely at run-time. Such storage must be subject to reclamation at an appropriate time.

storage allocation and reclamation actions must occur at predictable times and must be accomplished in a bounded amount of time.

## 4.3 Composition of Program Units

One of the principal design goals of Ada was to support the development of programs from separately compiled units while providing the same degree of checking as for a program compiled as a whole. Experience with Ada 83 has shown that Ada's rules for checking separately compiled units can sometimes make it difficult to minimize recompilation costs when programs are modified. Moreover, it is important to make it easier for programmers to compose programs by specializing and extending existing units. The needs and requirements expressed in this section address different aspects of these problems.

**User Need U4.3-A: Reduced Recompilation:** When a program unit is changed in a way that does not logically affect the behavior of other units, recompilation of these units should not be required or should be easy to avoid.

**Discussion:** From a user point of view the need is clear — changes that the programmer believes should have no effect on dependent units (e.g., the addition of new subprogram declarations to a package specification; a change to the initial value of a variable; the introduction of a new type declaration; a change to a subprogram body) should not require recompilation of other units. But Ada's rules make it difficult for a compiler to decide that a particular change will have no effect on dependent units: adding a new subprogram declaration could change the result of overloading resolution in dependent units; changing the initial value of a variable could lead to a change in the object code if a compiler performed optimizations based on its knowledge of the initial value; the introduction of a new type or object declaration could change the visibility of a name in a dependent unit; changing the body of a subprogram in a package usually means recompiling the whole package body, and it is not always easy to turn such subprograms into subunits because subunit names cannot be overloaded; changing the body of certain generic units could lead to recompilation of all units that instantiate the generic unit since in some cases, these instantiations could now be illegal. In short, Ada 83's recompilation rules, while ensuring that collections of units are consistent in their interdependences, have in practice made it complicated for implementations and programmers to avoid logically unnecessary recompilations.

**Study Topic S4.3-A(1) — Reducing the Need for Recompilation:** Ada 9X recompilation and related rules should be revised so it is easier for implementations to minimize the need for recompilation and for programmers to use program structures that reduce the need for recompilation.

**Discussion:** The Mapping/Revision Team should determine what changes would make it easier for implementations to avoid logically unnecessary recompilations. Some of these changes might affect how programmers use Ada. For example, allowing subunit names to be overloaded would allow programmers to use subunits more freely, helping to ensure that any change to a body will not result in recompilation of other units belonging to the same package body.

This requirement is categorized as a Study Topic because it is not clear to what extent Ada 9X can change Ada's recompilation rules without introducing possibly subtle semantic changes into existing Ada programs. Solutions to the next requirement, which deals with the need to adapt and

**4: Support for Programming Paradigms**

extend existing units without physically modifying them, may also serve to reduce the need for recompilation.

**User Need U4.3-B: Programming by Adaptation of Existing Units:** When adapting an existing package to new uses, programmers typically change just a few properties of the package. For example, the package might be adapted to new uses by adding several subprograms or by modifying the implementation of an existing subprogram. Similarly, an existing record type and its operations might be reused by extending its declaration. An increasing number of programmers want to program in this style.

**Discussion:** This User Need expresses one of the benefits of "object-oriented" programming, namely, the ability to adapt existing code to new uses by extending type declarations and adding new operations or modifying existing ones. Although Ada 83 supports this need to some extent, improvements are needed. (See [12] for a more detailed discussion of some of the difficulties encountered when attempting to use Ada 83 in this style.)

**Study Topic S4.3-B(1) — Programming by Specialization/Extension:** Ada 9X shall make it possible to define new declared entities whose properties are adapted from those of existing entities by the addition or modification of properties or operations in such a way that:

• the original entity's definition and implementation are not modified;

• the new entity (or instances thereof) can be used anywhere the original one could be, in exactly the same way.

**Discussion:** The statement of this requirement is taken from [2, p. 30]. The kinds of entities for which specialization and extension are required include types, subtypes, subprograms, packages, and generic units.

An important concept in software reuse is that a software component may be parameterized by a type. A parameterized component should work not only for a given type but also for any of a number of related types constructed from the original type. The advantage of constructing related types by specialization and extension of existing types is that there are broad conditions under which operations defined for the original type continue to be meaningful for the constructed types. This means that common underlying capabilities can be implemented and shared easily among related types in a layered fashion. When the construction of related types is combined with the ability to dynamically select a subprogram to be called (as specified in Study Topic S4.1-A(1) on page 17), the result can be a form of polymorphism.

This requirement is specified as a Study Topic mainly because of concern about the amount of change that might be required to support it effectively and the possible difficulty of integrating such changes smoothly into the existing language. Nonetheless, satisfying this requirement is considered to be important as a means of increasing Ada's ability to support software reuse.

Although the inspiration for the User Need and Study Topic arises from the so-called object-oriented languages, these generally provide more than is called for here. However, what is required here will go a long way toward improving Ada's support for software reuse.

**User Need U4.3-C: Library Support:** When developing large systems, developers need to exploit the program library in complex ways. For example, developers need to use multiple libraries in conjunction with version control systems, and they need the ability to partition a library so not all library packages are necessarily visible.

**4: Support for Programming Paradigms**

**Study Topic S4.3-C(1) — Enhanced Library Support:** Ada 9X shall make it easier for implementations to provide improved library management support and when possible, shall improve the uniformity with which such support is provided.

**Discussion:** The Ada concept of a program library exists primarily to ensure that separately compiled units can be combined with the same degree of checking as if they had been compiled as a single unit. In attempting to specify this goal, the standard uses words that sometimes seem to limit unnecessarily the services an implementation can provide to a user (see RR-0091, for example). On the other hand, implementations vary considerably in the library management services they provide. For example, some implementations support multiple libraries and can support multiple versions of units while others are quite restricted in their capabilities. These differences cause difficulties in porting Ada programs across compilers. Although Ada intended to provide wide implementation freedom in support for libraries, some improved standardization would be useful and may be possible.

This requirement is classified as a Study Topic because it is uncertain what library management functions are sufficiently proven that they should be specified at least in an Ada 9X annex.

## 4.4 Generics

There are three broad areas of user needs for generics. One is support for development of reusable components; this requires a facility with expressive power and general parameterizability. The second is separation of concerns between the users and the implementer of a generic unit. The third area is code space efficiency, sometimes known as code sharing.

There are conflicts among some of these needs, and Ada 83 offers one particular compromise. In the light of user experience, the Mapping/Revision Team should examine the tradeoffs that were made, identify which if any language improvements are required, and make the necessary revisions.

**User Need U4.4-A: Support for Reusability:** The design of a generic unit involves abstracting from particular instances to a general template, where the variability across the instances is reflected in the values passed as parameters at instantiations. A fundamental need, then, is for the language to supply sufficiently general generic parameterization to allow the definition of wide classes of reusable components such as data structures (lists, queues), graphics packages, etc.

**Study Topic S4.4-A(1) — Generic Formal Parameters:** Ada 9X should enhance generics to liberalize the uses of generic formal parameters within the template, and/or to allow more kinds of formal parameters, in the interest of improving the language's abstraction facilities.

**Discussion:** The so-called "contract model" (see below), coupled with requirements for staticness in a number of contexts in Ada 83, has resulted in situations where generics do not provide all the expressive power that would be desired. For example, it is not possible to use a generic formal **in** object or an attribute of a formal generic type where a static value is required. Relaxing the contract model or the requirements for staticness would make it easier to write certain useful kinds of generics (for example, a generic math package where the precision of a local type depends on the precision of formal type).

A related issue is generalization of the kinds of entities allowed as generic formal parameters. For example, if exceptions were allowed, exceptions raised by formal subprograms could be handled more appropriately within the generic unit (see RR-0383). However, a major reason for Ada 83's disallowance of formal generic exceptions is that such a facility could incur a run-time penalty by preventing an implementation from composing static tables for handlers. Such interactions need to be considered by the Mapping/Revision Team.

**User Need U4.4-B: Independent Use and Implementation of Generics:** A generic specification ought to serve as a "contract" between the users and implementer of a generic unit. An appropriate contract promotes *separation of concerns*, allowing a user to instantiate a generic unit without regard to the contents of the generic body and allowing an implementer to write a body without regard to the ways in which the unit will be instantiated. It also facilitates early detection of errors: if an instantiation is compiled before the generic body, then all semantic errors in the instantiation will be detected when the instantiation is compiled.

**Requirement R4.4-B(1) — Dependence of Instantiations on Bodies:** A user must have the ability to compile a generic instantiation before compiling the corresponding generic body. In those cases where a body is compiled before the instantiation, the user must have the ability to ensure the unit containing the instantiation is not dependent on the generic body.

**Discussion:** The ability to prevent the establishment of a compilation dependence is important in order to control the need for recompilation. If a dependence is established (e.g., if a generic unit is compiled inline at the point of instantiation), any modification of the generic body will generally require recompilation of all units containing an instantiation.

**Study Topic S4.4-B(2) — Tighten the "Contract Model":** Ada 9X should ensure that compatibility of a generic instantiation with the corresponding generic body is based solely on the compatibility of each with the generic specification. That is, there should be no cases where the legality of an instantiation depends on how a generic formal is used within the generic body.

**Discussion:** In a small number of situations, it is possible in Ada 83 to have the legality of a generic instantiation depend on how a generic formal parameter is used. One example is passing an unconstrained array type as an actual parameter to a formal private or limited private type. Such an instantiation is correct only if the generic template contains no declaration of a variable having that type, since it is illegal to declare a variable having an unconstrained array type. Tightening the contract model would eliminate such anomalies.

Note that the discussion of Study Topic S4.4-A(1) above suggested that the contract model should be relaxed rather than tightened, in order to satisfy other needs. This conflict with Study Topic S4.4-B(2) needs to be resolved by the Mapping/Revision Team after an analysis of the tradeoffs.

**User Need U4.4-C: Code Space Compactness:** A direct implementation of generic instantiation results in replicating the code for the expanded template. In some environments such code replication is undesirable, and it is preferable to have a single version of the template, with run-time parameterization to identify instantiation-specific information.

**Requirement R4.4-C(1) — Generic Code Sharing:** Ada 9X shall provide a mechanism (for example, a pragma) requesting the sharing or replication of generic code templates. An imple-

**4: Support for Programming Paradigms**

mentation may place restrictions on the kinds of generic units for which sharing will be performed.

**Discussion:** Several situations are candidates for code sharing. One is a generic template parameterized by subprogram (for example, a generic function for mathematical integration). This is the Ada 83 style for what in other languages is done by passing subprograms as run-time parameters; such an implementation is desired by many users. Another situation is a generic template taking, for example, a formal access-type parameter. Instantiations with types sharing the same machine representation can often share the same code. A third example is a generic body that depends only on certain attributes of a formal type, such as its 'SIZE attribute. This situation arises in cases such as block moves and I/O interfaces.

## 4.5 Exceptions

<u>User Need U4.5-A</u>: **Exception Name:** When an unexpected exception is raised, many applications require that at least its name be logged to help in tracing what went wrong.

**Requirement R4.5-A(1) — Accessing an Exception Name:** The simple name of the most recently raised exception shall be available as a string in an exception handler. If additional information (such as the name of the unit where the exception was raised) can be made available at little implementation cost, this would also be helpful.

**Discussion:** Nine revision requests, from a variety of sources, mentioned a need to have at least the name of a raised exception available in a standard way in an exception handler, and several implementations already support this capability. Ideally, additional information concerning the unit in which the exception was raised would also be made available. There was no strong demand for any additional information to be made available in a handler.

## 4.6 Input/Output

<u>User Need U4.6-A</u>: **Interactive Text Input/Output:** Applications typically require the ability to communicate with users via interactive devices.

**Requirement R4.6-A(1) — Interactive TEXT_IO:** Ada 9X shall improve the ability of Ada programs to communicate with users via interactive devices. Among the capabilities to be considered are:

- The ability to output text and receive input on the same line.
- Ensuring that column, line, and page numbers reflect use of the same device for input and for output.
- The ability to continue executing other tasks while one task is waiting for input.

**Discussion:** In principle, the current definition of TEXT_IO allows programs to output text and receive input on the same line (as illustrated by the example given in section 14.7 of the standard). But in practice, many TEXT_IO implementations buffer their output until a call to NEW_LINE is given, thereby making it impossible to query a user and receive input on the same line. Moreover, because text files cannot be opened in mode IN_OUT, the column, line, and page

**4: Support for Programming Paradigms**

numbers for input and output operations are maintained separately, and therefore are not useful when interacting with a single device. Finally, if a GET procedure is called in a task, some implementations do not allow any other task to execute until the GET procedure returns. This is often unsatisfactory for applications.

**User Need U4.6-B: Various Input/Output Functions:** Experience has indicated that there are a few simple additional I/O functions that would make the input/output packages more useful to users.

**Requirement R4.6-B(1) — Additional Input/Output Functions:** Ada 9X shall augment Ada's input/output functionality in ways that make the capabilities easier to use. In particular, the following functions shall be considered for inclusion in Ada 9X:

- The ability to check whether a file exists (without having to open it).
- A standard way to open a file for appending data to it.
- The ability to determine the maximum line length and page length for a given text file.
- The ability to read or write different types of data to the same external sequential file.

**Discussion:** The listed capabilities are among those that have been requested by Ada users. The ability to test for the existence of a file without having to open it is just a matter of providing a standard function for performing this useful operation. The ability to open a file so data can be appended to it is already allowed in Ada 83 (see AI-00278), but in an implementation-dependent manner. The ability to read and write different types of data to the same external file is required in many applications. In such files, the type of an item is often determined by the content of earlier items in the file. Such a file structure can be supported in Ada 83 by opening the same external file with different data types, but most implementations do not support such a use of "shared" files, and in any event, the behavior of such files is almost entirely implementation-dependent.

In short, the purpose of this requirement is to provide modest functional improvements to Ada's input/output capabilities.

# 5 Real-Time Requirements

This chapter deals with requirements posed by real-time applications, i.e., applications in which it is important to have precise control over *when* some action is taken. Other requirements of potential interest to the real-time community are addressed in Chapter 6, Requirements for System Programming (interrupt handling), in Chapter 7, Requirements for Parallel Processing (shared variables), and in Chapter 8, Requirements for Distributed Processing. Many real-time applications are safety-critical; safety-critical requirements are addressed in Chapter 9.

## 5.1 Time

<u>User Need U5.1-A</u>: **Time Measurement:** Real-time systems typically need to measure time in two distinct ways [8, p. 124]. Computations of time-based physical parameters such as velocity and acceleration depend on the measurement of *elapsed time*. The key property of elapsed time is that its value increases monotonically at a known rate (from some convenient starting point, e.g., mission start time).

On the other hand, for interfacing with external entities such as other processors, devices, and human operators, the *time of day* is needed. The time of day does not necessarily increase monotonically at a fixed rate, since it may have to be adjusted to account for time zones or leap seconds, or to synchronize with other clocks on a local area network. Such adjustments may cause the time-of-day value to retrogress, while retrogression is never allowed for measurements of elapsed time.

The precision of the two kinds of timing measurement may differ; a clock used to control and monitor elapsed time may be updated at a faster rate than the time-of-day clock when elapsed time measurements are used to control physical processes in tight feedback loops.

**Requirement R5.1-A(1) — Elapsed Time Measurement:** Ada 9X constructs that deal with time shall support two abstractions of time — monotonically increasing elapsed time and the time of day. The time of day abstraction shall be compatible with the Ada 83 package CALENDAR and may be maintained with different precision from that of elapsed time.

**Discussion:** The time defined in Ada's package CALENDAR is the time of day (see AI-00195). While real-time applications must sometimes be synchronized with the time of day, more frequently such applications need to use measurements of elapsed time. Baker [7, 8] discusses in more detail why both kinds of time measurement are needed.

<u>User Need U5.1-B</u>: **Periodic Computation:** Many real-time applications must perform certain actions at precise periodic intervals.

**Requirement R5.1-B(1) — Precise Periodic Execution:** Ada 9X shall provide a standard way to control the periodic execution of a sequence of statements with respect to elapsed time and the time of day. The method provided shall allow the period to be changed during the execution of a program and shall ensure that the statements are scheduled for execution at precisely the specified time.

**5: Real-Time Requirements**

**Discussion:** The current **delay** statement is not generally suitable for precise periodic scheduling because the computation of the necessary delay can be preempted at critical moments, leading to inaccurate periodic execution (see [7]).

This requirement is phrased neutrally with respect to whether precise periodic scheduling is provided by a pragma, a special call to the run-time system, or new syntax. In any case, performance constraints on implementations targeted to real-time applications will have to be specified to ensure that the specified solution is supported in usable fashion. Indirect solutions to this requirement could also be satisfactory. For example, the Third International Workshop on Real-Time Ada Issues [8] suggested that a **delay until** statement could be used to achieve this requirement. Another approach is being explored by the Ada Run-Time Environment Working Group (ARTEWG) with their Catalogue of Interface Features and Options (CIFO), which is currently under development.

**User Need U5.1-C: Overrun Detection and Response:** Real-time programmers need ways of specifying deadlines and ways of specifying what action is to be taken when a deadline is missed. Among the actions typically taken are: log the overrun and continue processing, stop the overrunning activity from continuing its execution (restarting it at an appropriate point and time), temporarily changing the rate of execution, etc.

**Requirement R5.1-C(1) — Detection of Missed Deadlines:** Ada 9X shall facilitate the detection of missed deadlines and the ability to initiate an appropriate response.

**Discussion:** Although watch-dog tasks can be used to detect overruns,[6] when an overrun is detected, it is sometimes important to quickly stop the activity that has missed its deadline so other processing can be started. In general, this requires an asynchronous transfer of control (see Requirement R5.3-A(1) on page 30).

## 5.2 Task Scheduling

**User Need U5.2-A: User-Controlled Scheduling:** Scheduling algorithms determine when a task is selected for execution. Scheduling decisions are associated with entry queues (selection of the next call to be serviced), selective waits (selection from among calls waiting at open alternatives), attempts at task synchronization via entry calls (how is the priority of the called task affected), the expiration of a delay, the priority, deadline, or execution time of a given task in relation to other tasks, etc. Specialized scheduling algorithms giving improved performance are sometimes needed to take advantage of an application's expected use of tasking constructs. Since the same scheduling algorithm is not suitable for every real-time application, application developers must be able to determine the algorithm to be used for a particular application.

**Requirement R5.2-A(1) — Alternative Scheduling Algorithms:** Ada 9X shall allow real-time programmers to determine the scheduling policy and algorithm to be used for a particular program.

---

[6]Such tasks execute timed waits. If an appropriate entry is not called before the delay expires, an overrun has occurred.

**5: Real-Time Requirements**

**Discussion:** This requirement intentionally avoids specifying how a scheduling policy will be specified by the user. One possibility is that Ada 9X will specify a set of standard scheduling policies plus a means of selecting which policy/algorithm to use for a given program. Another approach is for Ada 9X to specify low-level primitives or a standard run-time interface from which scheduling policies and algorithms can be built. In either case, scheduling alternatives that are not of general interest could be described in a real-time annex.

Many in the real-time community favor the low-level or standard interface approach because of the flexibility it can provide. But it is not yet clear that a standard interface or set of primitives can be exploited efficiently for all potential target machines — any given interface always seems to be biased in favor of some class of hardware architectures or some anticipated pattern of use which may not be right for a given application. Even compiler vendors sometimes find it difficult to stick to a self-imposed standard run-time interface when highly efficient performance or specialized optimizations are demanded.

The advantage of having Ada 9X specify some standard scheduling policies (e.g., in a real-time annex of the standard) is that the policies could provide a standard framework for designing and implementing real-time applications. The potential disadvantage, of course, is that applications requiring some other policy or some adjustment to a scheduling algorithm may be unable to use Ada tasks. Moreover, there is little agreement on what such policies must be. Nonetheless, specifying a few standard scheduling policies could help reduce the difficulty of porting real-time applications.

Given that Ada's current scheduling rules are relaxed to clearly allow the use of alternative scheduling algorithms, some feel that sufficient flexibility is provided simply by giving application developers access to vendor-supplied Ada run-time systems. This is not an entirely satisfactory solution since a given compiler vendor may not provide compilers for all the target configurations of interest to the application developer. In such a case, an application developer prefers to develop a portable executive that can be interfaced efficiently with different Ada compilers.

**Requirement R5.2-A(2) — Common Real-Time Paradigms:** Ada 9X shall ensure that common real-time programming paradigms can be implemented with predictably efficient performance. Among the paradigms to be considered are: controlling access to data shared among different tasks, resetting task priorities in response to a mode change, critical regions, and asynchronous communication (see User Need 5.4-A).

**Discussion:** The requirement mentions a number of real-time programming paradigms. Although the Ada tasking model can generally be used to support these programming requirements today, many in the real-time community feel that special language constructs are needed to express these paradigms clearly and to ensure they are implemented with appropriate efficiency. Others feel that special language features are not needed, that pragmas can be used to advise implementations that certain programming paradigms are associated with certain tasks, and that this information is sufficient to ensure acceptably efficient implementation support. But there is no disagreement that these paradigms must be supported with particular efficiency.

Some real-time programming paradigms are discussed in the Proceedings of the Third International Workshop on Real-Time Ada Issues [23]. For example, a monitor task (also called a

---

**5: Real-Time Requirements**

passive task) is a specialized tasking idiom that allows rendezvous to be performed for essentially the same cost as a procedure call. To achieve this performance, different implementations today impose different constraints on the structure and content of such tasks (e.g., the task body is required to consist of a single select statement in a single loop, and it can only call other passive tasks). Ada 9X could improve this situation by specifying standard restrictions that ensure no scheduler intervention is required to execute a rendezvous (assuming the entry call is not blocked) and by requiring that implementations document tasking performance parameters. On the other hand, given the frequent need for such operations, it might be best to provide a special language feature to support it.

Application developers also sometimes restrict their uses of tasking constructs in ways that permit special execution efficiency. For example, tasks in embedded real-time systems are often declared only at the library package level, meaning there is a fixed number of tasks and there are no dependent tasks. Under these conditions, the performance of various scheduling operations can be significantly improved. For example, task abortion and termination is simplified because there are no dependent tasks. The Mapping/Revision Team should consider whether such usage restrictions deserve standardization in a real-time annex.

## 5.3 Asynchronous Control of Execution

<u>User Need U5.3-A</u>: **Asynchronous Control of Execution:** There are many situations (e.g., mode change, dynamic reconfiguration, system restart) where it is useful to terminate one sort of processing and continue processing in a new place, based on the asynchronous occurrence of some event. For example, it is sometimes necessary to stop a process in response to a user interrupt because there is no longer any need for the activity and resources must be released to do something else (e.g., aborting an autopiloted landing). Similarly, it is sometimes necessary to stop a process when it has overrun a deadline.

**Requirement R5.3-A(1) — Asynchronous Transfer of Control:** Ada 9X shall allow the execution of a sequence of statements to be abandoned in order to execute a different sequence within the same task. The event causing this transfer might be, for example, an external interrupt from a timer or a call from another task. It shall be possible to abandon the execution quickly, even if execution is suspended at an entry call or an accept statement. In balancing the need for immediate response with the need for safe and predictable execution (e.g., the ability to release resources held by the abandoned code) (see Guideline **G-2**), it shall be possible to identify certain sections of code in which a request for asynchronous transfer of control will not be honored.

**Discussion:** Events requiring an asynchronous transfer of control can arise under conditions where they must be handled within strict time constraints. It must be possible to stop the computations of certain tasks quickly. Suspension is not enough because when a task resumes execution it must continue at a different execution statement. (For example, if an autopiloted landing is aborted, the responsible tasks should be restarted from some earlier point (with fresh data) the next time a landing is attempted.) In some cases, the transfer of control must be immediate. This requirement conflicts somewhat with other needs, e.g., the need to ensure that data structures hold valid values, the need to ensure that allocated storage is released when no longer needed, etc. The Mapping/Revision Team must find an appropriate way of satisfying these conflicting requirements.

**5: Real-Time Requirements**

The design of Ada in 1980 provided an asynchronous exception for asynchronous transfer of control. This mechanism was removed from the final design because various significant difficulties were discovered (see RR-0196 and [24] for a full discussion). The relevant difficulties have been mentioned in the above requirement to ensure that they are addressed in developing proposed solutions.

## 5.4 Asynchronous Communication

<u>User Need U5.4-A</u>: **Asynchronous Message Passing:** The ability to send data to a task without waiting for it to be received is an important and common paradigm in real-time programming. For example, device drivers in an embedded system must be able to send data to tasks without any scheduler intervention that might cause interrupts to be missed. Similarly, non-blocking operations are used when sending large amounts of information to relatively slow recording devices.

The message-passing paradigm is also appropriate for computer systems that do not have shared memory and for massively parallel systems. Finally, in some applications, messages with different priorities need to be sent to the same task; the messages need to be processed in priority order.

**Discussion:** Real-time programs could be easier to understand and maintain if the non-blocking communication paradigm were directly expressible in the language. Most real-time operating systems provide direct support for non-blocking communications (e.g., mailboxes), so real-time programmers are accustomed to having this capability available. Non-standard, implementation-dependent mechanisms are currently being used to support asynchronous communication needs. To reduce implementation dependencies and increase maintainability and portability, Ada 9X needs to specify standard asynchronous communication mechanisms.

**Requirement R5.4-A(1) — Non-Blocking Communication:** Ada 9X shall support non-blocking, asynchronous communication between tasks in an Ada program. In particular, from the viewpoint of the sending task, the maximum time to execute an asynchronous communication operation shall normally be independent of the state of the receiving task.

**Discussion:** Agent tasks that accept messages to be queued are the standard Ada construct for attempting to support non-blocking communications. Since all agent tasks have the same priority, service order is not guaranteed by Ada 83 rules. Moreover, if agent tasks are to be used for this purpose, the overhead that is apparently involved in creating and terminating them must be somehow be avoided, since fast service is especially important when an interrupt handling routine needs to store data very quickly and predictably in a buffer. For all these reasons, agent tasks have not proven to be a very satisfactory solution to this requirement.

From a programmer viewpoint, providing the capability with a standard package would probably be satisfactory, but Ada's current generic unit capabilities make the use of such a package awkward (different generic units are needed for asynchronous calls with different numbers of parameters; see [6]). It is possible that other Ada 9X changes to generics (see Section 4.4) would make it easier to provide an efficient message-passing package. On the other hand, considering these difficulties, direct support for a new language construct might prove to be the best solution.

**5: Real-Time Requirements**

<u>User Need U5.4-B</u>: **Asynchronous Multicast:** The ability to send messages to a group of tasks (without waiting for a reply) is sometimes necessary. Similarly, the ability of a receiver to determine its own eligibility to receive such a message is sometimes useful.

**Study Topic S5.4-B(1) — Asynchronous Multicast:** Ada 9X shall support asynchronous communication from a single sender to multiple receivers as well as the ability of potential receivers to control their eligibility to receive a message.

# 6 Requirements for System Programming

## 6.1 Unsigned Integer Operations

<u>User Need U6.1-A</u>: **Unsigned Integers:** Many coding algorithms (for example, checksums and cyclic redundancy checks) are formulated most naturally in terms of operations on unsigned integers. It should be possible to express such algorithms efficiently and directly in Ada.

**Requirement R6.1-A(1) — Unsigned Integer Operations:** Ada 9X shall provide efficient support for operations on unsigned integer data. In particular, unsigned arithmetic, logical operations, and shifting operations shall be supported.

**Discussion:** AI-00402 explains why unsigned integer types cannot be predefined types in Ada 83. AI-00597 and RR-0460 discuss the benefits of unsigned integer types and how they might be provided by careful interpretation of the current standard. However, it would be best if Ada 9X supported such types clearly and directly.

## 6.2 Data Interoperability

<u>User Need U6.2-A</u>: **Data Interoperability:** Many applications require the ability to interchange data with other programs and systems when the required format of the data is not under the control of the application.

**Requirement R6.2-A(1) — Data Interoperability:** Ada 9X shall provide a means to specify the exact representation of data in memory and on external files so that interoperability with other systems can be facilitated.

**Discussion:** Ada's representation clauses were intended to allow the complete specification of an object's representation. However, existing implementations do not always fully support representation clauses. The Mapping/Revision Team needs to ensure that methods for specifying data representations can and will be supported more uniformly.

## 6.3 Interrupts

<u>User Need U6.3-A</u>: **Interrupt Handling:** Interrupts typically need to be serviced with little or no run-time overhead. In addition, an association between interrupt-handling code and a source of interrupts must sometimes be changed at execution time.

**Requirement R6.3-A(1) — Interrupt Servicing:** Ada 9X shall ensure that an interrupt can be serviced with minimal (and predictable) run-time overhead. Ada 9X shall allow interrupts to be processed at an appropriate priority.[7]

---

[7]The appropriate priority will or could depend on the hardware architecture, the scheduling policy, and the application's view of the relative importance of processing the interrupt.

**6: Requirements for System Programming**

**Discussion:** Among the issues to be considered in satisfying this requirement are the ability to:

1. Permit the interrupt handling code to mask its triggering interrupt, e.g., while it is manipulating hardware that may cause the interrupt to occur or while it is not ready to accept or handle the interrupt.

2. Handle interrupts with minimal scheduler overhead when data must be passed to tasks executing at a lower priority or when the occurrence of an interrupt serves as a signal that some task can be released for execution.

3. Permit the handling of nested interrupts when the hardware architecture makes this feasible.

In addition, it is consistent with the requirements for user-controlled scheduling (Requirement R5.2-A(1)) that the priority associated with interrupt processing not be dictated by the language but instead be subject to the scheduling policy developed for a particular application, the hardware architecture, and the overall software design.

Ada implementations today that are aimed at embedded applications generally provide special implementation-defined capabilities to support interrupt handling [15]. Even when targeting the same processor, implementations from different vendors can vary widely in their support for interrupt handling code [15]. If possible, Ada 9X should bring more uniformity to how implementations support interrupt handling.

**Requirement R6.3-A(2) — Interrupt Binding:** Ada 9X shall allow the association between an interrupt and its interrupt-handling code to be modified during program execution.

**Discussion:** An interrupt binding may need to be changed dynamically for a variety of reasons, e.g., to recover from a hardware fault or to respond to an operational mode change. Ada 83 does not support such changes because the method for associating interrupts with interrupt handling code can only be invoked when a task is activated. There is no standard way of later changing the association, although implementations sometimes provide non-standard ways of doing so.

Ada 83 implies that the notation for specifying a memory location is the same as the notation for identifying an interrupt that is to be associated with handler code (since address clauses and the type SYSTEM.ADDRESS are used for both purposes). Although considerable flexibility is allowed by the language in the notation used for an "address" and hence, for specifying an interrupt binding, the Mapping/Revision Team should consider whether improvements are needed.

## 6.4 Dynamic References to Global Objects

**User Need U6.4-A: Dynamic Access to Global Objects:** In embedded applications, data may be pre-allocated by mechanisms other than the Ada program that needs to use the data (e.g., the data may be stored in read-only memory or may be created and loaded prior to program execution). The selection of which data to access may need to be determined at run-time (e.g., see RR-0018 and RR-0726).

**Requirement R6.4-A(1) — Access Values Designating Global Objects:** Ada 9X shall allow the use of access values that designate objects declared in library packages. Operations using such access values shall maintain the reliability and safety of Ada 83 access types.

## 6: Requirements for System Programming

**Discussion:** The ability to use access values to designate objects that have not been created by allocators is essential in some applications. Such designated objects are typically created and initialized by external mechanisms or are stored in read-only memory, so allocators are not a usable means of creating access values designating the objects. In addition, the selection of an access value must often be done at run-time, e.g., it must be possible to store such access values in data structures (such as arrays) that permit dynamic selection of an appropriate designated object.

Address clauses, the ADDRESS attribute, and unchecked conversion can often be used today to obtain access values that can be used in the desired manner, but such usage is more implementation-dependent than it needs to be.

**User Need U6.4-B: Low-Level Manipulation of Access Values:** Low level system programming, such as writing special-purpose storage allocation routines, require the ability to manipulate pointers, including the ability to obtain pointers to local objects and to perform address arithmetic.

**Study Topic S6.4-B(1) — Low-Level Pointer Operations:** Ada 9X shall provide low-level mechanisms for manipulating pointers.

**Discussion:** Ada 83 provides some capabilities for manipulating pointers via use of the ADDRESS attribute and unchecked conversion between access values and ADDRESS values. However, these techniques are potentially non-portable, although in practice, many implementations support these operations in a fairly portable fashion. WG9's Uniformity Rapporteur Group has been addressing these issues.

# 7 Requirements for Parallel Processing

The use of parallel computers, in which a single computer consists of a (possibly very large) number of identical processors, is an important architectural trend that must be accommodated by Ada 9X. Not only can we expect to see greater use of tightly coupled multi-processors for computationally intensive tasks, but individual processors will increasingly turn to chip-level parallelism as a path to increasing instruction throughput.

The tasking mechanism in Ada 83 provides an important starting point for building Ada programs for such parallel environments, but a number of shortcomings have been identified that makes it difficult to map Ada tasking programs to parallel machines. In other languages, such as C or FORTRAN, vendors have addressed these problems by adding specialized extensions, which are often non-portable. This approach is not desirable for Ada compilers.

An important part of the problem is that there is a wide variety of parallel computing architectures, differing in such regards as the availability and treatment of shared memory and the extent to which separate processing elements are distinct. On the one hand, vector machines allow for massive parallelism without separately identifiable threads of control, whereas MIMD machines provide separate threads of control much nearer to the Ada tasking model. There is no clear consensus on what constitutes the best design approach, and indeed a most likely scenario is that widely differing architectures will continue to prove applicable to different problem domains. This means that any solutions proposed for Ada 9X must be able to accommodate a variety of architectures.

## 7.1 Shared Memory

**User Need U7.1-A**: **Control of Shared Memory:** It must be possible to write Ada programs that efficiently map onto parallel machines with a range of architectures from systems with no shared memory to those where shared memory is available and must be efficiently accessible.

**Requirement R7.1-A(1) — Control of Shared Memory:** Ada 9X must permit an Ada programmer to control accesses to shared memory and to make full use of shared memory.

**Discussion:** In Ada 83, objects are shared by default. In general there is no way for a compiler to determine at compile time, or even at link time, which variables are actually shared (i.e., accessed by more than one task). In systems with no shared memory (such as hypercube architectures), shared memory must be simulated by message passing and is typically significantly more expensive than direct memory references. A programmer writing an Ada application for such a system must be able to minimize the use of shared variables and it must be possible for the compiler to determine which variables are shared.

In parallel systems that do provide shared memory, it is important that Ada programs be able to take full advantage of shared memory algorithms. As discussed in the Ada 9X Special Study on Shared Variables [13], the current facilities in Ada 83 are inadequate. For example, there is no provision for asynchronous shared access to elements of composite objects. Even in parallel systems with shared memory, it is typically the case that individual processing elements have local memory or caches; taking full advantage of such an architecture also requires the ability to clearly distinguish between shared and non-shared data.

### 7: Requirements for Parallel Processing

It is not in general possible to write efficient programs for parallel systems that are completely unaware of the architecture. Although it will continue to be possible for any Ada 9X program to run on any computer supporting Ada 9X, maximally efficient execution often involves a choice of algorithms and layout that are architecture dependent. Requirement R7.1-A(1) specifies that Ada 9X must provide features that allow a program to clearly specify its requirements for using shared memory.

Shared memory also plays an important role in Ada applications intended to run on a single processor. Solutions to Requirement R7.1-A(1) should also provide for improved control of the use of shared memory on conventional processors.

## 7.2 Massively Parallel Architectures

**User Need U7.2-A: Large Numbers of Tasks:** If Ada tasks are used to describe threads of control, and if a program is run on a massively parallel system with many processors, then the resulting program must be able to handle a large number of tasks in an efficient manner.

**Study Topic S7.2-A(1) — Managing Large Numbers of Tasks:** Ada 9X must provide for the efficient creation, initialization, execution, and termination of large numbers of tasks.

**Discussion:** A critical requirement for efficiency of large scale parallel applications is that there be no "serial bottlenecks," i.e., points at which the execution time depends on executing serial code whose execution time is dependent on the number of processors.

Ada 83 does provide many of the needed facilities to meet this requirement. Tasks can be initiated in parallel, and terminated in parallel (using the terminate alternative). However, there is no easy way to give tasks an identity so that the tasks that are initiated in parallel can work on separate parts of a problem without communicating with some master controlling task.

There are a number of possible approaches to solving this problem. One approach is to provide a task with the ability to directly determine its own identity (for example, its index in an array of tasks). Another approach is to provide some kind of mechanism for parameterizing tasks.

## 7.3 Vector Architectures

**User Need U7.3-A:** Support for Vector Architectures: Ada 9X compilers must be able to efficiently exploit vector machines and other architectures requiring statement level parallelism.

**Study Topic S7.3-A(1) — Statement Level Parallelism:** Ada 9X should accommodate compiler techniques for efficiently mapping sequences of Ada statements, including particularly appropriate loops, onto vector architectures.

**Discussion:** Although Ada permits the use of tasks for explicitly describing parallelism, this is much too heavy a mechanism for loop level parallelism. In other languages, approaches to this problem have involved automatic recognition of loop parallelism by compilers and the introduction of specialized loop constructs explicitly specifying parallel execution.

Compiler techniques for mapping sequential code onto vector architectures are well known. However, there is some difficulty in applying these techniques to Ada because of exception semantics. The relaxations permitted by section 11.6 of the Ada standard are insufficient to permit vectorization to the desired degree. For example, a simple loop that adds the elements of two vectors together cannot be vectorized since Ada requires that an exception occurring in the first loop prevent further iteration of the loop.

## 7.4 Configuration of Parallel Programs

<u>User Need U7.4-A</u>: **Configuration of Parallel Programs:** Control is needed over the mapping of tasks to processors in multi-processor machines in order to achieve maximum performance.

**Study Topic S7.4-A(1) — Configuration of Parallel Programs:** Ada 9X compilation systems should permit the programmer to optionally control the assignment of Ada tasks to separate processing elements in a multi-processor system.

**Discussion:** There are two situations in which this kind of control is required if programs are to achieve maximum performance.

First, in some architectures, the communication between separate processors is not uniformly efficient. Certain processors may be "nearer" to other processors, allowing more efficient access between them, or processors may be arranged into groups, with more efficient communication within a group than between processors in separate groups. In such situations, it should be possible, though not required, for the programmer to control the placement of Ada tasks to optimize inter-task communication.

Second, there may be more tasks than processors, in which case multiple tasks must be mapped onto a single processor. In such situations, it may typically be the case that communication between tasks on a single processor may be considerably more efficient. For example, such tasks may be able to efficiently access the local memory of a processor to give shared memory effects between one another, even though there is no system-wide shared memory. Again, such architectures require that the programmer exercise control over task placement.

Another factor to be considered is the effect of priorities. Depending on the architecture, the effect of priorities might be quite different on tasks residing on the same processor and on different processors. Similarly, whether tasks can migrate from one processor to another must be considered and, if necessary, controlled in designing an application.

# 8 Requirements for Distributed Processing

The use of distributed multiple computers to implement large-scale resource-intensive applications has increased significantly since the adoption of Ada in 1983. In the future, this use is expected to proliferate as the advantages of distributed execution become economically attractive to more applications. Typically, distributed applications use dynamic configuration facilities to optimize the use of available computing resources. Furthermore, fault tolerance must be addressed, since an important motivation for the use of distributed systems is the construction of survivable systems that can continue operation even if one or more of the distributed components ceases to function. Applications for which distributed processing support is essential include command and control systems, fault-tolerant systems, trusted systems, safety-critical systems, and information systems.

To the extent that a distributed computer system is similar to a parallel computing system, the considerations in the preceding section on parallel processing apply. In particular, control over shared memory is even more important, since typical distributed systems have no shared memory and simulation by message passing can be prohibitively expensive. Similarly, the ability to partition tasks across processors is important if a single Ada program is to be distributed.

However, distributed processing introduces a number of additional complications that must be addressed. In particular, a distributed system may be heterogeneous, involving different processors and different operating systems, and it may also require dynamic configuration, in which parts of the system are replaced or modified as the program is running. The Ada model of binding together a single large application statically into one program may well not be applicable in such situations.

Currently, Ada 83 can be used to program applications for multiple computers. A variety of approaches are used in practice. Most commonly, an application is treated as an interacting group of independently executing Ada programs. Less frequently, an application is written as a single program whose parts are allocated across target architectures. In each approach, applications rely upon different degrees of extra-lingual support, thereby compromising dynamic control and safety among the program units comprising the application. Moreover, the lack of specific language support degrades portability.

Ideally, Ada 9X should specify an approach to distributed programming that minimally extends the language to accommodate both the logical and physical separation of an application for distributed execution. The extensions must not preclude the continued use of existing approaches.

## 8.1 Distribution of Ada Applications

<u>User Need U8.1-A</u>: **Distributing an Application:** It must be possible to structure the code for a given application so it can be executed using multiple separate computers. This requires the ability to partition code into parts that need to be executed on a single computer. After distributing the parts among separate computers, the resulting code must retain the same degree of type safety as for a single program.

**8: Requirements for Distributed Processing**

**Requirement R8.1-A(1) — Facilitating Software Distribution:** Ada 9X shall facilitate the distribution of Ada code across a homogeneous distributed architecture. Enhancements to facilitate distribution might include, for example:

1. The specification of the exact semantics (behavior and timing, including failure modes) of timed and conditional entry calls, potentially remote subprogram calls, and exception propagation.

2. The specification of semantics to deal with hardware failure and recovery.

3. Treatment of the existence of independent clocks with possibly different timing precisions.

**Discussion:** Distributed Ada systems will become more prevalent in the future. One form of software for a distributed system is a single program that is partitioned so that parts of it can be distributed to separate processing elements (e.g., see [16]). The advantage of this approach is that type safety is automatically retained since the normal compile-time checks are performed.

A second form of distribution is to have multiple programs that run on separate computers, with perhaps more than one Ada program running on a given computer. In this case, a standard interface for inter-program communication and synchronization is needed. Many systems today use this model of distribution.

It is beyond the scope of Requirement R8.1-A(1) to deal with the distribution of a single program across heterogeneous systems. The problems introduced by multiple representations of data and by operating systems with incompatible semantics make it difficult to accommodate the normal Ada model that does not recognize such possible differences. In particular a problem arises in dealing with the system dependent definitions introduced in multiple versions of package SYSTEM.

The semantics of entry calls and subprogram calls are oriented towards non-distributed execution in that no provision is made for the existence of multiple clocks or for the possible failure of remote computers or communication links. These problems must be addressed if Ada 9X is to directly support distributed application programming.

## 8.2 Dynamic Reconfiguration of Distributed Systems

**User Need U8.2-A: Configuring an Ada Application:** It must be possible to control the allocation of code to the computers upon which an Ada application executes. This control includes specifying both the initial configuration and subsequent configurations so as to optimize the use of available computing resources.

**Requirement R8.2-A(1) — Dynamic Reconfiguration:** Ada 9X shall allow for the possibility of dynamic reconfiguration of a distributed applications. It shall be possible to replace or modify individual components of a distributed application without recompiling or restarting the entire application.

**Discussion:** The fundamental model of Ada 83 execution is to bind together a single large program, elaborate its library packages, and then elaborate the program. This model is somewhat at odds with the requirement to be able to dynamically reconfigure parts of an application while it

**8: Requirements for Distributed Processing**

is running. Issues to be considered here are the pre-elaboration of packages, and also the possibility of state-free packages for describing interfaces between components of an application (e.g., see [16]).

A minimal solution to this requirement might be simply to rephrase certain of Ada's rules to allow for the kinds of reconfiguration activities that are, in practice, being supported today.

# 9 Requirements for Safety-Critical and Trusted Applications

Safety-critical and trusted applications, including those that control aircraft, medical equipment, and nuclear reactors, often have special requirements arising from the need for predictable execution, certifiable code, and the enforcement of safe programming practices.

## 9.1 Predictability of Execution

<u>User Need U9.1-A</u>: **Constraining the Possible Meanings of a Program:** Developers of safety-critical and trusted applications need to be able to determine, by examination of program text, the precise effect of executing a program. When language rules allow implementations to make choices that affect program behavior, determining the behavior of a program is more difficult. Programmers of safety-critical and trusted applications need ways of controlling such choices or the ability to determine what choices will be made under given circumstances.

**Study Topic S9.1-A(1) — Determining Implementation Choices:** Wherever Ada 9X *explicitly* allows implementation-defined choices that affect program behavior, implementations shall be required either to document the choice that has been made (or the situations that control what choice is made) or Ada 9X shall provide a mechanism for controlling the choice.

**Discussion:** While Requirement R2.4-A(1) on page 11 calls for minimizing implementation dependences in Ada 9X, some implementation freedom is beneficial. Such freedom allows the language to accommodate a wide variety of target architectures and implementation techniques. For example, Ada today allows implementations to choose the range associated with the predefined INTEGER type, the parameter passing method to be used in subprogram and entry calls, and the value (if any) that is associated with uninitialized variables. Each of these implementation-dependent choices potentially affects the behavior of programs.

Given that some aspects of a program's behavior will continue to vary from one implementation to another, developers of safety-critical and trusted systems require at least the ability to predict how a program will behave under a *given* implementation. Some aspects of implementation-dependent behavior (such as the policy used for rounding real numbers midway between two whole numbers to integers) may be reportable in a document like Appendix F of the Ada 83 reference manual. Other aspects (such as the mechanism chosen for passing composite parameters) may have to be reported, upon request, on a case by case basis by the compiler. A safety-critical/trusted-system annex might specify constraints on such choices or standard methods for controlling some of them.

This requirement is stated as a Study Topic because it may not always be possible or reasonable to provide useful documentation or methods of controlling every explicitly allowed implementation choice. For example, Ada explicitly does not define the order in which subprogram arguments are evaluated. Study Topic S9.1-A(1) therefore says that the choice of a particular order of evaluation must either be documented or controlled. However, it could be argued that an optimizing implementation cannot usefully or easily document the algorithm it uses when evaluating the arguments of a subprogram call, and since programmers can easily avoid the use of arguments for which evaluation order has an effect, there may be little value in specifying a pragma that requires, say, left-to-right evaluation. Documenting or controlling the possible ef-

## 9: Requirements for Safety-Critical and Trusted Applications

fects of erroneous executions may also be problematic in some cases. In short, although the principle of being able to determine the precise effect of program execution seems essential in safety-critical/trusted-system applications, it may prove to be difficult to ensure that all the necessary information and control is provided by Ada 9X. In any event, the generated code can always be examined to determine the precise effect of some portion of a program (see User Need 9.2-A, below).

**Requirement R9.1-A(2) — Ensuring Canonical Application of Operations:** Ada 9X shall provide a mechanism, applicable to a region of program text, for restricting any freedom otherwise allowed to reorder, replace, or remove actions involving predefined operations.

**Discussion:** The intent of this requirement is to allow a programmer to curtail the semantic effects currently allowed by section 11.6 of the standard. The currently allowed freedom to reorder operations, to use operations with increased numeric accuracy, and to suppress checks for predefined exceptions can be detrimental to the development of safety-critical and trusted systems because it enlarges the set of possible effects of program execution, thereby complicating formal or informal reasoning about program behavior.[8]

## 9.2 Certifiability

**User Need U9.2-A:** **Validation of Generated Code:** Developers of safety-critical and trusted systems do not rely on compilers to generate code that correctly reflects the intent of a high-level-language programmer. Moreover, the complexity of translating any reasonably high-level language into object code makes it unlikely that a program performing that translation could ever be completely relied on. It is common practice when writing safety-critical and trusted software in a high-level language to certify the correctness of the generated object code rather than that of the source code, treating the source code as documentation of the object code. Those who certify safety-critical and trusted systems by examining the generated code require a clear correspondence between the source code and the generated code.

**Requirement R9.2-A(1) — Generating Easily Checked Code:** Ada 9X shall provide a mechanism for advising a compiler that code should be generated in a style that allows it to be checked against the source text with reasonable effort.

**Discussion:** The style of code generated by a compiler is not a meaningful concept in the definition of a programming language. Therefore, there is no appropriate way to specify what it means for a compiler to obey advice about the style of generated code — obedience cannot be enforced. In this respect, the mechanism called for by Requirement R9.2-A(1) is like the Ada 83 pragma OPTIMIZE, which allows a programmer to indicate whether the preferred criterion for generating code is optimization of execution time or optimization of space. In essence, Requirement R9.2-A(1) identifies a third criterion — clarity of the relationship of the generated code to the source code.

---

[8]See AI-00315 for a discussion of some effects of section 11.6 that can be quite surprising to programmers.

**9: Requirements for Safety-Critical and Trusted Applications**

There are legitimate reasons why a compiler might ignore such a request. For example, implementations targeted to RISC architectures must schedule instructions in unintuitive orders to exploit the full power of the machine. Even compilers for conventional architectures may be so strongly oriented towards the production of efficient code that optimization algorithms are not easily separated from normal code generation. On the other hand, the notion of what constitutes a clear relationship to source code can be affected by the tools that are available for analyzing this relationship. For example, a tool could reorganize the generated code to help display its relationship to the source text.

In the future, safety-critical and trusted software may be certified by other means, such as by validating intermediate-level code whose translation into machine language is straightforward enough that a translation program could be certified as trustworthy, e.g., see [10, 26, 27]. Nonetheless, validation of object code is likely to remain a common practice for some time to come.

## 9.3 Enforcement of Safety-Critical Programming Practices

<u>User Need U9.3-A</u>: **Restricting the Use of Ada Features:** Use of certain language features is often incompatible with the development and certification of safety-critical and trusted software. Often a requirement is imposed that safety-critical and trusted software be written in a "safe subset" of a programming language.

**Discussion:** There are a variety of reasons for excluding the use of a feature from a safe subset. For example, a feature might be excluded because it has nondeterministic behavior and the effect of safety-critical and trusted code must be predictable. Exclusion of a feature from a "safe subset" does not suggest that a feature does not have legitimate uses in other applications or that it should be excluded entirely from Ada 9X. However, developers of safety-critical and trusted code must be able to ensure that such code is written entirely within a prescribed subset.

**Requirement R9.3-A(1) — Allow Additional Compile-Time Restrictions:** Ada 9X shall allow a mode in which a compiler enforces adherence to coding practices beyond those imposed by the rules of the language.

**Discussion:** Ada 83 intended to allow such freedom to implementations, but the emphasis on no subsets (which was intended only to prevent the appearance of implementations unable to support the full language) has led some implementers and users to conclude that Ada 83 does *not* permit such modes. The point of this requirement is to ensure that this confusion is resolved in Ada 9X.

This requirement has utility beyond its use for safety-critical and trusted applications. For example, program developers might wish to forbid use of certain implementation-defined pragmas and attributes to enhance program portability.

## 10 Requirements for Information Systems

Information systems typically need to deal with character data in a flexible manner and with large currency amounts. In addition, many information systems applications use non-ASCII character sets (often EBCDIC), and these alternate character sets must be fully supported in Ada without loss of efficiency.

## 10.1 Handling Currency Quantities for Information Systems

**User Need U10.1-A: Support for Currency Quantities:** Information systems programs that deal with currency amounts need to perform exact arithmetic, with control over rounding. At least 18 digits of decimal precision are needed.

**Requirement R10.1-A(1) — Decimal-Based Types:** Ada 9X shall support fixed point types whose value of *small* is a power of ten. Such types shall have at least 18 decimal digits of precision. It shall be possible to ensure that intermediate results for expressions of such types are not computed or stored with extra precision, and that rounding is under programmer control.

**Discussion:** The current fixed point model in Ada does not meet this requirement in a number of respects (see [14]):

- It currently appears that implementations need not support non-binary values of *small* since most validated implementations do not do so. The reason for this lack of support is, at least in part, due to implementation issues stemming from Ada's accuracy requirements for numeric computations, particularly for operations on fixed point types with incompatible values of *small* and for conversions of fixed point values to integer and floating point types (e.g., see RR-0592).

- Ada fixed point is oriented to its use as a replacement for floating point, where exact results are not required. Consequently, the model for fixed point is close to that of floating point, whereas the arithmetic facility required for information systems is closer to scaled integer arithmetic. In particular, neither stored values nor intermediate results should be permitted with extra precision in this context. Extra range is of course permitted (actually required) for intermediate results.

- Deterministic semantics with control over rounding are required for currency computations as opposed to model number nondeterminism.

**Study Topic S10.1-A(2) — Specification of Decimal Representation:** Ada 9X information system implementations shall provide a mechanism for specifying decimal representations for decimal-based fixed point types.

**Discussion:** Information systems applications typically make heavy use of decimal representations (both 8-bit character and 4-bit packed decimal) for decimal scaled data. There are three reasons for supporting this feature in Ada:

- On many architectures used for information systems applications, the instruction set directly supports arithmetic using these representations. Ada 9X should facilitate use of this hardware.

- It commonly arises in this type of application that quantities are manipulated in contexts requiring external decimal representations (for example, for input/output), so

**10: Requirements for Information Systems**

the internal use of decimal representations can be efficient even in the absence of hardware support.

• Interfacing to COBOL (including files generated by COBOL programs) and to other related tools, including most data base managers, requires support for decimal representations.

The issue of whether representations of this type should be usable throughout a program, or more restricted (concentrating on the interface requirements) needs to be evaluated by the Mapping/Revision Team.

## 10.2 Compatibility with Other Character Sets

**User Need U10.2-A: Alternate Character Set Support:** Many information systems applications must interface smoothly with applications based on character sets other than ASCII, particularly EBCDIC.

**Study Topic S10.2-A(1) — Alternate Character Set Support:** Ada 9X information-system implementations shall provide for the extension of the set of graphic symbols to obtain input/output facilities and IMAGE attributes for alternate character sets (specifically, for EBCDIC) comparable in both functionality and performance with the features provided for the built-in character set.

**Discussion:** It is expected that this requirement will be satisfied by capabilities specified in an information systems annex. This requirement is also related to the international requirements described in Section 3.1 on page 13.

## 10.3 Interfacing with Data Base Systems

**User Need U10.3-A: Interfacing Ada Programs to DBMSs:** Information systems programs written in Ada must often interface with Data Base Management Systems (DBMSs). Such DBMSs are typically designed to interface with COBOL programs.

**Study Topic S10.3-A(1) — Interfacing with Data Base Systems:** It should be relatively easy to write Ada 9X programs that interface smoothly with DBMSs.

**Discussion:** The intent here is not to specify a standard for interfacing with data base management systems from Ada, but instead to ensure that it is not unduly difficult to specify such standards. For example, existing non-Ada DBMS interfaces assume that the data base manager can call a specified "trap" procedure in exception situations. If Ada 9X supported subprograms as objects, it would be easy to specify how such subprograms could be passed to the DBMS as a trap procedure (e.g., see [11] for a discussion of this and other issues).

## 10.4 Common Functions

**User Need U10.4-A**: **Standard Data Manipulation**: The manipulation of varying-length strings and "picture-based" editing of strings is commonly required in information systems applications.

**Study Topic S10.4-A(1) — Varying-Length String Package**: Ada 9X shall provide a standard varying-length string package.

**Discussion**: The manipulation of varying-length strings is common in information system applications as well as in other applications. If Ada 9X specified a standard package for performing such manipulations, some implementers would find it easier to support the specified capabilities with considerable efficiency, perhaps even generating optimized machine code. On the other hand, it is not easy to agree on what standard functionality should be provided, nor is it easy to agree on how varying-length strings should be represented, since different representations are appropriate depending on how the strings are to be used, performance requirements, etc. Therefore this requirement is classified as a Study Topic.

**Study Topic S10.4-A(2) — String Manipulation Functions**: Ada 9X shall provide a standard package of general string manipulation functions such as a function for finding a pattern in a string, a conversion function, and functions for creating formatted data in the style of "picture" formats as specified in languages such as COBOL and PL/I.

**Discussion**: The presentation of values in "edited" format is a common requirement in information systems processing. It does not seem reasonable to support such a capability directly in Ada 9X, given the goals of the 9X revision effort. However, a generic package of editing functions could be specified as part of an information systems annex in order to ensure standard support for such string processing needs in information systems applications.

## 11 Requirements for Scientific and Mathematical Applications

### 11.1 Floating Point

**User Need U11.1-A: Common Mathematical Functions:** Users need standard support for common elementary functions such as sine, cosine, square root, logarithm, etc. Developers of numerical software also need standard primitive subprograms that allow them to develop portable implementations of scientific and mathematical software.

**Requirement R11.1-A(1) — Standard Mathematics Packages:** Ada 9X shall provide a standard package of elementary functions such as square root, logarithm, sine, cosine, etc. In addition, Ada 9X shall provide a standard interface to subprograms that are useful in developing portable implementations of mathematical functions.

**Discussion:** A standard package of elementary functions is currently being considered for adoption as an ISO standard [17]. It would be sensible for Ada 9X to incorporate this standard by reference (assuming that it becomes an ISO standard; if not, it should be incorporated directly). Similarly, a package of primitive functions and procedures [18] is beginning the ISO standardization process and could also be referenced by the Ada 9X standard.

**User Need U11.1-B: Floating Point Support:** Numerical analysts require predictable use of a machine's floating point hardware.

**Study Topic S11.1-B(1) — Floating Point Facilities:** Ada 9X shall require that the results of floating point operations be predictable from the documentation provided for any given implementation. Ada 9X shall also allow implementations to fully support the IEEE floating point standard [20].

**Discussion:** The Ada 83 formal model for floating point uses nondeterminism to allow implementations sufficient freedom to conform to almost all floating point architectures. Subsequent experience has indicated that it is preferable to require deterministic results that are well-specified for any given architecture, with the language providing a framework for, and constraints on, these specifications. The proposed ISO Language Compatible Arithmetic Standard (LCAS) is an example of such a framework.

In addition, Ada 83 makes it difficult to accommodate certain features of the IEEE-754 standard, such as output of -0.0 and input of infinities. There are few such constraints, and they should be easy to relax.

### 11.2 Representation of Arrays

**User Need U11.2-A: Ordering of Array Components in Memory:** Programmers of numerically intensive computing applications need to be able to determine how a compiler has chosen to allocate array components in memory (row-major order or column-major) for at least two reasons: (1) to foster locality of reference in paged and cached systems and (2) to ensure that when interfacing with subprograms written in FORTRAN or C, successive array components in memory correspond with the expected index values.

### 11: Requirements for Scientific and Mathematical Applications

**Study Topic S11.2-A(1) — Array Representation:** Ada 9X shall allow programmers to determine whether arrays are organized in row-major or column-major order.

# References

**1.** *Ada 9X Project Plan.* Office of the Under Secretary of Defense for Acquisition, Washington, D.C. 20301, 1989.

**2.** *Ada 9X Project Requirements Workshop.* Office of the Under Secretary of Defense for Acquisition, Washington, D.C. 20301, June 1989.

**3.** *Ada 9X Project Revision Request Report.* Office of the Under Secretary of Defense for Acquisition, Washington, D.C. 20301, 1990.

**4.** *Ada Board's Recommended Ada 9X Strategy.* Office of the Under Secretary of Defense for Acquisition, Washington, D.C. 20301, 1988.

**5.** *Approved Ada Language Commentaries.* Published by Grebyn Corporation, Vienna, VA. See also the up-to-date files kept by the Ada Information Clearinghouse; these files are also available on the AJPO machine (ajpo.sei.cmu.edu).

**6.** Real-Time Tasking Semantics Working Group. "Asynchronous Communication Between Tasks". *Ada Letters X*, 4 (Spring 1990), 35-39. Proceedings of the Third International Workshop on Real-Time Ada Issues.

**7.** Baker, T. "Fixing Some Time-Related Problems in Ada". *Ada Letters X*, 4 (Spring 1990), 136-143. Proceedings of the Third International Workshop on Real-Time Ada Issues.

**8.** Baker, T. "Timing Issues Working Group". *Ada Letters X*, 4 (Spring 1990), 119-135. Proceedings of the Third International Workshop on Real-Time Ada Issues.

**9.** Brender, R. F. Character Set Issues for Ada 9X. Software Engineering Institute, October, 1989. Ada 9X Project Report.

**10.** Carré, B. A. and Jennings, T. J. SPARK — The SPADE Ada Kernel. University of Southampton, England, March, 1989.

**11.** Chastek, G., Graham, M. H., and Zelesnik, G. The SQL Ada Module Description Language — SAMeDL. Tech. Rept. SEI-90-TR-26, Software Engineering Institute, November, 1990.

**12.** Cohen, S. Ada Support for Software Reuse. Software Engineering Institute, October, 1990. Ada 9X Project Report.

**13.** Dewar, R. B. K.' Shared Variables and Ada 9X Issues. Software Engineering Institute, January, 1990. Ada 9X Project Report.

**14.** Dewar, R. B. K. The Fixed-Point Facility in Ada. Software Engineering Institute, January, 1990. Ada 9X Project Report.

**15.** Fowler, K. J. A Study of Implementation-Dependent Pragmas and Attributes in Ada. Software Engineering Institute, November, 1989. Ada 9X Project Report.

**16.** Gargaro, A. B., Goldsack, S. J., Volz, R. A., and Wellings, A. J. A Proposal to Support Reliable Distributed Systems in Ada 9X. Tech. Rept. 90-10, Computer Science Department, Texas A&M University, June, 1990.

**17.** *Generic Package of Elementary Functions for Ada.* ISO-IEC/JTC1/SC22/WG9 (Ada) Numerics Rapporteur Group, 1990. Being submitted as a Proposed Standard.

**18.** *Generic Package of Primitive Functions for Ada.* ISO-IEC/JTC1/SC22/WG9 (Ada) Numerics Rapporteur Group, 1990. Being submitted as a Proposed Standard.

**References**

**19.** Ichbiah, J. D., Barnes, J. G. P., Firth, R. J., and Woodger, M.. *Rationale for the Design of the Ada Programming Language.* Honeywell Systems and Research Center, Minneapolis, MN, 1986.

**20.** *IEEE Standard for Floating Point Arithmetic.* ANSI/IEEE Standard 754-1985 edition, 1985.

**21.** *7-Bit Coded Character Set for Information Processing Interchange.* ISO 646-1973 edition, 1973.

**22.** *8-bit Single-Byte Coded Character Sets.* ISO 8859-1987 edition, 1987.

**23.** Real-Time Tasking Semantics Working Group. "Real-Time Performance Standard". *Ada Letters X*, 4 (Spring 1990), 40-45. Proceedings of the Third International Workshop on Real-Time Ada Issues.

**24.** Quiggle, T. J. "Ramifications of Re-introducing Asynchronous Exceptions". *Ada Letters X*, 4 (Spring 1990), 25-31. Proceedings of the Third International Workshop on Real-Time Ada Issues.

**25.** *Ada 9X Revision Issues.* Release 2 edition, Office of the Under Secretary of Defense for Acquisition, Washington, D.C. 20301, 1990. Ada 9X Project Report.

**26.** Smith, M. K., Craigen, D., and Saaltink, M. The nanoAVA Definition. Tech. Rept. 21, Computational Logic Inc., June, 1988.

**27.** Wichmann, B. A. Low-Ada: An Ada validation tool. Tech. Rept. NPL Report DITC 144/89, National Physical Laboratory, August, 1989.

## Appendix A:  Efficiency, Simplicity, and Consistency Issues

Section 2.2 requests simplifications to Ada 83 but does not spell out specific problems to be addressed.  Examples of such problems are given in this Appendix.  These examples are to be considered suggestive rather than exhaustive.

## A.1 Efficiency of Executed Code

This section lists some examples of Ada rules that might be changed to make it easier to generate efficient object code.

### A.1.1. Access to a Task Outside its Master

In Ada 83 there is only one situation in which a task can be accessed from outside its master. AI-00867 points out that this consequence of Ada's rules poses a burden on implementations without any functional benefit to users.

### A.1.2. Null Ranges

The difference between the upper and lower bound of a null range can exceed one.  This possibility increases the overhead of index checks, particularly for machines with hardware index checking based on the lower bound and the length.

## A.2 Understandability

User Need 2.2-B on page 8 calls for simplifying rules that appear to be confusing or error-prone. This section lists some of the rules that should be considered for improvement.

### A.2.1. Elaboration Order

Ada's requirements for library unit elaboration and rules restricting access to an entity before its elaboration contribute to the language's apparent complexity from a user's viewpoint. RI-4017 [25] provides a thorough analysis of the problems these rules are attempting to solve and the problems that have been experienced with the rules, and lays a basis for possible improvements.

### A.2.2. Later Declarative Items

Ada 83's distinction between basic declarative items and later declarative items was motivated mainly to prevent mixing large and small textual items [19, pp. 19-20].  Despite this motivation, the rule has proven to be confusing to users and should be reviewed to see if the intended benefits are indeed worth the costs.

### A.2.3. Visibility of Literals and Operations

Ada 83 provides facilities to control the visibility of declarations.  However, the rules do not provide visibility of literals and operations in certain situations where the type itself is visible.  It is a common programming error to believe that being able to declare an object of a type means the literals and infix operations of the type are directly visible.

A: Efficiency, Simplicity, and Consistency Issues

### A.2.4. Obsolete Optional Bodies

Section 10.3(5) of the standard requires that an obsolete unit be recompiled (unless the implementation can deduce that compilation is not required). If a package body that is optional becomes obsolete, because of compilation of either its specification or of some other unit it depends on, the compilation system must delete it from the library. If the body is required by the logic of the application (even though it is "optional" by Ada's rules), this behavior can cause a hard-to-find bug.

### A.2.5. OTHERS Clause in Aggregates

The rules for use of OTHERS in array aggregates cause great confusion among programmers. See RR-0029, RR-0571 and RR-0605 for examples of the problems.

## A.3 Generality

Requirement R2.2-C(1) on page 8 calls for minimizing special-case restrictions or omissions in Ada 9X. This section gives examples of restrictions that might be relaxed as well as examples of omissions that might be remedied.

### A.3.1. IMAGE and VALUE for Real Types

The IMAGE and VALUE attributes can currently only be applied to integer and to enumeration types. Allowing these attributes to be applied to real types seems a natural generalization to most users.

### A.3.2. Exception Handlers in Accept Statements

Accept statements look very much like subprogram bodies to users, but an exception handler cannot be written as part of the syntax of an accept statement.

### A.3.3. RANGE Attribute for Scalar Types

It seems quite natural to users that they should be allowed to apply the RANGE attribute to a scalar type.

### A.3.4. Permit "raise ... when <condition>"

For consistency with the syntax of the **exit** statement, the syntax of Ada 9X could allow a similar structure for the raise statement.

### A.3.5. STORAGE_SIZE for Task Objects

Ada 83 allows a storage size specification only for a task type, but it would be reasonable to allow it to be specified for a single task as well.

### A.3.6. Explicit Type Conversions in Static Expressions

An explicit conversion of a static expression is not itself static. This can lead to unexpected programming problems (see RR-0099 for examples). This restriction was introduced into Ada because of a pathological case — if one writes INTEGER(1.5) as a choice in a case statement, the legality of the case statement will depend on an implementation's decision about how to round 1.5. Given the problems described in RR-0099, it is probably worthwhile to revisit this decision.

### A.3.7. Use of a Subprogram Name in its Specification

Section 8.3(16) of the standard forbids use of of the identifier that is a subprogram's simple name in the specification or generic instantiation of that subprogram. AI-00370 discusses the motivation for this rule, but even so, the result of the rule is to forbid generic instantiations that are in fact quite useful, e.g.:

```
with PACKAGE_1;
package PACKAGE_2 is
    procedure PROCEDURE_1 is new PACKAGE_1.PROCEDURE_1;   -- illegal
end PACKAGE_2;
```

The second use of PROCEDURE_1 is illegal.

### A.3.8. Default Names for Generic Formal Parameters

Ada 83 permits a default name or expression for all generic formal parameters except formal types.

### A.3.9. Ability to Redefine "="

Although Ada 83 apparently restricts the ability to redefine the equality operator, in fact, it is possible to declare an equality operator for any type. Given that this is possible, it might be reasonable to remove the current restriction on direct redeclaration of the equality operator.

### A.3.10. Reading Out Parameters

In general, a variable can be read after it has been assigned a value, but this is not true for **out** parameters. There was a lengthy discussion concerning the validity of this restriction during the initial Ada design. It might be worthwhile to revisit this discussion to see if the motivation for this special-case rule is still considered sound.

### A.3.11. Implicit Subtype Conversions

The lack of an implicit array subtype conversion in record and array aggregates is a continuing source of surprise to programmers (e.g., see RR-0734 and RR-0749). While it is not clear that this rule can be revised in an acceptably upward-compatible way, its revision should be considered.

### A.3.12. Negative Literals in Loops

New users are surprised to discover that constructs such as

```
for N in -1 .. 1 loop
```

are illegal. This restriction exists because of a pathological overloading resolution case discovered during Ada's design. The rationale for this rule should be reconsidered to see if the rule can be relaxed.

### A.3.13. Naming Syntactic Items

Two features of Ada 83 help to make Ada programs easier to comprehend: the optional name permitted on loop and block statements, and optional identifiers at the end of various constructs. It is particularly helpful that the latter (if present) are required to match the name of the unit.

### A: Efficiency, Simplicity, and Consistency Issues

Similar labeling of other syntactic constructs is often required by coding standards and seems consistent with Ada's existing rules, but is not allowed by the language. The Mapping/Revision Team should consider whether it is worthwhile to permit additional kinds of statements (**if**, **case** and **select**) to be labeled with matching end names. It would also be reasonable to permit matching end names for record declarations.

## A.4 Usability of Ada

This section is concerned with small changes to Ada that will ease its use.

### A.4.1. Completion of Subprogram Declarations

Ada 83 requires that the body for a subprogram specification be supplied by a subprogram body. However, it is often desirable to define the implementation of a subprogram by renaming another subprogram or by generic instantiation; doing so is not permitted in Ada 83. Although this restriction can be circumvented by placing the renaming or instantiation in a package specification, doing so reveals an implementation detail that should be concealed in the body. RR-0470 gives good arguments for why this capability is useful.

### A.4.2. Completing Incomplete and Private Types by Subtype Declarations

Ada 83 requires that an incomplete type declaration or a private type declaration be completed by a type declaration. Relaxing this rule by permitting a subtype declaration as a completion will simplify coding.

# 19

# Ada references

## 19.1 Calendar of events for 1991

February
UK

**Ada UK 1991 Ada Exhibition**

Contact: Helen Byard, Ada Language UK Ltd
PO Box 322, York YO1 3GY, UK
Tel. +44 904 412740

March 3–7
USA

**9th Annual National Conference on Ada Technology**

Contact: Ms Kay Trezza, HQ, CECOM,
Center for Software Engineering,
ATTN: AMSEL-RD-SE-CRM,
Ft. Monmouth, NJ 07703-5000

April
USA

**Symposium on Environments and Tools for Ada (SAETA2)**

1990 Contact: Joan Staunton, ACM Headquarters
11 W 42nd Street, New York NY 10036
Tel. +1 212-869-7440

May 13–17     **Ada-Europe, Athens, Greece**
Greece

> Contact: Apostolos Coucouvinos, Intrasoft SA,
> 2 Mesgion Str, Athens Tower, GR–11527 Athens.
> Tel. +30-1-7701692, Fax. +30-1-7782444,
> E-mail: mcvax!ariadne!intra!ada

June          **Washington Ada Symposium (WAdaS) 91**
USA

> 1990 Contact: Chris Braun, Contel Technology Center
> 15000 Conference Center Drive
> Chantilly, VA 22021

July          **5th International Real-Time**
UK            **Ada Issues Workshop**

> Contact: Helen Byard, Ada Language UK Ltd
> PO Box 322, York YO1 3GY, UK
> Tel. +44 904 412740

August        **6th Annual Ada Software Engineering**
USA           **Education and Training (ASEET) Symposium**

> 1990 Contact: Catherine W. McDonald
> Institute for Defense Analyses
> 1801 N Beauregard St, Alexandria, VA 22311
> Tel. +1 703-824-5531
> E-mail: mcdonald@ajpo.sei.cmu.edu

August        **Summer SigAda Meeting**
USA

> 1990 Contact: Hal Hart, TRW R2/2062
> One Space Park, Redondo Beach, CA 90278
> Tel. +1 213-812-0661

October       **Ada UK International Conference**
UK

> Contact: Helen Byard, Ada Language UK Ltd
> PO Box 322, York YO1 3GY, UK
> Tel. +44 904 412740

November   **4th Annual NASA Ada User's Symposium**
USA

   1990 Contact: Shiela Alban, The MITRE Corp.
   1120 NASA Road 1, Houston, TX 77058
   Tel. +1 713-333-0910

November   **7th Annual Conference on**
USA        **Artificial Intelligence and Ada**

   1990 Contact: AIDA '90
   Department of Computer Science
   George Mason University
   4400 University Drive, Fairfax, VA 22030
   Tel. +1 703-323-2713
   E-mail: AIDA@gmuvax.gmu.edu

December   **Tri-Ada '91**
USA

   1990 Contact: Dennis Ahern, Aerospace Software, M/S 432
   Westinghouse Electronic Systems Group
   P O Box 746, Baltimore, MD 21203-0746
   Tel. +1 301-993-6234
   E-mail: ahernd@eclus.bwi.wec.com

December   **Ada-France**
France

   1990 Contact: M. Michel Gauthier
   Departement d'Informatique, 123, avenue Albert Thomas
   F-87060 LIMOGES Cedex, FRANCE
   Fax. +33-55-457301

## 19.2   Booklist

### 1986

**Ada: an introduction to program design and coding**
Amoroso, S.
Howard W Sams and Co

**Introduction to Ada**
Claverly, P.
Brooks.Cole Co

**Ada as a second language**
Cohen, N.
McGraw-Hill

**Embedded programming in Ada**
Elbert, T.F.
Van Nostrand Rheinhold

**Ada, a first introduction**
Ledgard, H.F.
Springer-Verlag

**Data structures of Pascal, Algol 68, PL/I and Ada**
Lewi, J.
Springer-Verlag

**Applied Ada**
Mohnkem, G.L.
Tab Brooks

**Ada – a programmer's guide with microcomputer examples**
Stanley, J., Fung, J., Krantz, D. & Stachour, P.
Addison-Wesley

**Introduction to Ada**
Texel, P.
Wadsworth

**Practitioner's Guide to Ada**
Wallace, R.H.
McGraw-Hill

**Ada: managing the transition**
Proceedings of the Ada-Europe Conference, 1986
Wallis, P. (ed)
Cambridge University Press

## 1987

### Software engineering with Ada
Booch, G.
Addison-Wesley

### Software components with Ada – structures, tools and subsystems
Booch, G.
Benjamin/Cummings Publishing Co

### A review of Ada tasking
Burns, A., Lister, A.M. & Wellings, A.J.
Springer-Verlag

### UNIX Ada programming
Gehani, N.
Prentice-Hall

### Problem solving methods with examples in Ada
Lomuto, N.
Prentice-Hall

### ANNA: a language for annotating Ada programs
Luckham, D.C., Henke, F.W. & Krieg-Bruckner, B. (eds)
Springer-Verlag

### Software development with Ada
Sommerville, I. & Morrison, R.
Addison-Wesley

### Ada components: libraries and tools
Tafvelin, S. (ed)
Cambridge University Press

### Ada programming with applications
Vasilescu, E.N.
Allyn and Bacon

### Ada, Language & Methodology
Watt, B., Wichmann, B.A. & Findlay, W.
Prentice-Hall International

## 1988

### Ada for distributed systems
Atkinson, C., Moreton, T. & Natali, A.
Cambridge University Press

### The professional Programmers guide to Ada
Dawes, J.
Pitman Publishing

### Ada from the beginning
Skanholm, J.
Addison-Wesley

## 1989

### Ada: the design choice
Alvarez, A. (ed)
Cambridge University Press

### Programming in Ada, Third edition
Barnes, J.
Addison-Wesley

### Ada: an advanced introduction, Second edition
Gehani, N.
Prentice-Hall

### Ada in action – with practical programming examples
Jones, D.
John Wiley and Sons

### Understanding Ada with abstract data types
Shumate, K.
John Wiley and Sons

### Programming in Ada
Tremblay, J.-P. & Friesen, V.J.
McGraw-Hill

## 1990

### Distributed Ada: developments and experiences
Bishop, J.M. (ed)
Cambridge University Press

### Ada: sources and resources
Nyberg, K.A.
Grebyn Corporation

### Resources in Ada
ACM Press

# 19.3   Publications

Two publications are worthy of mention for the wealth of information they contain relating to Ada.

## Ada: sources and resources

by Karl A. Nyberg is available from the Grebyn Corporation, Post Office Box 497, Vienna, VA 22183-0497, USA. The 1990 edition is over 60% bigger than the 1989 edition, running to 268 pages.

## Resources in Ada

with an introduction by Gerry Fisher, ISBN 0-89791-374-4 is available from the ACM Press, New York. It has almost 100 pages of indexes as well as reviews and bibliographies.

There are many regular journals, magazines and newsletters devoted to Ada. These carry articles, views, reports of meetings and conferences as well as advertising for compilers, courses, software etc. Some of the most effective are listed here. Some of the subscription prices are quoted approximately, and can be obtained more precisely from the contact point.

## Ada Companion Series

A series of books on special Ada topics, published in conjunction with the Commission of the European Communities. Includes the proceedings of the Ada Europe Conferences. Individual copies < $100. Contact: Cambridge University Press, The Edinburgh Building, Shaftesbury Road, Cambridge CB2 2RU, UK. Phone: +44-223-315052.

## AdaData

Newsletter with emphasis on commercial significance of new Ada developments and the Defense Department's policies. Monthly. Subscription > $200. Contact: International Research Development, 21 Locust Avenue, #1C, New Canaan, CT 6840-4735, USA.

## Ada Information Clearinghouse Newsletter

This is the official publication of the Ada Joint Program Office (AJPO). It contains news about Ada's official progress, events and lists of validated compilers. Quarterly. Free. Contact: Ada Information Clearinghouse, c/o IIT Research Institute, 4600 Forbes Boulevard, Lanham, MD 20706-4320, USA. Phone: +1-703-685-1477.

## Ada Letters

One of the most useful Ada publications, with articles, reports, events, tutorials and compiler information. Published by the ACM's Special Interest Group on Ada (SIGAda). Bimonthly. Subscription $37 to

non-members, $15 to members, $17 outside USA. Contact: Ada
Letters, ACM Headquarters, 11 W 42nd Street, New York, NY 10036,
USA. Phone +1-212-869-7440.

## Ada Strategies

Newsletter focusing on competitive strategies in the Ada marketplace.
Monthly. Subscription > $200. Contact: Cutter Information Corp. 1100
Mass Ave, Arlington, MA 02174, USA. Phone: +1-617-648-8700.

## Ada User

Publication of Ada UK with information of events and products
connected with Ada. Quarterly. Subscription £70.00 (EC), $125.00
(USA/Canada), £77.00 (rest of world). Contact: Chapman and Hall,
2–6 Boundary Row, London SE1 8HN, UK. Tel. +44-71-865-0066, Fax.
+44-71-522-9621.

## Info-Ada Newsletter

A newsletter that contains information on current events in the Ada
community, plus lists of validated compilers. Monthly. Subs < $100.
Contact: Karl A Nyberg, Grebyn Corporation, P O Box 1144, Vienna,
VA 22180-1144, USA. Phone: +1-703-281-2194, E-mail:
karl@grebyn.com

## Journal of Pascal, Ada and Modula-2

A journal that provides an international forum for research,
developments, applications and new products in these languages.
Bimonthly. Subscription < $ 50 (individual). Contact JPAM Corp, P O
Box 968-B, Ft Washington, PA 19034, USA. Phone: +1-800-345-8112.

## La Lettre Ada

Published in French, with information about products and events in
France and Europe. Monthly. Contact: Jean-Claude Rault, EC2,
269-287 rue de la Garenne, 92000 Nanterre, France. Phone:
+33-47-8-70-00.

# 19.4    Address list

Mrs Mandy Covers
## Alsys
Partridge House
Newtown Road
Henley-on-Thames
Oxon. RG9 1EN
UK

Tel. +44 491 579090
Fax. +44 491 571866

## Christine M. Anderson
Ada 9X Project Manager
Department of Defense
Department of the Air Force
Air Force Armament Laboratory
(AFSC)
Eglin Air Force Base
Florida 32542-5434
USA

## Jesus Aragoneses
Teice Control
Castillejos, 34
E-28039 Madrid
Spain

Tel. +34 1 450 5300
Fax. +34 1 450 5159
Email: jaragoneses@teice.es

## Association for Computing Machinery, Inc
11 West 42nd Street
New York
NY 10036
USA

## Judy Bamberger
"Ada Follies"
Software Engineering Institute
Pittsburgh, PA 15213
USA

Tel. +1 412 268 5795
Fax. +1 412 268 5758
Email: bamberg@sei.cmu.edu

## John G.P. Barnes
Chairman, Ada UK
Alsys Ltd
Partridge House
Newtown Road
Henley-on-Thames
Oxon. RG9 1EN
UK

Tel. +44 491 579090

## Dr Judy M. Bishop
Department of Electronic
    and Computer Science
University of Southampton
Southampton
SO9 5NH
UK

Tel. +44 703 593565
Fax. +44 703 593045
Telex: 47661
Email: jmb@ecs.soton.ac.uk

**Jean-Paul Bossavit**
SEMA Group
Division Energie
BP 104
38243 Meylan Cedex
France

Tel. +33 76 90 71 11
Fax. +33 76 90 67 63
Telex: 980 750F
Email: JeanPaul.Bossavit@semagr.uucp

**Frank Bott**
Department of Computer Science
University College of Wales
Penglais
Aberystwyth
Dyfed
SY23 3BZ
UK

Tel. +44 970 622424
Fax. +44 970 617172
Telex: 35181
Email: mfb@cs.aber.ac.uk

**John Buchan**
Cray Research (UK) Ltd
Oldbury
Bracknell
Berkshire
RG12 4TQ
UK

Tel. +44 344 485971
Fax. +44 344 426319

**Helen Byard**
Ada UK Administrator
Ada Language UK Ltd
PO Box 322
York YO1 3GY
UK

Tel. +44 904 412740

**David Callahan**
Commission of the European
    Communities
DG XIII/A/4
Rue de la Loi 200
B-1049 Brussels
Belgium

Tel. +32 2 236 2349
Fax. +32 2 236 1948

**Russell M. Clapp**
Advanced Computer Architecture
    Laboratory
Department of Electrical Engineering
    and Computer Science
The University of Michigan
Ann Arbor
MI 48109-2122
USA

**Ed Colbert**
SIGAda, Vice Chair for Liaison
Absolute
4593 Orchid Drive
Los Angeles, CA 90043-3320
USA

Tel. +1 213 293 0783
Email: hermix!colbert@rand.org

## Commission of the European Communities

Karel de Vriendt
A25 7/3
Rue de la Loi 200
B-1049 Brussels
Belgium

Tel. +32 2 235 7769

## Apostolos Coucouvinos

Ada-Europe Conference, Athens
Conference Chair
Intrasoft SA
2 Mesgion Str
Athens Tower
GR-11527 Athens
Greece

Tel. +30-1-7701692
Fax. +30-1-7782444
Email: mcvax!ariadne!intra!ada

John Buchan
## Cray Research (UK) Ltd

Oldbury
Bracknell
Berkshire
RG12 4TQ
UK

Tel. +44 344 485971
Fax. +44 344 426319

## Martin Davies

BSI Quality Assurance
PO Box 375
Linford Wood
Milton Keynes
Bucks MK14 6LE
UK

Mr Palle Andersson
## DDC International

Gl. Lundtoftevej 1B
DK-2800 Lyngby
Denmark

Tel. +45 42 87 11 44
Fax. +45 42 87 22 17
After 13 April 1991:
Tel. +45 45 87 11 44
Fax. +45 45 87 22 17

## Kenneth W. Dritz

Mathematics and Computer Science
    Division
Argonne National Laboratory
Argonne, Illinois 60439
USA

Email: dritz@gov.anl.mcs.antares

The Secretary General
## ECMA

114 Rue du Rhone
CH-1204 Geneva
Switzerland

Tel. +41 22 735 3634
Fax. +41 22 786 5231

Vincent Rich
## Encore Computer

Marlborough House
Mole Business Park
Leatherhead
Surrey
KT22 7BA
UK

Tel. +44 372 363363
Fax. +44 372 362926

**Peter Fitzpatrick**
VSEL
Combat Systems Division
Barrow-in-Furness
Cumbria
LA14 1AF
UK

Tel. +44 229 873993
Fax. +44 229 873846

**Mark S. Gerhardt**
SIGAda Chairperson
ESL Inc., MS M507
495 Java Drive
Sunnyvale, CA 94088-3510
USA

Tel. +1 408 752 2459
Email: gerhardt@ajpo.sei.cmu.edu

**G. Giannino**
Chief ADASCC
NACISA
NATO
Rue de Genève, 8
B-1140 Brussels
Belgium

Tel. +32 2 246 8111
Fax. +32 2 242 1022
Telex: 25931

**J.G. Glynn**
Company Secretary, Ada UK
Ferranti Computer Systems Ltd
Ty Coch Way
Cwmbrân
Gwent NP44 7XX
UK

Tel. +44 633 871111
Fax. +44 633 873974
Telex: 497636

**Ken Hayter**
IEPG, Programme Co-ordination
    Committee Chairman
Royal Signals and Radar Establishment
St. Andrews Road
Great Malvern
Worcs. WR14 3PS
UK

Tel. +44 684 892733

**John Hole**
Publicity Director, Ada UK
Racal Communications Systems Ltd
Western Road
Bracknell
Berks. RG12 1RG
UK

Tel. +44 344 483244

**Paul D. Kenward**
National Physical Laboratory
Queen's Road
Teddington
TW11 0LW
UK

Tel. +44 81 977 3222
Email: pdk@seg.npl.co.uk

**Anton B. Leere**
Norwegian Defence Research
    Establishment
P.O. Box 25
N-2007 Kjeller
Norway

Tel. +47 6 807394
Fax. +47 6 807212
Email: leere%dione.ndre.uninett@
    nac.no

## Dr Fred W. Long

Department of Computer Science
University College of Wales
Penglais
Aberystwyth
Dyfed
SY23 3BZ
UK

Tel. +44 970 622440
Fax. +44 970 617172
Telex: 35181
Email: fwl@cs.aber.ac.uk

## M.J. Looney

Defence Correspondent, Ada UK
AXC Division
MoDPE, ARE
Portsmouth
PO6 4AA
UK

## Barry Lynch

Generics Software Ltd
Clonard House
Sandyford Road
Dublin 16
Republic of Ireland

Tel. +353 1 954012
Fax. +353 1 954011
Email: lynch@genrix.uucp

## Myer W. Morron

Environment Director, Ada UK
STC Technology Ltd
London Road
Harlow
Essex
CM17 9NA
UK

Tel. +44 279 29531
Fax. +44 279 441551
Telex: 81151

## Chris Nettleton

SD-Scicon UK Ltd
Pembroke House
Pembroke Broadway
Camberley
Surrey
GU15 3XD
UK

Tel. +44 276 686200
Fax. +44 276 683511

## Tony Orme

AEG (UK) Ltd
Engineering Division
Eskdale Road
Winnersh
Wokingham
Berks. RG11 5PF
UK

Tel. +44 734 698330
Fax. +44 734 699607
Telex: 848696

## M.J. Pickett
Financial Director, Ada UK
SEMA Group
Orion Court
Kenavan Drive
Reading
RG1 3DQ
UK

Tel. +44 734 508961

## Jean-Marc Poulet
SEMA Group - Energy Division
Chemin du Vieux Chene
BP 104
38243 Meylan Cedex
France

## Juan A. de la Puente
ETSI Telecomunicacion
Ciudad Universitaria
E-28040 Madrid
Spain

Tel. +34 1 5495700 x.379
Fax. +34 1 2432077
Email: jpuente@dit.upm.es
Alternatives: jpuente@goya.uucp

## Prof. Ian Pyle
Founder, Ada UK
SD-Scicon UK Ltd
Abbey House
Farnborough Road
Farnborough
Hants. GU14 7NA
UK

Tel. +44 252 541402
Fax. +44 252 549340
Telex: 859095

## REST Transition Services
Software Engineering Institute
Carnegie Mellon University
Pittsburgh, PA 15213
USA

## Vincent Rich
Encore Computer
Marlborough House
Mole Business Park
Leatherhead
Surrey
KT22 7BA
UK

Tel. +44 372 363363
Fax. +44 372 362926

## Jean-Pierre Rosen
ADALOG
115 avenue du Maine
75014 Paris
France

Tel. +33 1 43 22 44 50
Fax. +33 1 43 21 72 21

## Colin Rolls
European Space Research
     and technology Centre
Postbus 299
2200 AG Noordwijk
The Netherlands

Tel. +31 01719 86555
Fax. +31 01719 17400
Telex: 39098

## Daniel M. Roy
Chairman, PIWG
Software Engineering Institute
Carnegie Mellon University
Pittsburgh, PA 15213
USA

Ian Pascoe
## SD-Scicon UK Ltd
Pembroke House
Pembroke Broadway
Camberley
Surrey
GU15 3XD
UK

Tel. +44 276 686200
Fax. +44 276 683511

## Dr Mel Selwood
Siemens Plessey Defence Systems
Grange Road, Somerford
Christchurch
Dorset BH23 4JE
UK

Tel. +44 202 404341
Fax. +44 202 404221

## Jorge Serrano
Ada-Spain
P.O. Box 50.403
E-28080 Madrid
Spain

Fax. +34-1-450 5159
Email: jorge@teice.es

## Jun Shimura
Treasurer, Japan SIGAda
Head, Systems Development Sec
Kozo Keikaku Engineering Inc
4-38-13m Honcho, Nakano-ku
Tokyo 164
Japan

## Prof. D. Simpson
Academic Liaison Director, Ada UK
ITRI, Brighton Polytechnic
Lewes Road
Brighton
BN2 4AT
UK

Tel. +44 273 600900

## Software Engineering Institute
Carnegie Mellon University
Pittsburgh, Pennsylvania 15213-3890
USA

Tel. +1 412 268 7700
Fax. +1 412 268 5758

## Dr John Solomond
Ada Joint Program Office
The Pentagon
Room 3E114
Washington, DC 20301-3080
USA

Tel. +1 202 694 0208
Email: solomond@ajpo.sei.cmu.edu

## Bill Taylor
Ferranti Computer Systems Ltd
Ty Coch Way
Cwmbrân
Gwent NP44 7XX
UK

Tel. +44 633 871111
Fax. +44 633 873974
Telex: 497636

## Mike Taylor

RADE Systems Pty Limited
PO Box 136
Watson Bay
NSW 2030
Australia

Tel. +61 2 337 0542

## B.C. Tooby

Director — Applications, Ada UK
High Integrity Systems
Astras Centre
Edinburgh Way
Harlow
Essex CM20 2BE
UK

Tel. +44 279 450000


Peter Fitzpatrick
## VSEL

Combat Systems Division
Barrow-in-Furness
Cumbria
LA14 1AF
UK

Tel. +44 229 873993
Fax. +44 229 873846

## John Walker

Ada Joint Program Office
The Pentagon
Washington, DC 20301-3080
USA

Tel. +1 703 685 1477
Email: walkerj@ajpo.sei.cmu.edu

## Dr Alison Wearing

Industrial Liaison Director, Ada UK
Evisa Systems
17 Orford Avenue
Disley
Cheshire
SK12 2BH
UK

Tel. +44 663 63317

## John T. Webb

Rex, Thompson & Partners Limited
Systems Integrity Division
'The Barbican'
East Street
Farnham
Surrey GU9 7TB
UK

Tel. +44 252 711414
Fax. +44 252 735633
Telex: 858623/858393

## Brian A. Wichmann

National Physical Laboratory
Queen's Road
Teddington
TW11 0LW
UK

Tel. +44 81 977 3222
Email: baw@seg.npl.co.uk

## Herr Wilde

Der Bundesminister der Verteidigung
Rü T IV 1 – Az 62-03-02
Postfach 13 28
5300 Bonn
Germany

Tel. +49 2 28 12 68 31
Fax. +49 2 28 12 53 57
Telex: 886575

# Index of Ada systems and tools

# Feed back page

Please send comments, on any aspects of this book, to the editor at the address given below. All suggestions about what should, or should not, be included in future issues are welcome. If there is something you particularly like, or dislike, about the way the book is presented, please let us know. For example, the idea to use different fonts and layout styles for the two parts of the book was a bit of an experiment. We would appreciate hearing your opinions on whether this experiment was a success, or not.

If you have any comments or suggestions, please send them to:

### Dr Fred Long
Department of Computer Science
University College of Wales
Penglais
Aberystwyth
Dyfed
SY23 3BZ
UK

Tel. +44 970 622440
Fax. +44 970 617172
Telex: 35181
Email: fwl@cs.aber.ac.uk